ULTIMATE GUIDE
OF PURCHASER

ULTIMATE GUIDE OF PURCHASER

Fundamental Definitions, Concepts,
and Techniques for a Procurement Professional

JAMES K. HAWKINS

ULTIMATE GUIDE OF PURCHASER
FUNDAMENTAL DEFINITIONS, CONCEPTS, AND TECHNIQUES FOR A PROCUREMENT PROFESSIONAL

iUniverse books may be ordered through booksellers or by contacting:

iUniverse
1663 Liberty Drive
Bloomington, IN 47403
www.iuniverse.com
844-349-9409

Because of the dynamic nature of the Internet, any web addresses or links contained in this book may have changed since publication and may no longer be valid. The views expressed in this work are solely those of the author and do not necessarily reflect the views of the publisher, and the publisher hereby disclaims any responsibility for them.

Any people depicted in stock imagery provided by Getty Images are models, and such images are being used for illustrative purposes only.
Certain stock imagery © Getty Images.

ISBN: 978-1-6632-5289-0 (sc)
ISBN: 978-1-6632-5290-6 (e)

Library of Congress Control Number: 2023908130

Print information available on the last page.

iUniverse rev. date: 05/19/2023

CONTENTS

INTRODUCTION

A clever observer notices how a company's purchasing areas evolve rapidly. A few decades ago, the tools accessible to professionals were simple, without electronic sophistication, and took days to receive a proposal.

The focus was on sales for a long time, without appreciating support areas. The purchasing area was part of that group. Currently, selling without competitive costs is impracticable. No consumer pays more for a product because its manufacturer is ineffective.

Organizational changes occur everywhere. The structures are lean, the paradigms have changed, and professionals must have a vision of the company's activities and the skills required to occupy the position.

It is unacceptable for a purchaser to buy a good or contract a service without evaluating the impact of the acquisition on other processes in the organization's production or operational chain.

Indeed, ensuring the availability of necessary materials is essential. In this context, as James Stevens[1] points out, managing the entire supply chain is indispensable: "Supply chain management is one of the most important things you can learn in business, and at the same time, it is one of the most overlooked. Hundreds if not thousands of companies have failed because they did not understand the basics of supply chains, and therefore did not know how important it was to manage them".

The *Ultimate Guide of Purchaser* scrutinizes acquisitions in industrial, service, and commercial organizations. It offers insights on the topic, valuable for both beginner professionals and those with years in the field.

It is essential to highlight how the backbone of procurement procedures is similar across different branches. Any differences derive from the peculiarities of the varied sectors of the economy.

Because of its comprehensiveness, the *Ultimate Guide of Purchaser* is also helpful for students willing to learn about how an organization's supply or logistics area works.

---

[1] STEVENS, James. Supply Chain Management: Strategy, Operation & Planning for Logistics Management (Logistics, Supply Chain Management, Procurement). USA: Shepal Publishing, June 15, 2016

PART I

CONFIGURATION OF THE PURCHASING AREA

CHAPTER 1

PURCHASING IN THE CONTEMPORARY BUSINESS CONTEXT

"All organizations can deliver better results."

Jim Collins[2]

The above quote fits like a glove for the purchasing area, which has undergone profound changes globally in recent years.

As a result of this development, the area has achieved prominence, with prestige equivalent to finance, sales, or production. The area has gained valuable participation in the strategic decisions of organizations. No winning organization can give up the contribution of the purchasing/supply department in preparing the strategic plan.

It is possible to compare changes between past and current activities, as shown in the table in Figure 1.1.

Past	Present
Managed with scattered information	Has information management
Perceived as an isolated function, commonly linked to production	Integrated part, frequently subordinated to senior management
Issued short-term purchase orders	Negotiate and accomplish long-term contracts
Named the internal public as a user	It values the internal public by calling them internal customers

---

[2] Jim Collins is the author of best-selling leadership and business books such as Good to Great. The quote highlights how competition and longevity in the market starts internally.

Manual operation or using precarious computer systems	It has integrated management systems, frequently connected to suppliers
Recognized as a necessary nuisance	Appreciated as a competitive advantage
Reactive, focused on crisis management	Initiative-taking, anticipating problems, and developing solutions
Enlisted various suppliers	Interacts with a few suppliers
Quality inspections were necessary	Use quality assurance
Professional identified as issuer of orders	Categorize the professional as an entrepreneur
Used to strive only to cut prices	Plans and acts to optimize costs

Figure 1.1.: Table comparing the profile of Purchases
in the past with the current model

The comparisons in Figure 1.1. show the changes in the area. As a result, the description of the tasks and activities of purchasing professionals has also evolved.

Even the job title received a designation more suitable to the recently stipulated requirements, such as purchasing analysts, procurement analysts, or strategic sourcing professionals. Companies seek specialists with technical, commercial, management knowledge, and entrepreneurial characteristics.

Without prejudice to other activities, those who work in the purchasing area must develop new products, research, and manage supply sources, focus on cost management, and seek long-term partnerships.

The intended profile changed, and various companies started to pay variable remuneration as an incentive mechanism. The purchaser can receive bonuses in addition to the salary if the performance exceeds predefined goals.

Almir[3] points out the achievement of the goals: "It is important, however, to observe that the supply chain management and its respective strategy must be an integral part of the company's largest, global strategy."

---

[3] SANTOS Almir G, ELIA Bruno de S, MAGALHÃES Eduardo, PINTO Geraldo. Gestão da Cadeia de Suprimentos (Supply Chain Management). 1st edition. Brazil: FGV Management October 1, 2014

The purchaser, individually or as a team, performs the following activities:

a) Acting in the decision analysis between producing internally or purchasing a material;
b) Communicate material specification changes;
c) Contribution to the determination of purchasing policies;
d) Contribution to the development of supply strategies;
e) Development of market research and assessments;
f) Formulate cost projections;
g) Involvement in defining stock levels;
h) Long-term purchase planning;
i) Look for the desired quality;
j) Material requisition analysis;
k) Monitor and evaluate supplier performance;
l) Negotiation of prices and other commercial aspects;
m) Participate in the improvement of material specifications;
n) Participation in actions to increase productivity;
o) Prepare multiple reports;
p) Presence in the standardization of materials;
q) Selection of suppliers;
r) Solving problems with sellers;
s) Value analysis.

The list already incorporates recent activities because, in the past, the purchaser's attributions practically ended with the choice of the supplier. Currently, acquisitions are essential tools for organizations to gain a competitive advantage. Why do companies need to gain a competitive advantage?

The answer depends on the understanding that there is a rapid movement towards a unified world economy for the following reasons:

- Continuous improvements in information technology simplify and accelerate the transfer of data and information;
- Evolution of means of transport and consequent reduction in the costs of transferring goods from one place to another;
- Newly booming markets globally;
- Reduction of trade barriers by forming economic blocks on different continents.

To survive and prosper, companies must stand out and work hard to compete for Market Share. The main priorities in a battle for competitiveness are quality, delivery, flexibility, services, and price.

The goal is to align the company's performance with customer needs. The central question is: how can the purchasing area increase the company's competitiveness?

By analyzing the five competitive priorities mentioned, it is possible to discern how purchasing activity influences everyone, positively or negatively, as detailed below:

Quality

The quality of a product must satisfy the requirements and expectations of those who use it. In a company, the quality of products directly results from the purchased materials and/or services. The successful selection of suppliers will mean, as the main consequence, the receipt of materials according to the desired quality.

Lead Time

The supplier's time to deliver goods to the customer significantly impacts the overall replenishment period and influences the total time. Therefore, the delivery period must comply with the contracted party, and ensuring this condition requires the purchasing area to monitor the supplier actively. Notably, having raw materials in stock is essential for production to meet the planned schedule!

Flexibility

The origin of the word flexibility is the term flexible, which in the dictionary indicates something that bends easily and is malleable. In the business environment, flexibility is an essential competence, showing the condition of professionals and the group to which they belong to change their behavior or adapt to a new situation when it is critical to the project's success. A well-equipped and correctly dimensioned purchasing department contributes to a company's agility activities. Companies sometimes lose sales due to reduced flexibility to change their production or operation.

Service

Successful companies provide excellent services at all relationship stages: before, during, and after obtaining customer orders. The most common behavior is to offer good service until the supply authorization is in hand.

Purchasing area has a considerable influence on customer service to exceed expectations. Companies often delay the performance of warranty services because their purchasing departments are slow to provide replacement parts for the sectors responsible for performing the services, for example.

Price

The importance of the purchasing area in determining product prices is unquestionable, especially in commerce or industry. When a company buys at lower values, it has an advantage over competitors as it can offer highly competitive prices in the market.

An ever-present subject addresses the fundamental importance of purchasing activities in an organization. Comments abound on the merits of purchasing/materials for excellent or bad organizational performance.

However, many believe that purchases do not deserve the same credit as sales or production areas. As the saying goes: "if you don't produce and sell, you don't need to buy."

For others, the purchasing area is at the heart of the business universe, a department with the potential to generate huge profits.

Neither view is accurate. The purchasing department is essential to an organization's excellent performance. Nevertheless, its relevance is relative for several reasons, such as the nature of the organization or the degree of dependence on third parties.

Following this understanding and studying the purchasing sector and its position in the supply chain, it is unacceptable to ignore that even winning or losing a war results from efficiency in obtaining supplies at decisive moments.

David Burt[4] explains how purchasing is essential in the context of the supply system: "purchasing is the foundation of supply management, which in turn is the foundation of supply chain management. By acquiring goods, services, and equipment from other organizations, a chain of upstream suppliers is formed - a supply chain".

Undoubtedly, the importance of purchases in the context of a large industry differs from that experienced by a bank or company specializing in cleaning and maintenance services.

In any case, there is no longer any discussion about the great earnings potential of the purchasing area when it fulfills its attributions. Thus, when a purchaser goes to work, he must always be aware of the importance of his effort to the company's results.

---

[4] BURT, David N; PETCAVAGE, Sheila; PINKERTON, Richard. Proactive Purchasing in the Supply Chain: The Key to World-Class Procurement. 1ˢᵗ edition. USA: McGraw Hill, December 6, 2011

CHAPTER 2

WHY COMPANIES NEED A PURCHASING AREA

*"Customers can fire everyone in a company, from the top
executive down, simply by spending their money elsewhere."*

Sam Walton[5]

This proposition emphasizes the importance of retaining customers, and the purchasing department is active in this endeavor. To properly understand this point, it is worth asking: what is the purpose of the area?

In a more general understanding, it is reasonable to state that the purpose of the purchasing area is to acquire goods and services of the desired quality, at the right time, for the lowest possible cost and quantity demanded. Such a view is classic, as Sollish[6] reinforces: "This follows the adage that the Procurement Department's role is to deliver the right material (or service) in the right amount to the right place at the right time and the right price."

The purchasing department is an essential part of the supply chain system. James Stevens[7] defines this context: "A supply chain comprises all participants involved in ensuring that customers get what they want, whether directly or indirectly involved in the request made. Knowing this definition, people immediately imagine suppliers or manufacturers, retailers, and wholesalers, believing that the chain covers only them. However, supply chains include transporters, warehouses used for storage, and even the end-users themselves".

Materials are essential for supplying the company's production and operational lines (direct or productive materials) or the rest of the organization (indirect, non-productive, or auxiliary materials).

---

[5] Samuel Moore Walton was founder of the world's largest retail chain, Wal-Mart.

[6] SOLLISH, Fred; SEMANIK, John. The Procurement and Supply Manager's Desk Reference. 2nd edition. USA: Wiley, May 23, 2012

[7] STEVENS, James. Supply Chain Management: Strategy, Operation & Planning for Logistics Management (Logistics, Supply Chain Management, Procurement). USA: Shepal Publishing, June 15, 2016

Concerning the general services necessary for the organization, such as maintenance, cleaning, and surveillance, most companies also delegate negotiations to the purchasing department with procedures such as those used in acquiring materials.

Here is a glimpse of each item mentioned in the overview.

2.1 Purchasing goods and services of the desired quality

The purchasing area plays the "service provider's role" for the other company units without diminishing the importance of its contribution to the organization's performance. Purchasers act when requested; that is, when receiving a purchase order for any product, they must follow the instructions of the requesting department or material management area regarding the characteristics and specifications of the desired item. It is up to the purchasing professional to seek the most suitable alternative supply for the intended good.

Sollish[8] highlighted the essentiality of the details of the acquisition object: "Unless you can describe to a supplier exactly what you need, the procurement process will not be successful. As detailed below, this description often involves a specification for materials or a statement of work (SOW) for services. Most commonly, the internal user generates this information – often called a requirement – and the procurement professional must ensure that it is properly conveyed to the supplier in the procurement document (such as a purchase order or contract)."

As a result, the purchasing department cannot redefine a specification stipulated by the internal customer or purchase materials other than requested. However, it is possible to consummate a purchase at a better price. In the case of a more advantageous proposal but offering material different from the one originally intended, the purchaser should consult the requester, and he has the last word on the quality of the material.

Previously, quality was a reactive function; therefore, the inspection phase was essential to identify and separate the "defective" item. As a result, there were reworks and a high scrap rate, causing increased costs.

Today, quality is a proactive function that requires preventive actions to practically eliminate the risk of defects in material delivery. In the initial phase of the procedure, the quality costs can be slightly higher; however, there will

---

[8] SOLLISH, Fred; SEMANIK, John. The Procurement and Supply Manager's Desk Reference. 2nd edition. USA: Wiley, May 23, 2012

be a considerable gain in the benefits to the entire business in the long run. The following definitions are helpful in the process:

a) Characteristics: General aspects of a product, such as dimensions, fuel, or colors. For example, a hybrid vehicle has the potential to attract customers by offering low consumption and being environmentally sustainable;

b) Conformity: Check the adherence of the item under examination with the characteristics specified for a given product. For example, merchandise supplied as defined in the purchase order;

c) Durability: Life expectancy of a product. For example, electronics manufacturers can offer a long customer warranty period;

d) Performance: the product's behavior in relation to the essential characteristics of the operation. For example, the fuel consumption of foundry equipment per ton produced;

e) Reliability: The probability that a product will not perform as expected owing to the use time. For example, the period of operation of aircraft engine;

f) Service: ease of repairing the product, agility in meeting requests, competence, and courtesy. For example, technical assistance for appliances goes to the customer's place to fix a product covered by the warranty.

2.2 Purchasing goods and services at the right time

When preparing a material request, the applicant sets a delivery deadline according to the work schedule.

The delay in the item's arrival compromises all the elaborated schedules and causes losses of different natures. Internal and external customer dissatisfaction are common effects.

In addition to general disapproval, if the product is unavailable on the intended date, it may be unnecessary on another date, causing losses. Working in harmony with different users and serving them at the established time is essential.

If a chain store buys thousands of wool sweaters for the winter collection, but the delivery takes place in the spring, they are useless, and low sales and a waste of money are the consequences.

To avoid such constraints, the purchasing department must act to prevent delivery problems. As soon as it notices that there will be delays, immediately inform the requesting sector. This approach allows everyone to assess the potential consequences of late delivery and to study alternatives to overcome this problem.

2.3 Purchasing goods and services at the lowest achievable cost

After fully complying with the above requirements, the purchaser should pursue the lowest possible cost for buying the product or contracting the desired service.

Before there are guarantees of meeting the conditions of quality and terms, analyzing the cost is a fundamental error with negative consequences and does not satisfy the company's interests.

When addressing the cost issue, it is always helpful to emphasize that price is a fundamental, but not exclusive, part because payment terms, taxes, freight, and packaging, among other variables, are cost components.

Frazelle[9] was very clever when explaining why focusing on price alone and disregarding other variables is a mistake: "In the name of "cost reduction," the acquisition that seeks only the lowest price may cost twice as much with hidden stock and loss of sales due to poor quality, transportation, and other costs."

Professional purchasers must invest efforts to search for the lowest possible cost but pay attention to other commercial conditions.

2.4 Purchasing goods and services in quantity requested

The quantity topic is like quality, as supply will not meet needs if there is a discrepancy between the delivery and contracted volumes.

The correct quantity deserves extra attention, as meeting the other purchase requirements will not matter if a lower volume than specified in the purchase order arrives.

---

[9] FRAZELLE, Edward H. Supply Chain Strategy, Second Edition: Unleash the Power of Business Integration to Maximize Financial, Service, and Operations Performance. 2nd edition. USA: McGraw-Hill, October 27, 2017

Sometimes, a supplier proposes a different quantity than requested, whether for productive, logistical, or packaging reasons. The purchaser sees the opportunity to gain under this new condition. However, even if the organization profits from the proposition, it is impossible to accept the offer without consulting the applicant. The recommendation is to make such a consultation exposing the situation and verifying if the suggested quantity is acceptable. The last word is from whoever asked for the material.

Occasionally, a different amount arrives. If there is a surplus, the recommendation is to return it unless there is authorization from the user sector to receive an additional volume.

If fewer quantities arrive, the purchase process will remain open until it reaches a balance.

CHAPTER 3

MAIN PURCHASE PROBLEMS

There are no easy methods for solving difficult problems.

René Descartes[10]

As with any routine and relevant activity, purchasing is subject to setbacks that affect the procedures and results. Eliminating undesirable situations is not feasible, but the duty to constantly seek measures to minimize the impact and frequency of occurrence is indisputable.

The initial step is identifying the problems associated with the company's purchasing activities and acting vigorously to improve the scenario. The following occurrences are the most significant.

3.1 Urgent purchases

Urgent purchases usually result from deficiencies in scheduling the replenishment of goods or delays in requesting services. Acquisition under these conditions is not favorable to purchasers because of the reduction in the alternatives of suppliers and difficulties in negotiating, causing higher prices and a great possibility of supply occurring after the desired date.

The adverse effects of these occurrences fall on the purchasing area, as it is up to it to locate suppliers that can meet the needs.

Shoshanah [11] goes straight to the point: "… many companies think about their supply chains only when something is wrong - high inventory levels, dissatisfied customers, or supplier problems, for example."

---

[10] René Descartes was a French philosopher, physicist, and mathematician. He gained mathematical recognition for suggesting the fusion of algebra and geometry, giving rise to analytic geometry and the coordinate system that bears his name.

[11] COHEN, Shoshanah. Strategic Supply Chain Management: The Five Core Disciplines for Top Performance. 2nd edition. USA: McGraw-Hill, June 14, 2013

There will always be emergency purchases because no organization can keep enough stock of all items to fulfill any material request.

Almir[12] explains this impossibility: "Fulfilling 100% of orders, for example, would immediately imply huge inventories, the cost of which could be considered unacceptable."

The mechanism to overcome this problem is to develop effective strategies to reduce emergencies without compromising the company's operations and avoiding a significant increase in the cost of inventories.

Therefore, planning actions to reduce the frequency of urgent requests is essential in the daily lives of organizations.

3.1.1 Develop control mechanisms

In the current stage of companies' informatization, it is not acceptable that a purchasing department does not have control tools, even for small and medium organizations.

Managers must know the scope of requests for materials and services, who issues the request, and how it is prepared, among other relevant information.

However, the demand for controls does not justify excessive bureaucratization. It is a mistaken view, divorced from the current business reality.

Controls assist in revealing incorrect procedures for subsequent reviews for the benefit of the purchasing sector and the business itself, including simplifying activities.

The existence of monitoring mechanisms makes it possible to develop better methods for evaluating the performance of activities in the area.

In sporadic cases of urgent purchases, the most effective action should focus on the source of the process: ordering materials. Therefore, it is wise to identify which areas are responsible for the highest incidence of urgent requests and then begin active work with them to reduce emergencies.

Figure 3.1. demonstrates how to proactively address urgent purchases in terms of control.

---

[12] SANTOS, Almir G; ELIA, Bruno de S; MAGALHÃES, Eduardo; PINTO, Geraldo. Gestão da Cadeia de Suprimentos (Supply Chain Management). 1st edition. Brazil: FGV Management, October 1, 2014

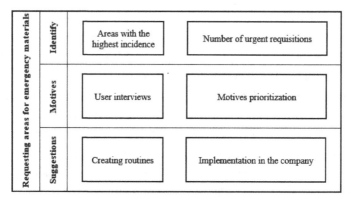

Figure 3.1.: Emergency control and action framework

In the identification stage, the professional researches which areas most required urgent purchases in the period and number of situations.

In the reasons stage, there is contact with managers from other areas to answer questions and allow diagnosing the causes of urgent purchases. Next, it is essential to prioritize the reasons for the emissions, as some will be of little relevance, and the contribution to the reformulation of the processes is insignificant.

In the suggestion period, ideas emerge to meet sector demands without compromising service deadlines. Taking suggestions from people in other areas is beneficial. Finally, implantation takes place.

3.1.2 Inform and raise awareness among managers

After identifying the focus of orders whose deliveries are "for yesterday," it is essential to contact, inform, and raise awareness to reduce the volume of such orders. The urgent ordering of materials usually results from the customer's lack of appropriate information.

It is common for professionals from other departments to be unaware of the procedures for conducting the purchasing activity, such as the time to perform the tasks or the difficulties inherent in purchasing less frequently requested materials.

If users have information about these factors, it is reasonable to assume they will change how they work.

Concerning awareness, exposing applicants to the consequences of demanding urgent purchases, including highlighting their effects on prices, usually influences future conduct.

This approach will encourage them to analyze ways to avoid this problem. By allowing professionals from other areas to express themselves, the expectation is that suggestions for improvement will appear, allowing for the progress of the purchasing process.

It is convenient to consider that this action has an immediate positive effect, which loses efficiency over time. As a recommendation, based on the information collected in the requisition control analysis, it is vital to reinforce communication with applicants periodically.

3.1.3 Develop Standards and Procedures Manual

The previous item showed how a lack of information about purchasers' procedures leads to repeated requests for urgent delivery.

David Burt[13] points out the potential consequence of purchases in the short term: "The stoppage of production is the most serious problem resulting from the insufficient acquisition lead time."

Many company activities are unclear, principally about "how to execute them." This situation highlights the usefulness of manuals of standards and procedures: to improve the performance of different sectors, interdepartmental relations, and individuals.

The standards and procedures manual facilitates an understanding of how each area works. It is so important that it will be the subject of a specific analysis. A manual details the execution of activities in each department and guides employees on how to carry out tasks and what regulations to follow.

The updating of manuals must be constant, and to be effective and produce positive results, they require intense action from top management to ensure compliance with the established standards.

Undoubtedly, the benefits of developing and using a procedure manual written with the participation of all involved are as follows:

---

[13] BURT, David N; PETCAVAGE, Sheila; PINKERTON, Richard. Proactive Purchasing in the Supply Chain: The Key to World-Class Procurement. 1st edition. USA: McGraw Hill, December 6, 2011

- Detailed flows: clarify doubts about procedures essential to the accomplishment of the sector's tasks and how applicants should proceed;
- Standardize activities: a crucial factor in the operation of each business, enabling employees to act similarly, avoiding the execution of similar tasks in diverse ways;
- Improvement of activities: when preparing or revising a procedures manual, ideas emerge to optimize flows and eliminate documents, simplifying the operations of the purchasing area and the company itself;
- Team training: having the manual contributes to the better performance of professionals, especially when hiring new employees.

Despite the apparent benefits of adopting manuals, it is prudent to be careful when preparing and disseminating them to avoid limiting employee creativity.

Another significant action is to study situations in which exceptions are necessary and how to manage procedural deviations, so they do not become routine.

During the preparation of standards, demonstrate "who," "when," and "how" to carry out the activities. However, writing long and tiring rules to detail a subject is unnecessary.

As the saying goes, less is more. Thus, the description of the procedure must be simple and didactic.

The intranet should host norms, such as those mentioned, available for consultation by all interested parties.

3.1.4 Establishing priorities

Experience confirms that part of the rush orders the purchasing department receives are not emergencies.

Every purchaser has experienced the frustration of struggling to locate and enable the delivery of an urgently requested material in record time and later discovering that the item remained untouched in the warehouse for days without the requester picking it up.

This situation, although illogical, occurs with irritating regularity. The following are some of the reasons for this recurrence.

The appeal to preference in attendance, a desire of many people, is one explanation for this unjustifiable action.

The higher the position of the requesting department in the organizational pyramid, the more pressure demand imposes. However, the manager is often unaware of the need for a quick purchase solution, as an assistant uses his name to speed up the acquisition.

It is worth highlighting the other side of the coin; several executives focused on the best for the organization and did not use their position in the chart to obtain advantages.

On the other hand, it is common to have acquisitions stuck on purchasers' desks, who have difficulty identifying which ones are a priority.

Because companies often have more demands than the processing capacity of purchasers, it is necessary to determine a hierarchy for each situation and, of course, address the most critical issues first.

For this purpose, material classifications help define the order of precedence.

3.1.5 Purchasing planning integrated with organizational strategic planning

The purchaser focuses on executing, postponing, or skipping the planning stage for urgent purchases. The execution of tasks without planning produces awful results that are unacceptable to the winning companies.

Ideally, procurement professionals should plan their actions, aligning them with the organization's general planning.

Companies pursue high-quality standards in processes. However, they do not always plan the execution of internal activities with the necessary competence, which leads to the opposite situation than desired.

No business activity can provide a well-thought-out plan for setting the course. Paraphrasing: If each professional in the company works in a different direction, achieving practical goals and succeeding in management will be challenging.

At this point, it is appropriate to compare the traditional closed planning model (present in countless organizations) with the current dynamic model (conquering space in the business world).

With a long-term focus, strategic planning defines the company's global guidelines, emanating from the organization's top management and adopted by everyone, serving as a guide in developing other planning phases.

On the other hand, tactical planning focuses on the medium-term, and its elaboration starts with strategic planning and points out the objectives necessary for its fulfillment. Professionals positioned in the middle range of the organizational context develop it.

Operational planning, emphasizing the short term, starts with the guidelines and objectives from the previous stages and stipulates which goals to pursue. The conception and execution are attributions of the companies' organizational base members. Figure 3.2. illustrates this point.

Figure 3.2.: Types of Planning

The contemporary business planning model does not exclude traditional steps. Decisions, even those from the top of the organizational pyramid, can result from actions initiated in any part of the company.

Making decisions in the "top-down" direction, typical of the traditional pattern, loses its strength.

In the new models, employees from any area can play a leading role in strategic decisions by simply exposing their points of view. This innovative way of acting makes the process more dynamic, participatory, and likely to succeed.

The graphical representation is in Figure 3.3.:

Figure 3.3.: Planning Model

Again, it is worth mentioning the decisive role of the purchasing area in formulating any well-prepared planning, as its actions are fundamental to the company's operation.

For example, a hypothetical company will exhibit at a trade show. At this stage, the marketing department developed ideas with the sales team and communicated only to the board of directors about the activities, materials, and services necessary to install and operate a fair stand.

The exhibition will begin 60 days after the presentation of the plans to the board.

Just days before the event starts, the commercial manager asked the purchasing area for various materials, equipment, and services necessary for the construction and operation of the stand, following the rules of the fair administrator.

The purchasing department consulted the suppliers and found that the delivery of most materials will take at least 90 days, which is incompatible with the beginning of the fair.

This resulted in an uncomfortable situation, and the leading cause was a lack of planning and teamwork.

The example, although fictional, illustrates the negative consequences of an absence of planning. Enabling event participation as per initial expectations will require issuing multiple rush orders, and even then, there are no guarantees that vendors will deliver all materials on time.

The most common benefits of meticulously crafting a business plan, regardless of the market segment, are:

- Develop action alternatives for the entire organization;
- Empower everyone involved to achieve superior results;
- Encourage synergistic behavior of organizational units;
- Encourage the involvement of professionals in complying with pre-established guidelines, goals, and objectives;
- Provide employees with the opportunity to step away from routine activities and think about the organization as a whole;
- Simplify and streamline the decision-making process;
- Transforming a reactive company into an initiative-taking company.

3.1.6 Create a communication channel and keep applicants informed

Sometimes, the internal public's dissatisfaction with the purchasing area is noticeable, mainly because of the lack of information about the progress of acquisitions.

Unfortunately, many complaints are valid, as few purchasing areas regularly inform internal customers about the status of material requests.

In addition to wear and tear, the absence of explanations increases the incidence of urgent purchase orders. It is a matter of expectation because if the user distrusts the efficiency of purchasers, he will resort to any means that assures him security.

When ordering an item, any requester imagines a period for receiving what they need. If a human resources analyst requests folders and pictures for a training that will take place in five days, two scenarios arise:

- The delivery takes 15 days, which is longer than the forecast; therefore, he will consider the purchasing area inefficient;
- The folders arrive in three days, a shorter interval than expected, and this alone will be enough for the HR analyst to perceive the purchasing area as competent.

In either case, the label would not be adequate, as it was the exclusive result of the user's expectations, which created them without any objective reason in the definition.

Avoiding unrealistic expectations is essential, and the prerequisite is constantly informing applicants and inhibiting erroneous predictions about the acquisitions.

Keeping in touch with the other areas wins the confidence of the company's internal public. Never forget that purchasers' lack of credit leads to urgent orders.

Today, companies with integrated management systems and efficient interdepartmental communication channels have no reason to keep internal customers unaware of purchase progress.

Many organizations have systems that allow the applicant to view the status of their application online.

Almir[14] explains how technology improves performance: "The optimization of all processes in the supply chain can be achieved with the appropriate use of information technology."

3.1.7 Properly dimension the team and improve its quality

Companies typically allocate a large volume of purchases to a small group of purchasers. This scenario encourages emergency and poorly planned expenditures. Using performance measurement tools in the purchasing sector can avoid such a situation.

Purchasing managers must monitor the volume of orders received daily against the number of purchasers available. For several reasons, with cost reduction in the spotlight, companies are reluctant to change their purchasing structure, even in the face of an increase in the number of requests received by the area.

Such action is a severe mistake, as purchase orders pile up, while the department will have fewer employees to perform tasks efficiently.

As Frazelle[15] puts it, "The complexity and scope of supply chain decision-making are increasing much faster than the decision support resources - models, metrics, education, methodology, management, and software tools - are developing."

---

[14] SANTOS, Almir G; ELIA, Bruno de S; MAGALHÃES, Eduardo; PINTO, Geraldo. Gestão da Cadeia de Suprimentos (Supply Chain Management). 1st edition. Brazil; FGV Management, October 1, 2014

[15] FRAZELLE, Edward H. Supply Chain Strategy: Unleash the Power of Business Integration to Maximize Financial, Service, and Operations Performance. 2nd edition. USA: McGraw-Hill, October 27, 2017

Another question concerns the qualifications of the purchasers. Some professionals lack the necessary and sufficient conditions to exercise the function. It is not their fault if training is insufficient.

A purchaser accumulates knowledge by frequently performing tasks as in any other activity. Together with the search for information and methods, this action helps improve their ability to carry out assignments. This behavior is essential for professional development.

Investing in frequent training of professionals subordinate to the purchasing area raises the level of the department itself.

David Burt[16] focuses on managing investments in supply system resources successfully: "The development and management of supply chains and supply networks require significant investment, mainly in the form of human resources. The proper selection, training, and education of the individuals involved in these activities and the application of software systems can reduce the necessary investments".

3.1.8 Analyze the quantities of emergency requests

A fundamental issue that purchasers constantly ignore is to confirm whether the requested amount is crucial for immediately responding to the situation's urgency.

Often, only part of the quantity must arrive in the short term, and if this is the case, the correct procedure is to buy only that volume quickly. Getting the balance is possible through a standard purchase procedure.

Hypothetically, a purchaser receives an urgent request for 200 units of a particular lamp. A brief analysis of the item's consumption profile is sufficient to prove that buying everything immediately is unnecessary.

When consulting the user, he finds that, from the order of 200 units, 50 are enough to meet the immediate need.

As this is a material whose quantity has little influence on the price, the purchaser must urgently buy only the 50 lamps that satisfy the urgent necessity.

[16] BURT, David N; PETCAVAGE, Sheila; PINKERTON, Richard. Proactive Purchasing in the Supply Chain: The Key to World-Class Procurement. 1st edition. USA; McGraw Hill, December 6, 2011

3.2 Situations with scarcity in the market

From an economic perspective, scarcity refers to an imbalance between the supply of goods by producers and customer demand.

This situation can result from a sudden or excessive increase on the demand side or an abrupt reduction in the availability of goods for consumption.

Occasionally, a mismatch occurs due to an event independent of the will or action of market agents, such as a natural catastrophe that paralyzes or eliminates means of production and, consequently, reduces supply.

Another possibility is that the market dynamics discourage the producer from offering a specific item, such as a moment of falling prices.

Whatever the cause of the shortage, its occurrence directly affects the purchasing department's performance. The significant repercussions are as follows:

- Stock shortage;
- Stoppage of productive or commercial activity;
- A vigorous rise in acquisition costs;
- Potential to leave unattended customers.

These consequences are undesirable, promoting losses for the company and discrediting the purchaser's image.

What actions can purchasing professionals take to mitigate the effects of a problematic shortage? Below are options:

- Achieving priority among the few suppliers with inventory: It is a big mistake to imagine that all customers are the same for the seller. Kindness opens doors, and a lousy approach pushes the customer to the end of the line. Factors such as the volume usually ordered, regular purchases, maintenance of long-term contracts, and good relationships with sales representatives are decisive in winning the supplier's preference over other customers, determining who gets the supply on time and who goes hungry. To minimize supply risks, ideally, the purchaser should consider the above factors when negotiating and deciding to whom to place the order.
- Existence of substitute materials: it is not the case of having various brands; instead, there is a product that is not the best but meets the minimum necessary and sufficient requirements to replace the selected

item, at least for a brief period. For example, let it be a raw material supplied in bulk and available in different grain sizes. A specific particle size leads to higher production efficiency, reduction in the consumption of energy sources, and lower costs. However, if such granulometry is scarce, others may meet the company's needs, despite the temporary sacrifice of performance parameters and the impact on the result.

- Development of new suppliers: Occasionally, scarcity occurs in a specific location. Suppose the search for a supply source extends beyond this region; the chances of overcoming the problem increase. Therefore, following the market, monitoring shortages, and determining where to find the material is necessary. It highlights the importance of restricting this action to materials essential to the company's activities. If there is a lack of stationery material, there will be no disastrous consequences for smoothly running the company's activities.

It is important to emphasize that shortages affect all market players. However, those that take longer to identify the event and seek alternatives for supply will be the most affected.

In this aspect, the purchaser needs to continuously monitor the supply of essential items for the company's activity to notice potential supply problems quickly.

When detecting a potential shortage early, it is essential to promptly inform the user and stock management areas of an eventual acquisition in volumes higher than usual to overcome the period of lack of supply in the market.

3.3 Incorrect specifications

Another frequent problem is that the requisition issuer incorrectly describes the material, creating uncertainty for both the purchaser and the seller.

According to Baily[17], the UK Department of Industry "identified that inadequate specification of needs and poor communication between the customer and the supplier are among the main causes of the subsequent problems."

---

[17] BAILY, Peter; FARMER David; CROCKER Barry; JESSOP David. Procurement Principles and Management in the Digital Age. Twelfth edition. USA: Pearson, October 21, 2021

Inaccurate specifications cause delays in completing the purchase, as they can influence the issuance of a purchase order containing a material different from that intended.

When this is the case, repairing the problem is undoubtedly complex and often fruitless, as it can be impossible to develop a solution. On these occasions, the interpretation will be that the purchaser failed.

For the accurate realization of the acquisition, the material specification must perfectly characterize the object of the contract, even to enable the proper transmission of information to the supplier.

When the requisition is incorrect or incomplete, the purchaser wastes valuable time exchanging messages with the requester to clarify the material to purchase.

Regrettably, however, it is when happens that the supplier identifies the flaw in the description when receiving a request for a proposal.

This situation is objectionable because it exposes an actual deficiency of the company (it cannot even reliably clarify the material it intends to acquire) and forces the process's restart.

The most harmful consequence of an incorrect specification is the chance of purchasing different and unusable material and the impossibility of returning it, either because of the supplier's intransigence or because it is an exclusive fabrication for that customer.

The occurrence of this nature harms the organization. With all the information and communication tools available, living with such a lack of professional preparation is unacceptable.

One point is undeniable: the purchasing area bears a significant share of responsibility for the recurrence of incorrectly specified requests.

This statement comes from the fact that it is trivial for a purchaser to continue receiving documents with incorrect information without worrying and taking steps to correct the situation.

In contrast to the common sense of inducing the attempt to execute the purchase, often trying to guess the actual object of the requisition, the appropriate action is the prompt return to the applicants of all incorrect orders, whether they originated electronically or not.

Although, at first sight, such an attitude seems rude, it aims to guide the applicant to be judicious in preparing any order and minimizing the risk of an unwanted conclusion in subsequent purchases.

Specification text faults are of diverse types, and the most common are:

- Incomplete description: the requested material is insufficiently described, preventing proper identification;
- Wrong material codes: it usually results from consulting outdated catalogs. Applicants should update the prospectus periodically, requesting suppliers or consulting the manufacturer's website;
- Wrong units of measurement standards: requests are unaware of measurement standards or make mistakes when preparing requisitions and ask for different quantities than desired.

Similarly, as discussed for urgent acquisitions, the purchaser must act permanently with applicants who incur the error of miswriting the specifications to reduce the incidence. This behavior will improve the results, and there will be less pressure at work.

3.4 Supplier failures

The usual relationship between purchasers and sellers is a challenging problem for those working on purchases, which can negatively affect their professional image.

This relationship suggests that both professionals are inseparable, and this perception makes the purchaser co-responsible for supply failures.

Negative repercussions arise from poor supplier performance. Usually, in deliveries assured by the seller, failures happen. The problems include unfulfilled deliveries, the supply of out-of-specification products, or even defective materials.

Whenever there is an incidence of failures of this nature, the purchasing professional faces difficulties explaining the actual delivery condition to his department's management or to his company colleagues eager to receive the requested material.

With exceptions, the biggest culprit for these adversities is the purchasing department, as it is the responsibility of this area to select the most appropriate suppliers for each case.

The following chapters address supplier selection, qualification, and performance evaluation, with suggestions for minimizing supplier failures.

3.5 Excessive bureaucracy

Purchasing departments manage large sums of money; each order implies a disbursement obligation with the supplier.

To ensure the integrity of the processes, companies prepare multiple steps to complete the acquisition, which is potentially unnecessary.

Because of this obsession with ensuring the fairness of acquisitions, the structure of the purchase flowchart for completing a process forces purchasers to work beyond reason!

Such a procedure definition is nonsense when successful companies focus on agile systems that enable them to overcome the difficulties imposed by the market in competing for survival.

From this perspective, disrupting the routine of those responsible for purchases with debatable procedures and without any relevant purpose does not help the company maximize its effectiveness.

Having prior planning of activities allows the use of techniques capable of providing agility and, at the same time, ensuring that the administration maintains control over the processes of the areas.

One of the objectives of this book is to examine ways of working in the described configuration, proposing tools to reduce bureaucracy in purchasing products and contracting services.

3.6 Interference

Eventually, employees from other areas believe they can acquire essential materials for their activities.

They confuse the skills required to make personal purchases with those essential to the professional field. Such a belief is unrealistic, as buying for oneself as an individual is entirely different from buying for an organization.

This false perception of knowing how to buy induces people from other areas to interfere in the purchasing department's activities. Often, they even deal with and decide on matters that are the exclusive competencies of the purchaser.

Management must stipulate strict rules to inhibit the occurrence of intrusions, even because they cause high costs.

In practice, it is, at the very least, illogical for companies to impose rigorous standards for purchasing professionals to develop and complete all acquisitions and to "close their eyes" when other sectors order products without complying with any criteria and employing methods prohibited to purchasers.

Frequently, to conclude the purchase, it is necessary to have at least three proposals. On the other hand, it is common for a user to request goods from a supplier and then send the invoice for regularization by the purchasing department as if this were the correct procedure.

Rejecting such conduct is essential, and it is up to the purchasing department to resist this interference.

3.7 Execution of tasks from other departments

Just as other departments should not perform activities assigned to the purchasing department, the opposite is true; a purchaser should never execute activities that are the exclusive responsibility of different sectors.

A purchaser's time is scarce, and when he is doing other people's work, there is a loss of opportunities to buy better and obtain beneficial results.

Sometimes purchasers need to perform tasks at odds with their roles. Various analyze invoices, calculate price adjustments, verify goods received, and perform other functions unrelated to the purchasing activity. Some readers may disagree and interpret such occurrences as reasonable for allowing purchasers to learn different activities.

Realistically, it may be impossible to escape the practice in small companies. On the other hand, in medium and large companies with multiple departments, it is not acceptable for purchasers to perform functions outside their responsibilities.

While a purchasing analyst examines an invoice, a typical financial activity, he fails to negotiate a purchase condition that could save money.

This concept does not eliminate purchasers' obligation to collaborate with other company units when such actions become necessary.

CHAPTER 4

CLASSIFICATIONS OF MATERIALS

With organization and time, you find the secret to doing everything and doing it well.

Pythagoras[18]

Organizing materials according to physical characteristics, use, value, or even from the source that makes them available is a valid instrument to increase efficiency in executing tasks in the procurement department.

This simple measure positively affects purchase processing, and the structuring of the registration of materials and suppliers will benefit.

The technical literature details systems designed to order items according to their characteristics. The ABC classification of materials is among those with the most significant potential to improve the productivity of purchasing professionals.

The ABC system is a quantitative criterion; it uses measurable attributes to propose an order and definition of importance.

Therefore, it is an objective procedure.

4.1 ABC Classification of Materials

The origin of the ABC classification or ABC curve dates back to the end of the 19th century in Italy, when the Italian scientist, sociologist, and economist Vilfredo Pareto (1848-1923) developed the method.

Pareto sought a way to represent income distribution among the inhabitants of Italy at the time. After extensive research, he devised a system demonstrating how a small portion of the Italian population accumulated much of the country's income while most had far fewer resources.

---

[18] Pythagoras (580-497 B.C.) was an important Greek mathematician and philosopher of antiquity. Author of the "Pythagorean Theorem"

Pareto achieved his goals with the developed work, successfully proving the phenomenon of income concentration.

Figure 4.1. shows a graphical representation of the work Pareto has done.

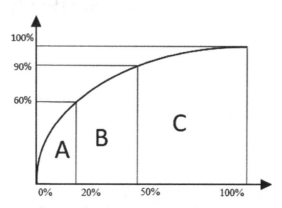

Figure 4.1.: graphical representation of the ABC curve

Decades later, in the middle of the 20th century, extending the concepts of Pareto studies to other areas of human knowledge proved feasible.

Specifically, in the case of materials management, Pareto findings have broad applications. A quantitative analysis of organizations' stocks helps identify a strong correlation with the results of ABC method analyses regarding statistical distribution.

Although structuring the ABC classification is simple, it will be more didactic to use an example, in this case, the fictional company Little Ice Food Industry.

Little Ice is an ice cream maker. The list of raw materials is in the table in Figure 4.2. The values presented correspond to the consumption of the last 12 months, in financial terms, resulting from the multiplication of the acquisition value by the amount consumed in the period.

Item	Consumption ($)
Pineapple	90.000
Lychee	11.000
Blueberry	9.000
Acidulant	5.000
Sugar	70.000
Cocoa	160.000
Cashew	19.000

Preservative	15.000
Vanilla essence	1.000
Hydrogenated fat	20.000
Banana	7.000
Orange	50.000
Milk	180.000
Condensed Milk	3.000
Lemon	120.000
Mango	30.000
Passion fruit	40.000
Strawberry	140.000
Cherry	13.000
Tangerine	17.000
Sum	1.000.000

Figure 4.2.: Little Ice raw materials

Building an ABC classification starts with sorting materials according to individual values.

The item with the highest financial consumption will occupy the first position, the second with the highest consumption will come next, and so on, until the last article, the one with the lowest consumption.

Building a second table derived from the first one with this criterion is possible. The results are in Figure 4.3.:

	Item	Consumption ($)	% Item	% Accumulated
1	Milk	$180.000,00	18,0%	18,0%
2	Cocoa	$160.000,00	16,0%	34,0%
3	Strawberry	$140.000,00	14,0%	48,0%
4	Lemon	$120.000,00	12,0%	60,0%
5	Pineapple	$90.000,00	9,0%	69,0%
6	Sugar	$70.000,00	7,0%	76,0%
7	Orange	$50.000,00	5,0%	81,0%
8	Passion fruit	$40.000,00	4,0%	85,0%
9	Mango	$30.000,00	3,0%	88,0%
10	Hydrogenated fat	$20.000,00	2,0%	90,0%
11	Cashew	$19.000,00	1,9%	91,9%
12	Tangerine	$17.000,00	1,7%	93,6%
13	Preservative	$15.000,00	1,5%	95,1%
14	Cherry	$13.000,00	1,3%	96,4%

15	Lychee	$11.000,00	1,1%	97,5%
16	Blueberry	$9.000,00	0,9%	98,4%
17	Banana	$7.000,00	0,7%	99,1%
18	Acidulant	$5.000,00	0,5%	99,6%
19	Condensed Milk	$3.000,00	0,3%	99,9%
20	Vanilla essence	$1.000,00	0,1%	100,0%
	Total	$1.000.000	100,0	

Figure 4.3.: List of raw materials ordered

The subsequent step involved grouping the materials into three sets. The most valuable materials belong to Class "A", approximately 20% of the items and equivalent to 60% of total consumption. They are essential in financial terms. In the example, items A would be the first four in the table.

After items A, there is a second group, including the products with considerable consumption value. They form Class "B".

Naturally, Class B materials are less economically significant than Class "A" materials, but they are still a fundamental part of the overall consumption. About 30% of the items are in group "B" and correspond to about 30% of the global consumption. In this case, it would be items 5 to 10.

Finally, the last set, Class "C", is formed by the least essential items on the list if the criterion is the consumption value.

Lower-value materials comprise about half of all items but account for approximately 10% of consumption. Here would be the last ten materials from the table.

One pertinent question is the benefit of this rating for a company such as Little Ice. The ordering by monetary criterion shows the variations in the values of the components of each group, confirming that they are items of variable merit. Because they are unequal, they deserve different treatment.

Class "A" materials concentrate more value; maintaining high inventories implies immobilizing considerable capital, an undesirable situation. Good management recommends keeping smaller stocks in this group, minimizing the immobilization of financial resources.

However, it is unwise to ignore the risk of shortages by maintaining product volume at lower levels. With reduced stock, the strategy to ensure service to users is to provide high turnover, that is, frequent inputs of materials in line with outputs, preserving the constant meeting of needs.

The reader noticed that managing inventory turns is a complex task. With the intense physical movement of products, strict control is essential, enabling synchronization between receiving and dispatching materials.

The approach for class "B" is similar. As they are materials that immobilize a significant part of financial resources, their stocks must remain below the average, with the constant movement of inputs, in line with consumption, and subject to a proficient level of control.

The conduct for items belonging to class "C" is the opposite. As this group is composed of materials with low consumption values, having larger volumes in stock will not cause significant immobilization of capital.

Working with larger volumes reduces the number of deliveries, with fewer goods receipts. Since storing more quantities minimizes the risk of material shortages, this is a valid strategy and does not require strict control.

Below is a summary of the exhibition:

- Class A:
  - o Low stock level;
  - o High inventory turnover;
  - o Strict control.
- Class B
  - o Low stock level;
  - o High/medium inventory turnover;
  - o Strict control.
- Class C
  - o Higher inventory level;
  - o Low inventory turnover;
  - o Less stringent control.

The purchasing department engages in successful inventory policies by establishing personalized relationships with key suppliers.

Sollish[19] details this possibility: "Other strategies developed with procurement can similarly support operational strategies. These include just-in-time (JIT) delivery, supplier-managed inventory (SMI), and a variety of other programs developed to enhance well-run operations and eliminate waste and non-value-added costs."

---

[19] SOLLISH, Fred; SEMANIK, John. The Procurement and Supply Manager's Desk Reference. 2nd edition. USA: Wiley, May 23, 2012

CHAPTER 5

PURCHASING ORGANIZATION

"Let's go invent tomorrow instead of worrying about what happened yesterday."

Steve Jobs[20]

C ompanies dedicate time and energy to identifying the best organization for their functional structures and defining the appropriate characterization of the attributions of each area.

The correct characterization of the tasks assigned to each professional and the best way to perform them are the fundamental premises for achieving high efficiency. This concern is also present in the purchasing sphere.

This chapter details suggestions for purchasing activities, emphasizing the expected benefits.

5.1 Centralization x Decentralization

With the constant growth of companies, often resulting from acquisitions and mergers, it is common to have units in geographically distant locations. Therefore, deciding between having a single centralized purchasing department in one of the units or having smaller purchasing departments in each one is tricky.

Both solutions have advantages and disadvantages. There is no single valid rule for this choice. The characteristics of each organization should guide managers in choosing the configuration to adopt.

Studying the advantages and disadvantages of each of the possibilities would be helpful. The table in Figure 5.1. provides this comparison.

---

[20] Steven Paul Jobs was an inventor and entrepreneur famous as co-founder and CEO of Apple, and for revolutionizing six sectors: personal computers, animated films, music, phones, tablets, and digital publications

TYPE	CENTRALIZED	DECENTRALIZED
Volume	Higher volume gives the purchaser more bargaining power, due to the economy of scale, in the manufacture and sale of products	Less quantity decreases purchaser power in negotiations with a direct effect on prices
Prices	Single price for each item, without interference from geographic location, ensuring uniform costs	Prices for the same material vary from unit to unit, making cost analysis difficult
Stocks	Better inventory management due to more control over the global volume of materials	Faster in meeting the needs of each unit
Shortages and emergencies	More chances of success to overcome shortages in the supplier market	Faster action on purchases in emergency conditions
Standards and power	Homogeneity in general purchasing procedures	Different procedures in each unit for the same type of acquisition
Authority	More power in the face of top management	More authority and responsibility for local administration.

Figure 5.1.: Contrast between centralization and decentralization of the purchasing department

Knowing the advantages and disadvantages helps to decide between models, considering the benefits and drawbacks of each one.

A widespread solution is to adopt a hybrid pattern of the two alternatives:

> A central purchasing department, responsible for the most relevant acquisitions, allocated to the most important or best-located unit and small purchasing sectors installed in the other units, solely for the supply of specific or low-value items.

In this decision, the concept that items of classes A and B, when purchased in a unique location, help to take advantage of negotiating a greater volume should have an expressive weight. A recommendation for this range of materials is to centralize purchases to generate more volume.

Material acquired by a unit with delivery in another does not constitute any management problem.

The allocation of low-value purchases in units uses human resources more effectively. David Burt[21] highlights how small purchases are a source of concern in purchasing management: "Small orders are a perennial problem in all organizations and a serious problem in some. An examination of a typical company's purchase order history reveals that a sizeable percentage (sometimes up to 80 percent) of its purchases involves an expense of less than $ 250. However, those purchases consist of a small percentage (rarely more than 10 percent) of the company's annual dollar expenditures."

5.2 Internal and external relations

Due to the nature of its attributions, the purchasing area maintains an intense relationship with the company's internal public. Actions to strengthen relationships are essential to ensure that the needs of various departments receive adequate attention.

The characteristics of procurement activity occasionally give rise to conflicts because of the differences between what requesters want and what purchasers can do without exceeding the limits stipulated for processing purchases.

Figure 5.2. shows a table in which spending impacts are critical and shows the natural antagonism of an organization's area objectives:

ANTAGONISM AMID THE OBJECTIVES OF THE AREAS		
AREAS	**AREAS GOALS**	**PURCHASING TARGETS**
SALES	Enable an increase in the number of customer orders using all necessary means	Meet demands arising from the volume of sales orders without breaching estimated costs
PRODUCTION	Produce within the deadlines and quality set with maximum productivity	Plan deliveries according to production schedule, but without exceeding costs

[21] BURT, David N; PETCAVAGE, Sheila; PINKERTON, Richard. Proactive Purchasing in the Supply Chain: The Key to World-Class Procurement. 1st edition. USA: McGraw Hill, December 6, 2011

MATERIALS	Reduce inventory levels and purchase materials at the lowest cost, ensuring the organization's supply	Acquire materials at the lowest cost, fulfilling the inventory delivery schedule
FINANCE	Manage the organization's financial resources to preserve cash flow	To be able to pay with a shorter term if the financial gain justifies

Figure 5.2.: Antagonism between purchasing and user objectives

It is always opportune to emphasize the pressures on the areas to conduct assignments with maximum efficiency and effectiveness. In this context, there is antagonism between individual objectives. However, the results will be positive with competent management of such a situation.

The purchasing analyst is the agent responsible for understanding users' aspirations and seeking the best practices to process requests, always complying with the conditions established by the company's rules and procedures.

The purchasing department acts as a supplier to the other areas of the organization, so colleagues expect more agility in meeting demands.

It is unreasonable to ignore that the department is an advisory body to other sectors, which are customers of the purchasing area. It is the concept of an internal customer always in evidence.

Nonetheless, the advisory function does not subordinate purchases to other areas. Purchasing independence is a prerequisite for guaranteeing the company's desired performance. The department must work cohesively in action but be independent in the decision.

5.3 The purchaser's functions

Departmental structures are subject to constant change. There has recently been a significant flattening of organizational charts, remodeling the traditional administration forms of areas.

The purchasing departments are not different. The major transformation is not in the position title but in the scope of the functions, eliminating the limits between domestic purchases and those made abroad.

Historically, an entire department conducted imports segregated from professionals responsible for national purchases.

The trend is to unify these two activities. When processing a material request, the same professional must research the local suppliers and those established abroad.

This new scenario requires more skills and qualifications. Knowing the administrative, bureaucratic, and legal activities of import processes is essential. Proficiency in other languages is one of the primary requirements.

Integrating all actions to work locally and globally becomes the biggest challenge.

Frazelle points out companies' inattention to developing their professionals[22]: "Less than 10 percent of supply chain professionals have any formal education or training in supply chain management, and this education is often outdated and/or impractical."

Purchasers are constantly subject to additional responsibilities, increasing their decision-making autonomy. In line with the addition of duties, demands on the professional's performance grow together.

Part of the traditional activities remains, even because they are indispensable. In Figure 5.3. are the most common:

DESCRIPTION	Relevancy
Advice on cost reduction programs	Medium
Develop new suppliers	Medium
Follow market trends and new product launches	Medium
Guide suppliers on the implementation of quality projects	Medium
Have material specifications filed in the system	Medium
Keep files of general documents (registration, proposals, orders) up to date	Low
Monitor supplier performance	High
Negotiate with suppliers the conditions for making purchases	High
Organize the computerized purchasing management system	Medium
Preserve suppliers' purchase history with records of deliveries, quality, and price	Medium
Process purchase requisitions	High
Qualify suppliers for registration purposes	High
Require corrective action from suppliers for materials and services delivered in breach of specification	High
Solve problems related to suppliers	Medium

Figure 5.3.: Purchaser's main activities

[22] FRAZELLE, Edward H. Supply Chain Strategy: Unleash the Power of Business Integration to Maximize Financial, Service, and Operations Performance. 2nd edition. USA: McGraw-Hill, October 27, 2017

5.4 Competencies framework

Specific attributions are naturally controversial, and it is possible to highlight the following:

- designate who can authorize a purchase;
- indicate who can approve a requisition for materials;
- establish the cases the purchaser has full autonomy to finalize;
- define who has the authority to approve high-value purchases.

These are all examples of the so-called "decision competence." The purchasing process requires decisions at every step, from issuing a material request to authorizing payment to the supplier.

In acquisitions that consume high values, the importance of decisions is significant, and the consequences for managers are serious.

In the previous chapters, we highlighted that each material has different importance. Analysis using material classifications reveals the need to adopt more sophisticated approaches for higher-value items.

Similar principles should guide the selection criteria for competency levels. Assigning the most critical decisions to senior managers generates the best results. Therefore, the lower hierarchical levels are responsible for decisions of lesser relevance.

A frequent mistake is to require senior management to review all cases, believing that this increases the security and integrity of processes.

There are two main effects of this type of requirement:

- The time required to complete the acquisition is exceptionally long, forcing the maintenance of more extensive stocks or increasing the risk of a lack of materials;
- Managers are overloaded and cannot examine the most critical cases with due rigor, as they need to analyze and release a large volume of purchases of insignificant amounts.

5.5 Manual of standards and procedures

The table of competencies is only valid and valuable if its existence and consultation forms are known to all internal customers.

These areas work through routines and rules that interface with other departments; the purchasing department is no exception. Therefore, what is the most efficient way to disclose various practices capable of interfering in each company area? The forum indicated for dissemination is the Manual of Standards and Procedures.

It is a compendium composed of routines and competencies defined for the company, with chapters covering all activities and the respective responsible.

The purchase procedures are part of a specific chapter that explains how to access the services provided to other sectors and details the appropriate way to use them.

The complete definition of the primary acquisition flow is a fundamental aspect of the list of issues in the purchasing area. This measure clarifies the internal customers about the entire document procedure, demonstrating the need for time to complete the process.

This information aligns with one of the most common sources of dissatisfaction among users of materials and services: the "excessive delay" in receiving the requested items.

Ignoring that everyone is familiar with the act of purchasing is a mistake. Internal customers buy personal items daily, which impairs their judgment about the purchasing professional's decision-making power and the speed of execution of an acquisition.

Usually, consumers are unaware of the steps the purchaser must follow until they receive the desired merchandise.

To remain valid, reviewing the manual's content must be ongoing. The current routine may not be suitable or may require modification.

It is worth highlighting the benefits arising from the adoption of information maintenance:

- Development of skills in performing functions: reading instructions improves knowledge of individual responsibilities and increases efficiency in performing various routine activities;
- Description of flows: detailing the sequence of activities to the various stakeholders, clarifies doubts, and streamlines administrative processes;
- Training and professional guidance: a manual provides tools to guide employees in the transfer process and promotions, at the beginning

of their careers, in short, those who change work areas. It avoids subjective guidelines;

• Standardization of activities: establishes an execution standard for each activity, ensuring that all company employees have the same conduct in similar situations and reducing errors due to lack of knowledge or misinformation.

The Standards and Procedures Manual must be available on a computerized system and accessible to all company employees.

5.6 Job rotation between purchasers

With rare exceptions, purchasers have a fundamental characteristic of performing their duties: they are generalists. In a moment, they purchase graphic products, and then it is up to them to buy a tool.

Minimizing uncertainties about the responsibilities of each professional will be easier with the division of purchasing areas by item family. However, structuring the process does not mean keeping the same people buying the same materials for a long time.

Relocating purchasers periodically and assigning different areas of activity optimizes professional development.

Job rotation makes it easier for everyone to know more about new segments of the supplier market.

The complexity lies in performing this rotation without losing quality in the performance of the functions. A period of adaptation for those involved in the process is helpful; consequently, the permanence time of each professional in managing the new supply segments should not be short.

Initially, professionals' efficiency in the new area tends to be lower. However, predecessors' support will minimize this phase and its associated difficulties.

The Bird Paper[23] lists helpful questions in the adaptation process for new functions: "Which user is the product for? Already ordered? When? How? In what quantities? Did he give any satisfaction? What is my freedom of maneuver concerning the express demand? Can I modify the lead time or the amounts to be ordered?"

---

[23] The Bird Paper. The Essential: Purchasing and Supply Chain Management. France: Douni.

Actions that generate valuable benefits in this process are:

- Follow-up and guidance from the supervisor or manager: in the weeks following the rotation, the supervisor must closely monitor the purchaser who switched the area, guiding him and ensuring the support of experienced colleagues in that segment.
- Maintain the same pattern of responsibilities: ensure that the new areas of activity have a level of importance like the previous ones and are compatible with the professional's capacity. Never transfer tasks from a purchasing assistant to a senior purchaser and vice versa.
- Periodicity: people should not change their areas of expertise frequently. They will not have the time to learn the new responsibilities, nor will they be prepared to transmit knowledge to future occupants. Setting a sufficiently extended period is essential for successful rotation.

Some colleagues criticize the rotation; however, this process has more benefits than disadvantages. Motivating professionals stagnant in their careers, breaking ties with salespeople, and reducing difficulties with continuing work on vacation, retirement, or leaving the company are sufficient reasons for adopting the tool.

CHAPTER 6

BASIC FLOW FOR PROCUREMENT PROCEDURES

"Labor is prior to and independent of the capital. Capital is only the fruit of labor and could never have existed if labor had not first existed. Labor is the superior of capital and deserves much the higher consideration."

Abraham Lincoln[24]

The performance of any company originates from the contribution of each activity area. To maximize an organization's results, it is essential to coordinate people's work and balance the actions of the various parties involved.

The correct distribution of people, the establishment of hierarchies between them, and the definition of the activities of each one, as well as their sequencing in the molds of a process, constitute the so-called organizational structure.

This ordering is a sine qua non condition for achieving individual (here, covered by sectors) and global (in terms of the company as a whole) objectives.

When it comes to the purchasing area, there is no way to be different, so the activities necessary to supply the organization must follow a process that prevents each professional from working at their convenience and compromising the area's performance.

For no other reason, as in any other area, purchases should have a previously established routine to ensure that the activities satisfy a basic dynamic.

Purchasing professionals should not have the authorization to conduct their processes without controls or rules.

Confidence that there is uniformity in procedures will depend on elaborating a compelling sequence of operations capable of agility in

---

[24] Abraham Lincoln (1809 - 1865) was the 16th president of the United States, between 1861 and 1865, and the first president of the US Republican Party.

acquisitions but without compromising the safety and integrity requirements in conducting the processes.

Efficient management of activities is essential for an organization to develop precisely according to needs.

David Burt[25] emphasizes how strategy and managerial quality are effective in the scope of supply: "To obtain the benefits of the supply chains, top administration must recognize the importance of supply chain management and support the necessary transformation to strategic status."

In this perspective, it is worth emphasizing appropriate steps to request the purchase of materials or services from the moment of need detection until the delivery by the supplier.

Therefore, in summary, we can list the following:

1. Identification of the need for resupply
   Any area finds that it is time to purchase a good or hire service and, to satisfy such demand, forwards a requisition to the purchasing sector.
2. The purchasing department researches the supplier market
   Having received or collected the essential information for the purchase (description of the desired item or service, code, quantity, packaging), the purchasing professional selects a list of suppliers and requests an offer.
3. Completion of acquisition or contracting
   Upon receipt of the proposals, it is essential to analyze them carefully to identify which best meets all the supply criteria. After this measure, it is up to the authorized persons to ratify the choice of the selling company.
4. Issuance of the purchase order or contract
   With the approval of the chosen proposal, authorization to deliver the material or the beginning of the execution of services occurs. This action results from preparing a document establishing a commercial link between the holder of the best offer and the client company.
5. Follow-up
   Monitor the delivery to ensure the deadline's compliance and confirm that the quality and quantity meet the established conditions.
6. Supply completed

[25] BURT, David N; PETCAVAGE, Sheila; PINKERTON, Richard. Proactive Purchasing in the Supply Chain: The Key to World-Class Procurement. 1st edition. USA: McGraw Hill, December 6, 2011

The delivery of the material or the execution of the service occurs. For this positive result, inspection is the only way to guarantee compliance with the contractual conditions.

7. Material or service is available to users

   Receipt of the material or service is insufficient to authorize its use by the requester. The assurance that the supply took place satisfactorily stems from an inspection process. Only after successfully completing this step will the applicant be able to utilize the product or service.

8. Pay the supplier

   The process will end when the supplier receives the amount stipulated in the purchase document, complying with the negotiated payment term.

A structured and well-defined flow is beneficial for minimizing doubts among all those involved in the acquisition, including internal customers, purchasing professionals, and suppliers.

Creating a flow but not publicizing it is fruitless. The recommendation is to communicate its availability for consultation to all areas to maximize benefits. To this end, the main steps for meeting the request deserve special attention, as well as the communication to those involved about the execution of activities after issuing the request for material.

This simple action avoids wearing out the purchasing area with other departments, which would judge the purchaser's work as unsatisfactory due to not knowing the procedures.

CHAPTER 7

REQUISITION OF MATERIALS

It is more important to do the things that must be done than to do the things as they should be done.

Peter Drucker[26]

Receiving material requisition in the purchasing department begins the acquisition process. It is worth clarifying that orders can be physical (on paper, increasingly outdated) or electronic.

Although issuing Material Requisition is not the responsibility of the purchasing area (except when the department is responsible for scheduling materials), it is incumbent upon it to carefully analyze the data provided and, with this simple measure, minimize doubts about the request objects. While all the details required for purchase are essential, evaluating specifications, terms, and quantities deserves particular emphasis.

Implementing a standardized form for requesting materials and services, with fields to specify the essential information in more detail, accelerates the process.

Even though it is reprehensible, the existence of companies in which the Purchasing Department admits that other areas request materials by any means, including telephone, is notorious.

Endorsing this practice implies the lack of standardization of procedures, leads to errors or omissions, and causes losses for the client organization and the seller.

Specific data are essential to start the purchase and are always present when ordering the materials. In Figure 7.1., there is a list of them:

Amount
Application or destination of the material
Budgeting or cost center unit

---

[26] Peter Ferdinand Drucker was an Austrian-born writer, professor, and management consultant, considered the father of modern management.

Cost estimate
Full description of the material
Identification of the person responsible for the requisition
Identification of the requesting area
Material code (internal or manufacturer)
Material lead time
Request date
Request identification (numeric or alphanumeric)
Unit of measure (mile, liter, bar, dozen)

Figure 7.1.: Information required for a material requisition

Regardless of its design, the material requisition form may not contain all the data. When existing fields are insufficient to record all essential information, specify what is missing in a separate document (catalogs, projects, descriptive memorials, reports, and attachments).

As mentioned in the chapter that studies the most frequent problems in the purchasing area, the number of requisitions filled out incorrectly is expressive. When there is critical inaccuracy capable of compromising the purchase, the recommendation is to return the document to the requesting sector. It is not a punitive instrument but an action to inform the issuer about inaccuracy in the record.

This action alone inhibits the possibility of future filling failures. Otherwise, the purchaser will waste time interpreting and correcting the wrong specifications.

The U.S. Government Accountability Office enforces the effects of misinformation on requisitions: "Military Standard Requisitioning and Issue Procedures (MILSTRIP) have improved the processing of requisitions. However, the maximum benefits of MILSTRIP have not been realized because many requisitions contain erroneous or incompatible data and cannot be processed routinely. One of the main causes of erroneous data being used was that current information was unavailable to the requisitioners."

A necessary step is to carefully observe the entry date for the requisition of materials in the purchasing department. Recording the entry date prevents future problems. Occasionally, several days elapsed between the issuance of the document and arrival at the purchasing department, usually due to bureaucratic actions in the sections before the purchases in the flow.

CHAPTER 8

DEVELOPMENT OF ALTERNATIVES

How you gather, manage, and use information will determine whether you win or lose.

Bill Gates[27]

The relationship between customers and suppliers has recently undergone a meaningful change. As a result, effective partnerships have multiplied, playing a fundamental role in the business environment.

Even in the face of this pattern change, it is foolhardy for a purchasing company to settle for only one supply source, especially when certain suppliers have exclusivity in delivering materials and providing services.

Customers should be aware of cases from single sources; it is up to the purchaser to analyze the list of suppliers and research possibilities for improvement. Thus, focusing on the number of registered companies is not mandatory. The competence of each supplier included in this registration deserves attention.

A formula for improving the list of supply sources is the search for promising new companies with the potential to deliver immediately or shortly.

However, in addition to finding new suppliers, purchasers should explore the possibility of developing alternative materials. This action is strategic as an instrument for improving supplier registration.

Identifying an alternative supply source allows gains in aspects not initially considered. Naturally, it is unreasonable to restrict the search for new sources solely to exclusivity cases. Shoshanah[28] highlights an advantage in the process: "Tax optimization is an additional consideration for some companies when it comes to locating sources ..."

---

[27] William Henry Gates III, known as Bill Gates, is an American entrepreneur, CEO, investor, philanthropist, and author known for founding, along with Paul Allen, Microsoft.

[28] COHEN, Shoshanah. Strategic Supply Chain Management: The Five Core Disciplines for Top Performance. 2nd edition. USA, McGraw-Hill, June 14, 2013

As a rule, the seller searches for new customers to increase the volume of business. The method of approach is invariable: the seller schedules a visit with the purchaser to present his product, extolling the material's qualities and emphasizing the company's reliability and relevant position in the market.

Customers constantly look for new sources of specific materials or services. Several large organizations incorporate specialized technical professionals who research new supply options to succeed in their missions.

In the case of small and medium-sized companies, it is not feasible to set up a separate structure to search for alternative suppliers. In such instances, the purchaser is responsible for performing the task.

Developing suppliers requires the involvement of other areas. The user can collaborate by passing on information, performing tests, and preparing technical specifications.

Regardless of who is responsible for the activity, criteria considering material relevance to the operation, whether in terms of value or importance of physical availability, must be the basis of the procedure.

It involves working with all the information available, even those of little utility, helping to find an alternative supply or discover a material to replace the one usually purchased.

The disadvantage of assigning the purchaser to search for new suppliers arises from the large volume of daily work. In this context, there is usually no time to manage non-routine activities.

In any case, someone must carry out the task, and the purchaser will be responsible if there is no alternative.

Suppliers can be located through catalogs, specific publications, fairs, or personal contacts resulting from visits made by suppliers.

In this endeavor, using the tools of Internet search engines is also valid, increasing the chances of finding suppliers anywhere in the country or, if applicable, in the world.

The search for new suppliers and the development of materials should not only focus on companies with the desired products. The most valuable form of development occurs when the purchasing specialist identifies a potential source that cannot deliver the desired product precisely but demonstrates that it can do so soon.

Naturally, the action described will depend on investments and research to obtain a product capable of replacing the current one.

From this perspective, involving colleagues from other areas is essential for obtaining the desired results. Davi Burt[29] emphasizes the importance of the participation of the quality management area in the process: "Quality professionals should be invited to participate in the supply management, from the development of new products, through the involvement in sourcing and the development of the supplier, aiming at minimizing quality problems during the current supply. The role and responsibilities of the quality area change significantly with the outsourcing of the manufacturing function. The quality department is relevant in qualifying potential suppliers. Then, it becomes responsible for monitoring the supplier's quality system and providing technical assistance if quality problems occur".

There are advantages when you have enough suppliers to compete to deliver needed items. Figure 8.1. lists the most important ones.

More security in stock replenishment
More bargaining power for the purchaser
Great possibilities of reduction in the price of the purchased product
Breaking of monopolies or cartels

Figure 8.1.: advantages of finding new suppliers or materials

Going deeper into the topic, it is worth analyzing the tendency to reduce the number of suppliers to improve procedures and manage cost reductions. Does the development of new suppliers go against this trend? It is possible to separate the answer to this question into two parts:

1. First, it is not valid to disregard cases involving signing long-term contracts with suppliers of certain materials and equipment, as in the automobile industry. A vehicle manufacturer contracts the entire production process through a few suppliers, who, in turn, purchase the necessary materials from other suppliers and, thus, successively form the so-called "supply chain."

2. Secondly, the development of alternative suppliers or materials does not conflict with the action above, being essential whenever necessary, whether for technical reasons such as costs, a change of supplier, or to have alternative materials available.

---

[29] BURT, David N; PETCAVAGE, Sheila; PINKERTON, Richard. Proactive Purchasing in the Supply Chain: The Key to World-Class Procurement. 1st edition. USA, McGraw Hill, December 6, 2011

CHAPTER 9

SUPPLIER QUALIFICATION

It is not the employer who pays the wages but the customer.

Henry Ford[30]

The benefits arising from the development of new suppliers may not exist if the purchaser conducts the process with companies of low credibility, interested only in profit in the short term.

Sellers who want to supply a product look for the person responsible for the purchasing department. Which purchaser has never been surprised by the annoying question: "But... what exactly are you buying?" Situations like this reinforce the importance of being cautious when starting a relationship with newly identified sources, especially for delivering essential goods.

Numerous suppliers eagerly seek to obtain the purchase order and only then begin worrying about delivering the requested item.

Consequently, as a matter of prudence, purchasing analysts should plan measures to work around unforeseen events when approving a new supplier company. Notably, regardless of the purchaser's good intentions when seeking an option, responsibility for any failure will be on the person who made the purchase.

The bird paper[31] addresses the possibility of a supplier not meeting expectations: "the risks are that the products or services provided by the supplier do not meet compliance or the implicit expectations of the client company."

To minimize the occurrence of delivery failures, suppliers must undergo a rigorous qualification process before registration.

---

[30] Henry Ford was an American mechanical engineer and entrepreneur, founder of the Ford Motor Company and author of the books My Philosophy of Industry and My Life and Work, and the first entrepreneur to use the concept of the assembly line to produce automobiles in large quantities, less time, and less cost.

[31] The Bird Paper. The Essential: Purchasing and Supply Chain Management. France, Douni

Throughout the procedure, it is mandatory to demand documentary evidence from sellers attesting to the required capabilities, including fully demonstrating that they are legally authorized to carry out the activity or supply materials subject to any restrictive legislation.

The purchaser must request certificates, contracts, and attestations, investigate suppliers' past performance, and visit the facilities, all according to the relevance of the object of the acquisition.

It is unnecessary to demand dozens of papers with needless information, from firms who apply to sell materials of everyday use and low value. In certain cases, the cost of documentation exceeds that of the acquisition itself.

The following is a suggestion for the qualification process without excluding the request for additional information that the reader deems pertinent:

- Current by-law: an essential document as it defines the company's activities, qualifications, and responsibilities. Reading by-laws helps identify who has the authority to decide on a company. Consider the problem if the customer believes it is hiring a specific service and finds that the professional who signed the contract did not have the competence to do so. In this situation, an agreement does not exist legally.
- Enrollment in the ENI - Employer Identification Number, also known as the Federal Tax Identification Number, is used to identify a business entity. It is one of the first steps in the process of starting companies.
- Proof of regularity before the Internal Revenue Service (IRS): documentation whose request is necessary because of the implications for the customer in case of supplier irregularity.
- Evidence of regular supply with quality and contracted volumes: this is an important check to determine if the candidate demonstrates experience in delivering the desired items and their standard of service in terms of quality, punctuality, and service to other client companies. The seller must provide certificates related to the materials it supplies, containing the necessary information about deliveries and quality. Connecting with the certificate issuer to ratify the information provides more security.
- Analysis of the supplier's installed capacity, comparing its backlog with the customer's needs: the supplier can manufacture excellent-quality products, but if it has reduced production capacity or is

committed to other customers, there is a risk of delivery failure. Therefore, the supplier must prove compliance with deadlines.

- Specific evidence related to the supplier's industry: products whose commercialization depends on authorization from government agencies, such as some medications. The seller must prove that it is legally authorized to supply such items.

- Examining the supplier's financial situation and analyzing the balance sheet and income statement for the last three years: qualified professionals must analyze the financial and accounting documents; preferably, accountants and economic analysts must oversee this evaluation. Balance sheets and financial information may indicate a company's inability to provide according to customer requirements. Naturally, the range of indexes resulting from the balance sheet is extensive, and the usefulness of each one depends on the analyst's purpose.

- Proof of Non-Bankruptcy: if the supplier does not present the certificate, it is worth considering excluding it from the process. Of course, this will depend on the restriction's severity and other factors.

- Relation of the company's monthly invoicing in the last 12 months: if the average monthly invoicing is incompatible with the value of the orders, there is a risk of contracting it because the difficulty in bearing the costs is a possibility. For example, a particular company has had an average monthly turnover of $150,000 for the past twelve months, and the usual order value for these items is approximately $400,000.00 monthly. With these data, the company would need a significant structural increase, so it would be imprudent to hire it, except for delivering small batches of materials.

These are simple measures that purchasers can implement to qualify suppliers. Acting cautiously, customers have suitable suppliers on their list.

CHAPTER 10

SUPPLIER MANAGEMENT

Basically, management means influencing the action.
Management is about helping organizations and units do what
needs to be done, which means action.

Henry Mintzberg[32]

Mintzberg's approach is beneficial when examining how best to manage suppliers. A competent purchasing department should contract the best suppliers and comply with all the procurement parameters.

In this context, what are the most appropriate objectives for ensuring success in supplier management? The following are suggestions.

10.1 Competitive costs

Shoshanah[33] revealed the difference between companies focused on costs and those that want only low costs: "Certainly, all companies need to keep an eye on costs. But this is different from competing in costs. Companies compete on cost-bid prices to attract cost-sensitive purchasers or maintain participation in a commodity market. This competition base requires highly efficient operations. The standardization of products and processes is fundamental, as well as the quality of suppliers and the control of production and stock".

Purchases of materials and services constitute the largest share of costs for most companies. Consequently, the issuance of the purchase order entails the compulsory allocation of part of the company's financial resources for payment to the beneficiary supplier of the operation.

---

[32] Henry Mintzberg is a Canadian author with over 170 articles and thirteen books published, the most famous being "The Rise and Fall of Strategic Planning".
[33] COHEN, Shoshanah. Strategic Supply Chain Management: The Five Core Disciplines for Top Performance. 2nd edition. USA: McGraw-Hill, June 14, 2013

Such a mandatory allocation generates a positive return if it contributes to cash generation more significantly than the amount invested. Naturally, any supply failure will cause a reverse effect.

In practical terms, selecting a company to supply stems from the actions incurred in the preceding phases. Efficiency in approving companies to be part of the supplier register and maintaining up-to-date information on previous purchases of the same item are prerequisites for a successful purchase decision.

Efficiently executing the previous steps increases the chances of finding a bidder that offers competitive costs.

At the time of purchase, numerous criteria are essential for choosing the best option: the lowest price, satisfactory quality, adequate delivery time, and desired quantity.

Cost-competitiveness, however, depends on going beyond these commonplace attributes in any acquisition. The shipping and packaging costs, price readjustment for some criteria, disbursements with technical assistance, and requirements to enjoy the product warranty deserve attention.

Correct assessment of the relative importance of each parameter and its contribution to the desired result are essential elements in choosing an alternative that offers the most competitive cost!

10.2 Share information with suppliers

Estimating the result of an activity is essential for good execution performance, as it allows the design of the process according to the objective.

This view also applies to the relationship between customers and suppliers. If Mintzberg's concept interprets management as an influencing action, an immediate conclusion is that sharing information with suppliers guides their efforts towards better satisfying customer expectations. Route planning depends on the starting and ending points.

Using a practical example, a company devises a strategic plan to increase sales by 20% annually. If the process is successful, sales will double in 4 years. In this planning line, it is reasonable to assume that suppliers must double the quantity they supply during this period. Are they prepared for the mission? Communicating the goal now will maximize the chances of success over time.

There are questions to share: increased production, the introduction of new products, and changes in projects are good points to analyze.

10.3 Identify inputs and services that are best suited to use

The market offers a wide range of products for the same application. The differences are in multiple aspects, such as performance, durability, appearance, practicality, and flexibility.

It is unrealistic to believe that information about all the new materials released always reaches internal customers. Commonly, material requisitioners prefer the best-known references, interpreted as more reliable, which constitutes an obstacle to introducing innovations.

Jeet Patidar[34] deals with the contribution of supplies in the search for options: "Materials department can help a lot in developing new materials and products. Its personnel regularly deal with suppliers responsible for new developments. Whenever they learn of anything of interest, they can call it to the attention of interested parties in manufacturing, engineering, or other departments".

The fact that the seller usually seeks the purchaser to present a new product favors development activities, but proactivity is essential for the permanent success of the process.

The natural tendency of a purchaser, when offered a new product for a customary purchase, is to refuse, concluding that there are enough approved materials to satisfy the needs of the requesting area.

However, professionals who anticipate development identify opportunities for improvement when they receive such suggestions.

These situations can potentially break with pre-established standards and contribute to the company's progress in technological updating.

It is always opportune to remember that an organization does not need to be the best company in the country; it must be better than its direct competitors!

10.4 Streamline the flow of products and services

Management competence consists of making resources available to obtain more agility in providing products and services.

Controlling the various stages of acquisition, guiding suppliers and users, and clarifying doubts contribute to increasing the performance of everyone

---

[34] PATIDAR, Jeet; JAIN, K C. Purchasing and Materials Management. S Chand, December 1, 2011

involved in the supply chain and enabling the continuity of deliveries at the desired pace.

If the objective is performance improvement, defining the leading performance indicators associated with this issue and stipulating targets will contribute to a shorter supplier response time to customer needs.

Maximizing the results by combining a clear and detailed definition of activities with a precise understanding of the expected result is essential.

Large-scale actions are unnecessary, and a few interventions aimed at the objectives are sufficient to enhance management and improve relationships with business partners.

10.5 Encouraging sustainability

Sustainable development refers to adopting measures that allow society to meet the needs of the current generation without compromising the satisfaction of the needs of future generations.

It is a development model focused on preserving natural resources, highlighting three major areas: social, environmental, and economical.

For each one, we can briefly emphasize the following:

- Environmental: scope related to the conservation of the planet's natural resources through conscientious use by society;
- Economical: linked to the production, distribution, and consumption of goods and services;
- Social: includes people and the community to which they belong: education, health, work, and leisure.

As a rule, purchasing analysts should research the evidence that contracted companies fulfill the rights of their employees, customers, and other parties involved in the commercial process.

Baily[35] points out the condition of sustainability as a requirement in acquisitions: "Recognition arose, perhaps belatedly, that it makes sense for businesses to be 'green' and to be seen as responsible in this regard. Recycling, specifying renewable raw materials, a greater concern with the effects of waste

---

[35] BAILY, Peter; FARMER David; CROCKER Barry; JESSOP David. Procurement Principles and Management in the Digital Age. Twelfth edition. USA: Pearson, October 21, 2021

and by-products, a broader concern with the use of returnable packaging, and many other related concerns have implications for purchase and are affecting the perception of function".

Regarding the social issue, it is also opportune to investigate the company's relationship with the community where it operates, its contributions, and its effects.

Central assessment should concentrate on the impact of activities and operations on environmental topics. Is there a good destination for industrial waste? Are pollutant emissions controlled and treated so they do not disperse into the atmosphere? Does a detailed examination of environmental certifications confirm that the company plans its activities to avoid damaging nature?

Finally, from an economic perspective, the assessment should allow us to understand how the company's performance impacts the territory in which it operates. Check whether the payment of taxes occurs under the required conditions and whether there is a priority in the relationship with other municipal or state entities to which they belong. All these data provide evidence of efficiency concerning this parameter.

10.6 Supplier Categories

Creating categories permits organizing, identifying, and ordering data or objects. In the case of larger groups of materials, it is beneficial to establish subdivisions or subcategories that serve a specific purpose.

The creation of categories simplifies the management of each subgroup and makes it possible to assess the importance of each set based on its specific characteristics.

Organizing the registration of suppliers and materials into classes and providing links between them accelerate the search, primarily when consulting multiple companies. The first condition is to define the most critical characteristics for grouping items.

One of these features is Master Data Management (MDM), an item cataloging system that allows for differentiating, detailing, and dividing materials. Allocating multiple items into similar material classes creates constructive interaction between the purchasing function and the organization's overall management.

Basing master data management on specific criteria and requirements:

- There must be standardization in the description;
- Eliminate obsolete items;
- Exclude similar items with different codes;
- Improve communication between users, inventory, and purchases through adequate channels;
- Identify materials with generic descriptions and rewrite specifications;
- Reduces costs and duration of purchasing processes;
- Unify bills of materials for multiple units.

The recommended methodology for structuring the process consists of analyzing the original description of the items, followed by the identification, ordering, and labeling of materials and services.

After the category constitution phase, allocating all approved suppliers to classes consistent with their characteristics and aptitudes is mandatory.

Adopting this action will make queries more straightforward and faster by delimiting the universe of proponents.

10.6.1 Industry - Direct Materials

The direct production materials group comprises raw materials, packaging, components, and all essential items for manufacturing and improving the appearance of the finished product.

They are plastic and metal parts, electrical and chemical materials, screws, bearings, and everything incorporated into the finished product and play a role in it at some stage of production.

The main category encompasses all materials for direct use. The structuring of subgroups considers the application, as seen in the first paragraph of this topic, based on the similarity between the materials, such as plastic and metallic, or depending on the manufacturing production process, such as cast, forged, and laminated.

Defining the subgroup individually will depend on the needs of each company, looking for an alternative capable of facilitating consultations by the purchasing department and contemplating the demands of the departments that consume materials daily.

10.6.2 Industry - Indirect Materials

As the terminology indicates, indirect materials are not directly incorporated into a company's products.

They are valuable items in the execution of auxiliary production activities but have no direct application or effective use in manufacturing products for sale.

How to organize the subgroups depends on the company's characteristics, seeking to simplify the research of the purchasing department and meet the needs of the departments that store or use materials daily.

All are important; otherwise, it would be unjustifiable to immobilize resources in their acquisition. However, when there is a lack of stock, there is no interruption in the industrial operation, and the assembly of products on the manufacturing line proceeds as usual.

The main application of the material guides the definition of categories, and as examples, we have maintenance parts, cleaning materials, and printed fabrics.

10.6.3 Categories in the commercial segment

The previous topic dealt with the industrial segment and relevant subdivisions. Creating groups to organize products is also essential for commercial activities, whether retail or wholesale.

Applying the item according to the customer's consumption type is a way to form divisions. Among countless possibilities, an easy-to-understand example is subdividing foods, grouped into beverages, frozen foods, flours, or grains. After it comes to toiletries, and so on.

Another categorization model is associated with the role of the product group and its ability to attract customers to commercial establishments:

- Destination: in the consumer's perception, the quality of the products is above average, and this interpretation works as a factor in attracting customers to the commercial point that offers them, as it is considered the best place to acquire such goods.
- Routine: all products for regular and routine consumption, such as rice, meat, and pasta. Consumers choose where to buy these products due to the ease of commuting to work or home. The main feature is

the high frequency of consumption over time, which maintains good sales at any moment.

- Occasional: products consumed on specific dates, giving them the condition of seasonality. They are associated with special occasions, such as turkeys during Thanksgiving celebrations. From the consumer's point of view, the choice of location depends on the greater probability of finding the product on these special dates.
- Convenience: Items designed to meet unique and specific consumer needs, such as beverages, frozen dishes, and snacks. The customer will decide the place of purchase based on practicality, proximity, and the expectation of always having the product, hence the characterization of convenience.

10.7 How to manage the categories

Supplier management needs to create categories. Based on these, it is feasible to elaborate evaluation instruments, promptly identify suppliers with a particular type of merchandise, and develop a more efficient process with the potential to reach the planned results.

10.7.1 Define items in each category

A good list of materials linked to the suppliers' register makes it possible to locate companies that provide the desired material quickly.

An excellent mechanism to accomplish this goal is to group materials with similar characteristics and applications into one category, linking all suppliers already qualified to sell these products.

This trivial conduct restricts the research universe and minimizes the chances of making a wrong choice. The sine qua non requirement for such an action to succeed is that material management and purchasing work integrated.

The main actions intend to define criteria for inserting and accessing information, establishing associations, and selecting cataloging methodologies.

10.7.2 Fix the importance of each category

One of the first rules good managers learn is not to use the same methodology to solve different problems. Each acquisition requires a specific procedure, although the process must follow a standard.

More specifically, are there a certain number of suppliers a purchaser should consult? Does setting the same number of proposals for $100 or $100,000 purchases make sense? The answer is undoubtedly no! In the acquisitions of small-value items, the resulting monetary impact will be negligible if the organization pays 10% more by mistake. The same 10% deviation in a $100,000 deal will mean wasting $10,000.00.

Based on the previous comment, the conclusion will be:

- Small value purchases (and in each company, the small value concept will be unique) can be carried out with a small number of consulted bidders because, regardless of the number of offers, the financial gain or loss will be negligible;
- Large-value purchases (the same interpretation applies here for small values regarding what this means in each company) must have a high number of bidders to maximize the gain.

Standardization consists of listing a few companies for retail purchases and inviting numerous suppliers to participate in significant purchases.

Financial factors must always be one of the criteria for differentiating the categories, giving greater importance to materials that produce a large outlay on purchase. Baily[36] accurately illustrates this: "The purchase price is probably the factor most often associated with purchasing responsibilities. The purchasing function plays an important role in judging the correct price for any purchase."

Likewise, it is advisable to devise criteria to individualize materials according to the effects of a lack of stock on operational activity.

Most materials and services unavailable at a specific time do not entail adverse consequences. Users consume them; however, temporary shortages are acceptable. In this case, simpler processes regarding the number of suppliers and proposal requests are the best options.

---

[36] BAILY, Peter; FARMER David; CROCKER Barry; JESSOP David. Procurement Principles and Management in the Digital Age. Twelfth edition. USA: Pearson, October 21, 2021

Receiving only formal proposals is not mandatory for purchasing items with such characteristics (of course, aspects related to legislation and company standards must allow) or the need for personal contact, which is unnecessary in most purchases.

On the other hand, the lack of stock of diverse types of materials has detrimental effects, from the interruption of the operation to the obligation to change the flow of activities to make work feasible during product shortages.

In the worst-case scenario, the entire production line could stop. In these cases, the number of bidders must be significant, and the professional must redouble the attention in the execution of the purchase.

Formal proposals and timely delivery guarantees are indispensable conditions for completing the process.

10.7.3 Establish evaluation criteria

The importance of indicators in management is indisputable. Often, due to insufficient knowledge or inattention, it goes unnoticed that the success of a measurement process depends on the correct choice of evaluation criteria.

Maintaining an updated history of monitoring parameters is essential to manage suppliers. This database makes it possible to identify the companies with the best performance.

An assessment tool simplifies consulting suppliers based on individual performance. The first step is to evaluate the most relevant indicators in the purchase process: payment period, delivery period, quality, quantity, and purchase price.

Depending on the priorities of each organization, other indicators may stand out. The goal is to classify all of them and identify the highlights in each category. It is essential to have a unique methodology to standardize the analysis of different suppliers.

10.7.4 Appoint management professional

A famous proverb states that a dog with two owners starves! If no one person is responsible for a task, it is impossible to ensure its execution.

In some companies, supplier management is one of the purchaser's tasks. It probably competes with follow-up for first place on the list of activities not executed due to insufficient time.

Various large companies have professionals specially appointed to register and monitor suppliers, ensuring the updating of performance indicators.

In the case of medium and small companies, it is feasible to implement instruments to monitor the performance of leading suppliers, even with fewer resources.

The area manager can designate a more experienced professional to inspect the process and appoint a purchasing assistant to carry out the related administrative activities, stipulating a time interval for reviewing the information processed in the period.

10.7.5 Prefer suppliers with more merits

One outcome of the efficient management of suppliers is to provide a hierarchy of sources, allowing the selection of the best ones.

Based on the information collected and tabulated, the professional can identify qualified bidders and include them in the group of regularly consulted ones. Adopting a performance-based benchmark ensures meeting terms in the next contract.

On the other hand, a competent purchaser knows the potential benefits of providing opportunities for new companies. With this attitude, they gather complete and realistic information about the product or service market.

Therefore, the ideal model is to merge these two types of actions. If a new supplier occasionally presents the best offer, the analyst should evaluate the advantage of offering to those who have regularly provided the chance to match the offer. The premise is that this approach offers the benefits of a better buying condition with the security of a seller with a good track record.

Conversely, if there is consistent evidence of the start-up company's ability to deliver according to pre-established requirements, joining the list of suppliers will be fair.

10.7.6 To elaborate Service Level Agreement

SLA – Service Level Agreement is a document that details the supplier's responsibilities in providing services or delivering materials.

In the most usual format, it lists the contracting party's obligations, points out performance indicators, describes the contract's object, and stipulates the transaction's general conditions and compensation in the case of non-compliance with the service performance parameters.

An attractive benefit is to provide an objective analysis of the services, define assessment instruments, and pursue improvements in the execution of services and delivery of required items.

The purchaser and seller must negotiate and periodically review the terms of this document to ensure their adequacy to the needs of those involved over time.

It is noteworthy that the focus of SLA is to certify the contracted quality standard upon delivery of the purchase object and detail the penalties for non-compliance with any of the agreed obligations.

It is mandatory to indicate the person responsible in the contracting entity, to inspect the various clauses of the Service Level Agreement, as there is no use in worrying about preparing the contract well if there is no effort to check its execution.

In general, inspection is the responsibility of a professional from the requesting sector, interested in meeting deadlines and qualified to carry out the necessary assessments.

10.7.7 Assess the supplier's ability to meet customer needs

Trust is a function of two things: character and competence. Character includes your integrity, your motive, and your intent with people. Competence includes your capabilities, your skills, and your track record. Both are vital

Stephen Covey [37]

---

[37] Stephen Richards Covey is an American writer, author of the bestseller The 7 Habits of Highly Effective People

This quote expresses the most relevant attributes for choosing a supplier worthy of receiving a purchase order.

Assessing the supplier's ability to ensure the delivery of goods or services under the exact conditions intended by the customer, even those with an impeccable track record, is a substantial part of the purchaser's professional activity.

An example is to verify whether it has sufficient productive capacity. Each company has the maximum volume it can produce depending on the equipment installed and the professionals that make up its team.

It is up to every purchaser to have reliable information about the quantity that a particular supplier can deliver without compromising lead time and quality. Never issue an order to a supplier whose capacity is incompatible with the purchase amount. It is a shortcut to disaster.

It may be successful, but the most likely scenarios are delays, quality failures, and intermittent deliveries, to mention the frequent effects. Sellers are unlikely to alert purchasers of this situation. The routine is to take the order and then worry about how to meet the defined terms.

Typically, the purchaser holds the supplier responsible for the failure. Nevertheless, a more detailed evaluation would demonstrate that researching the contractor's technical, financial, productive, and commercial conditions would avoid the problem.

In management, it is essential to scrutinize all the conditions necessary to guarantee the excellent performance of suppliers delivering the most critical materials from the purchasing portfolio.

An important aspect is that focusing exclusively on higher-cost cases to define priorities is a wrong strategy. All materials that can compromise the entire operation in the case of an out of stock require special monitoring.

10.7.8 Establish penalties for non-compliance with requests

Suppliers have orders from different customers on their backlogs. It is likely that some deliveries will not comply with the contracted conditions. The seller is aware of this situation and, because of this, establishes priorities for orders, choosing which ones to deliver in line with the purchase order.

Because of this possibility, the purchaser must be skilled and position his order in a preferential position on the supplier's delivery schedule. An effective stimulator is to apply a mulct to the supplier in proportion to the negative impact when non-compliance with contracted conditions occurs.

Jeet Patidar[38] listed the main objectives of material management and highlighted the following:

- "Continuity of supply. When supply occurs intermittently, excess costs are inevitable. Production costs increase, and higher shipping and transportation fees are likely. At the same time, continuity of supply is vital for highly automated processes, where costs are stiff and occur even if production stops due to a lack of materials.
- Quality consistency. Maintaining consistency of the quality of the materials with the lowest possible overall cost is another critical objective of the materials department."

Logic dictates that minimizing the risk of failure is essential when a supplier's actions are detrimental. As mentioned, the fine is efficient; however, prior discussion of its use during the negotiation phase is vital.

It is common for some suppliers to refuse this type of penalty and reject to close deals where this condition is compulsory. It is up to the purchaser to assess whether the conflict associated with this commercial requirement is worth the safeguarding it offers.

The supplier's refusal to conduct business subject to penalties does not imply that the supplier is unreliable. Due to internal rules, some organizations refuse sales whose contracts have potentially loss-causing clauses.

Just as it is the seller's right to refuse an order because of the possible occurrence of punishment, it is also legitimate for the purchaser to dismiss the penalty due to the positive history of the seller. Maintaining a high level of business relationship is also a valid reason for this.

It is evident that the existence of a penalty clause in a commercial contract significantly reduces the chance of supply failure. However, it is worth mentioning that the fine's incidence stems from irregularity in the supply, and it will hardly compensate for the losses in full.

Finally, in addition to the fixed forfeit in significant acquisitions, there must be a deadline to remedy quality or quantity defects, adapt the goods for use, and evaluate whether it will be the case to reduce the amount payable to cover the remaining losses.

---

[38] PATIDAR, Jeet; JAIN, K C. Purchasing and Materials Management. S Chand, December 1, 2011

10.8 Results of efficient category management

Conducting activities competently and efficiently generates positive results, often exceeding projections.

Adopting good practices raises expectations and creates a virtuous cycle, with the implementation of improvements, the generation of superior results, and the encouragement to continually research more measures to increase performance.

In category management, commonly pursued results are below.

10.8.1 Minimize financial, commercial, and brand risks

An acquisition involves choosing where to allocate capital. When a company orders a particular product or hires a specific service, the effect is to assign part of its cash flow in the process, intending that the resulting benefits outweigh the costs of the decision.

Any gains resulting from the parties' decision to establish an exchange relationship consist of receiving material or service when making cash payments.

In this type of system, incorrect decisions in sequence pose risks to the organization's financial health and compromise its ability to remain operational. On the other hand, when purchasing activities are well-coordinated, the gain will be a natural consequence, as well as a reduction in the risks of financial problems.

The commercial gains mentioned come from efficient relationship management with suppliers and customers.

In the case of suppliers, the benefits come from transparency in negotiations and the satisfaction of those involved with the commitments assumed.

Customers will feel better served with a continuous supply of materials and services without failures, as their purchases are necessary to meet their sales portfolio.

Finally, the brand, the most critical asset of any company whose value results from consumers' positive perception, will be more respected as satisfied business partners renew their transactions and strive to maintain a bond with a company recognized as high-performance.

A brand associated with the organization's name and established symbol add value to a product or service.

10.8.2 Providing lower costs

All purchasers, including career beginners, and therefore not experienced in the usual tactics and objectives, understand that the purchasing department's primary purpose is to reduce operating costs. The mistake of many lies in the means used to reach the goal. In Figure 10.1. there is a table of the central items comprising the acquisition cost.

DESCRIÇÃO DO COMPONENTE DE CUSTO		
Storage	Freight	Payment Term
Technical Assistance	Warranty	Price
Courier	Installation	Price Adjustment
Packaging	Movement	Transport Insurance
Financial charges	Deadline	Tax

Figure 10.1.: components of acquisition costs

Purchasing professionals obsessively seek material or service price reduction as the only method to minimize costs. They neglect relevant aspects available for negotiation with sellers, such as quantity, delivery time, payment terms, and quality. However, they are an excellent option for reducing costs and making good purchases.

High inventories immobilize resources excessively, and the scarcity of items for the operation leads to losses with unplanned stoppages and lost sales.

Poor-quality materials devalue the final product and cause delays, among other harmful aspects.

Effectively managing companies in charge of the supply avoids the unfavorable effects mentioned above. This results in savings with reduced stocks, availability of the necessary material at the right time, and the absence of problems resulting from the rejection of products. These are examples of advantages convertible into value and potentially lower total costs.

It is important to emphasize that, although essential, cost reduction should not be a single or exclusive condition when developing a long-term supply strategy.

Shoshanah[39]emphasizes how an effective response to adversity must be present in formulating the supply plan: "Resilience is a key characteristic of a robust supply chain strategy. Global networks built solely to optimize costs and inventory during ideal conditions may be unable to deliver in natural disasters, political turmoil, or financial stress."

10.8.3 Time savings with problems and meetings

The golden rule for any activity is that getting it right the first time saves time and money. To better understand the concept, consider a delivery with quality problems. In addition to the inconvenience and additional services for the other areas involved and necessarily affected by the error, the purchaser will need to perform different unnecessary tasks:

- Report the problem to the supplier;
- Discuss with him how to correct the failure;
- Arrange the return of the defective material;
- Monitor the replacement arrangements;
- Communicate to stakeholders the negotiated solution.

The actions listed above waste time and money in the area's routine! Suppose suppliers do it right for the first time. In that case, there will be no rework, which is an effect of the efficient management of the supplier register, identifying the most qualified companies, and encouraging them to offer better performance.

Conversely, with poorly performing suppliers with no prospect of progress, the recommended action is to exclude them from the register and keep records of their failures to avoid consulting such companies in the future!

10.8.4 Innovation in products and processes

Innovation refers to an idea, device, process, or product conceived and capable of breaking paradigms, initially developed, later implemented, and made available on the market.

---

[39] COHEN, Shoshanah. Strategic Supply Chain Management: The Five Core Disciplines for Top Performance. 2nd edition. USA: McGraw-Hill, June 14, 2013

The evolution of products provides superior performance in the functions expected by consumers. They want their business partners to pursue innovative technologies permanently and invest in research on more efficient processes.

Regarding the potential of innovative technologies to entirely change a market's profile, Shoshanah[40] states: "Disruptive technologies can introduce new players and dislocate existing ones, thereby changing the fundamentals of the value system. New technologies such as electronic delivery can make possible more frequent product launches, higher levels of customization, and less costly delivery of smaller orders, requiring changes in customer service, asset footprint, and operating models."

However, experience demonstrates how so many companies accommodate themselves, believing that the excellence of the current product line will be enough to guarantee the market share they now enjoy in the future. They forget that they also left behind competitors, unable to adjust to market evolution when they started.

Motivating suppliers that are part of the list of registered companies to innovate permanently is one of the main functions of purchasing analysts. When done well, it ensures the supply of the best products and services available for purchase.

For the formula to be successful, it is essential to encourage suppliers to maintain research and development departments. The customer must reward the advantages of the new products and agree to negotiate new commercial conditions if the current benefits exceed those offered by the previous product.

10.8.5 Improving the Contribution Margin

The calculation of the Contribution Margin consists of subtracting all variable costs from the total net revenue, which corresponds to the total sales of each product or service minus taxes and returns. The result of dividing the gross contribution margin by the quantity sold corresponds to the contribution margin of the unit.

The contribution margin provides the financial resources to pay fixed costs and generate profits. By defining the margin and considering the already accepted hypothesis that the amounts paid to suppliers are among the highest

---

[40] COHEN, Shoshanah. Strategic Supply Chain Management: The Five Core Disciplines for Top Performance. 2nd edition. USA: McGraw-Hill, June 14, 2013

costs of organizations, it is logical to conclude that the reduction in expenses directly and positively impacts the contribution margin.

The efficient management of suppliers reduces the costs incurred in acquisitions, and it is noticeable how much the contribution margin increases!

Baily[41] highlights how purchasing procedures are increasingly involved in companies' strategic decision-making process because the purchasing area acts powerfully to add value and not just to reduce costs. It influences the awareness of losses due to increased expenditure on materials and emphasizes the profit potential of purchases.

10.9 The Kraljic Model and its application in supplier management

Peter Kraljic, a former director of McKinsey & Company, an American organization in the business consulting market, gained notoriety for developing Matrix Kraljic, a company portfolio analysis tool.

This technique enables the development of acquisition strategies and increases earnings according to merchandise type. It assesses the correlation between the risks and costs associated with materials.

The matrix is an instrument available to purchasers to increase supply security and reduce disbursements by managing bargaining power.

The principle fits perfectly into the concept of strategic management of suppliers since, according to Kraljic, "the purchase must be a management of supplies."

The first step of the Kraljic tool is to group the inventory items into categories. For each material, the procedure involves calculating the supply risk and its impact on the company's financial results.

The risk is high when there is a limited supply of raw materials, either because the supply logistics are complex and subject to easy interruption or because there are few qualified suppliers.

The influence on profit is significant when the material has an enormous impact on revenue or is fundamental in the production process, having a prominent effect on the final product and its subsequent demand.

Combining these two factors results in the matrix shown in Figure 10.2.:

---

[41] BAILY, Peter; FARMER David; CROCKER Barry; JESSOP David. Procurement Principles and Management in the Digital Age. Twelfth edition. USA: Pearson, October 21, 2021

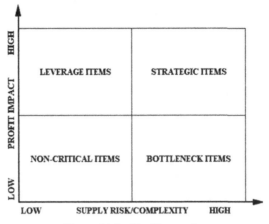

Figure 10.2.: Kraljic matrix

The four quadrants define certain conditions for the item under analysis, and based on them, it is possible to elaborate an adequate strategy to manage the purchase.

10.9.1 Leverage Items

The main particularity of the items in this class is that they significantly impact global results. At the same time, they have a wide range of supply alternatives (conclusions resulting from information about low supply risk). Figure 10.3. highlights the quadrant corresponding to these items.

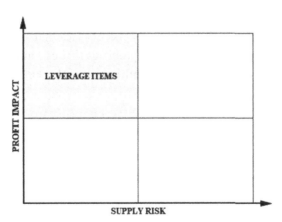

Figure 10.3.: Leverage Items

Even a less attentive observer realizes a considerable advantage to the purchasing professional when acquiring items from this group. There are many companies to consult, making it possible to choose whom to negotiate with and, depending on the range of existing options, allowing to interrupt a negotiation if a supplier demonstrates intransigence to start a conversation with another.

From this premise, bargaining power should guide the purchase process since multiple sources strengthen the customer's position.

In addition, the abundant supply allows the evaluation of the replacement of the material or supplier if any economic or commercial benefit results from this action.

It benefits the purchaser, encouraging competition between suppliers and sharply reducing costs. The initial move is to consult several companies to receive many proposals.

When formulating a trading strategy, the focus should be on reducing costs. A favorable situation allows the purchaser to obtain good discounts, improve payment terms, and create other ways to gain from the process.

Due to the potent effect on the business result, it is rational to evaluate potential gains if the volume is more significant, whether due to the scale effect or the possible scheduling of deliveries according to the need for receipt combined with the supplier's manufacturing possibilities.

10.9.2 Bottleneck Items

The main feature is the minimal impact on business results, whereas the chances of shortages are significant. The risk of a lack of material often stems from having few suppliers or logistical problems that can interrupt deliveries for a period. Figure 10.4. shows the identification of these items in the Kraljic matrix.

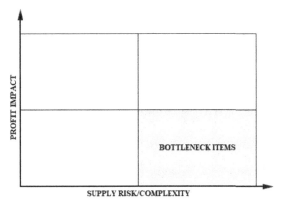

Figure 10.4.: Bottleneck Items

Even with the monetary impact on the business being small, the interruption in supply causes adverse effects, forcing the development of strategies to ensure that delivery occurs on time or having alternatives for the lack of items, such as substitute materials.

As supply security is the focus, the purchaser must act to guarantee the necessary volumes. Occasionally, to achieve this objective, the acquisition may occur at a higher price than planned, as the impact on the business is low due to the reduced financial volume involved in the transaction of these items.

It is helpful to suggest to the inventory management department to analyze the feasibility of increasing the safety stocks of these materials and minimizing the risk of shortages during the replenishment process.

Managing the purchases of bottleneck materials requires planning contingency actions for delays or non-occurrence of deliveries on scheduled dates.

The basic actions to overcome these difficulties include identifying alternative suppliers or products and, in the most expressive cases, imposing financial penalties in eventual situations of non-compliance with orders.

10.9.3 Strategic Items

Materials in this category are noteworthy for causing a significant impact on the business, and simultaneously, they have few supply options. Figure 10.5. shows the characterization of this category in the matrix.

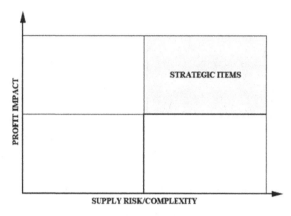

Figure 10.5.: Strategic Items

As they are essential materials, the purchasing analyst must continually check market conditions, seeking to identify in advance signs of scarcity or increased demand, with a consequent boost in suppliers' prices.

The most appropriate action would be to plan and implement strategic partnerships with carefully selected suppliers. Criteria such as delivery reliability and quality assurance deserve special attention when choosing a supplier.

Almir[42] explains how the reduction in the supplier base is a consequence of establishing partnerships: "Reduction in the number of suppliers since many are not prepared for the necessary process changes or are interested in them. Another aspect is the difficulty to manage process integrations closely, with associated services, with many suppliers."

Another sensible measure is to analyze the supply and demand trends in the market, anticipating moments of imbalance and issuing supply orders in advance. Alternatively, long-term contracts remain valid, with ongoing assessment of adjustments to commercial conditions.

Due to the difficulties arising from failures, acquisitions must include protective measures, such as imposing financial penalties and other types of sanctions in case of non-compliance with contractual clauses.

The same procedures proposed for critical items apply to them, with the provision of alternative actions (plan B) in the case of delayed deliveries concerning the scheduled dates.

[42] SANTOS, Almir G; ELIA, Bruno de S; MAGALHÃES, Eduardo; PINTO, Geraldo. Gestão da Cadeia de Suprimentos (Supply Chain Management). 1st edition. Brazil: FGV Management, October 1, 2014

Finally, for noncritical items, particular recommendations are dispensable due to their nature. They are the most common, and acquisitions should follow simplified processes, favoring agility because the cost is marginal, and the risk is irrelevant.

10.10 Ray Carter's 10 Cs model

Another prominent tool in supplier management is the 10 Cs model by Ray Carter, an American consultant and director of DPSS Consultants (Developing People Serving the Supply Chain), an international training and development consultancy.

The first publication of the model took place in the CIPS Supply Management magazine in 1995, making it popular among purchasing professionals.

The 10c model is a valuable tool for validating the reliability evidence provided by suppliers who intend to partner and maintain dependable business relationships.

The analysis procedure uses ten capabilities that candidate companies must demonstrate to provide materials and services and ensure that deliveries will occur precisely under the conditions agreed with the customer.

Below are all ten related and with brief comments on each one.

10.10.1 Competency

Presenting evidence of having the competence to supply strictly in compliance with the conditions stipulated in the contract is an essential verification in evaluating a supplier.

Every vendor claims to have a solid track record of delivery to the intended standard, but documentation must support such claims.

The following list indicates evidence that deserves analysis.

- Curricula and qualifications: availability of curricula and records of the capabilities and skills of the people essential in manufacturing the product. Although proving to have highly qualified individuals does not guarantee performance, it is a positive indicator;

- Vital professionals: should be identified and contacted when this type of action is feasible to assess their contribution to the supplier's performance and the potential to act excellently over time;
- Recruitment: are there documents on recruiting people for the most critical positions in the organization and pointing out the methodology used to select these people?
- Training and development: what are the means to verify if the supplier has a structured system with a training schedule for developing the team of employees? In this sense, the documents must prove established initiatives to make the supplier a model of excellence in the market.

10.10.2 Capacity

Knowing the status of the supplier's order book provides valuable information for deciding the assignment of an order. However, it is worth noting that the answer to this question requires a specific interpretation.

If the order book is almost complete, the initial conclusion is that customers trust the supplier and place orders. It is a good "indication" that it is an effective supplier.

In contrast, the same situation in the order backlog indicates that the supplier will face difficulties delivering new orders within the contracted term and with stipulated quality.

In this case, some analyzes are relevant to assess this competence.

- Capacity: what is the supplier's capacity? Will there be sufficient capacity to meet the current and future requirements if a new contract is signed?
- Operational Controls: does the supplier maintain a history of statistical data demonstrating control of quality or service level issues? ISO 9000 accredited suppliers must have available evidence for consultation. Non-accredited companies must confirm their past performances. It is worth emphasizing that a good track record in customer service does not guarantee good future performance;
- Forecasts: what are the supplier's sales expectations? Will sales volume be high? If the answer is yes, it is a sign of confidence from

current customers; however, will the supplier successfully serve a new customer in such a scenario?

- Administrative resources: does the supplier certify that it has the necessary systems and procedures to support the quality system and service level? Is there a sales management system sufficient to ensure efficient and effective order processing or manufacturing control to track the progress of a production order?
- Production facilities: scheduling visits to the production site must be an exclusive action for suppliers of essential materials because it is an effective and indispensable means of evaluating aspirants. The presence in the manufacturing facility makes it easier to analyze how the supplier's administration is or collect data about its capacity. These visits are also helpful for the purchaser to learn about the supplier's industrial processes and systems. For example, if the supplier indicates that it has the total capacity used, it does not make sense that its stock is out of the raw material.

10.10.3 Commitment to Quality

Is there evidence of suppliers' ongoing efforts to deliver high-quality products and services? Does it provide evidence that a structured and successful quality policy exists?

Verifying the existence of these points implies confirming that the supplier has methodologies such as those in the following list:

- SPC - Statistical Process Control is a statistical method used to measure the quality of the product and allows to identify if there are possibilities of exceeding the specified tolerance limits. SPC provides information for taking corrective action before a failure occurs. Contributes to improving quality and keeping associated costs low;
- TQM - Total Quality Management develops collective awareness of the importance of quality in an organization. This organizational culture is essential for ensuring better quality for end customers;
- CIP - Continuous Improvement Processes: does the organization prove that a system is in place in its structure to improve its processes continuously?

- Culture and Values: does the supplier have evidence of organizational culture and corporate values focused on quality and continuous improvement, and are the related procedures implemented and communicated to everyone?
- ISO 9000: is the supplier accredited to this standard? The standard does not guarantee the quality of products from certified companies, but it is a good guide and proves the existence of a solid quality system. Other vital standards are QS 9000 (a stricter version of ISO 9000 from American car manufacturers) and ISO 14000 (an environmental standard).

10.10.4 Consistency of Performance

Demonstrates competence to provide and maintain consistent levels of quality and service regularly.

It is essential to collect evidence on the supplier's ability to deliver repeatedly and with quality throughout the contract to ensure this condition.

The resource needed to verify this qualification is a sound supplier management system capable of elaborating corroborative indicators of this condition and measuring the supplier's performance over time.

Having a supplier employee available to witness this management process and to link the customer and supplier is beneficial.

10.10.5 Cost

Monitoring the total cost of goods or services takes place through a rigorous analysis of the cost spreadsheets presented by the supplier:

- Profit: are the supplier's operations profitable? A supplier whose operation generates insufficient profit may have to exit the market in the medium or long term. When a supplier goes through a significant financial crisis, the customer suffers from a lack of supply until it finds alternatives, spending time and money to obtain another source. A good purchasing analyst seeks to ensure that their suppliers remain profitable, although there are still some inexperienced professionals for whom the supplier's bottom line does not deserve attention.

- Variable costs: these are directly proportional to production, that is, their amount grows due to any increase in production. Among the variable costs, labor, raw materials, and other materials incorporated into the product during the manufacturing process, called direct costs, stand out.

- Analyze whether the supplier's workers' remuneration is competitive compared to the market if it does not delay the payment of wages and negotiates a fair price for the purchase of raw materials and components. The associated costs are high if the supplier pays exaggerated wages. However, spending remuneration below what would be fair demotivates employees and may lead to interruptions in activities with delays in supply. Likewise, spending too much on acquiring materials will increase input costs and boost the selling price, while paying too little may compromise the quality.

- Fixed costs: analyze the value of these costs, formed by expenses with indirect labor (employees who do not work directly in production), energy, insurance, and rent, among others.

- Evaluating the sales price contribution margin is essential, as it provides the necessary resources to settle the fixed costs. If it is too high, the selling price is excessive; if it is low, it suggests that the supplier is subject to financial problems.

- Profit margin: what is a supplier's profit margin? Profit margin measures a company's profits in relation to its sales, being a component of the price. Every company must make a profit; otherwise, there is a risk that they will go out of business and the customer will lose the supplier. The formula to calculate is: profit margin = profit / revenue x 100.

- Break-even point: the designation for a specific production volume in which total costs equal net revenue. Logically, producing above this volume will generate profit, and the supplier will lose if production is below. Knowing the supplier's breakeven point makes it easier for the purchaser to negotiate based on the ideal production quantity and pay a fair price.

James K. Hawkins

10.10.6 Cash and Finance

This criterion examines the supplier's financial situation, solvency, and payment capacity in the medium and long term. Certain information is beneficial in assessing this financial condition:

- Book balance: The company's cash balance is based on its accounting records, admitting that it includes transactions not yet settled in the bank account. Represents how much a company owns, or to paraphrase, permanent calculation of its cash balance, including all transactions, even those not yet reconciled by the bank.
- Income Statement: assessment of the supplier's operations in the previous year. It compares the company's revenue with the running and operating costs of the business and indicates whether the supplier has made a profit.
- Credit analysis: financial institutions evaluate companies' financial statements to determine whether they can receive credit and how much. An adverse credit rating serves as a warning and requires a detailed examination.

10.10.7 Communication

Does the supplier demonstrate evidence of organizing and maintaining efficient operational communication channels with customers?

Communication can occur in numerous ways, such as occasional or periodic meetings, face-to-face events, conference calls, or other resources such as instant messaging applications or electronic mail.

The supplier must demonstrate that it invests and conducts training to have a functional contact method and a consistent information recording system.

10.10.8 Control of Internal Processes

Effectiveness and efficiency in running a business are essential for its success. How does the supplier demonstrate its management level? Evidence includes information on the critical aspects of control, such as:

82

Stocks	Marketing
Operation	Purchasing
Quality	Distribution
Sales	EHS (Environment, Health, and Safety)

Ensuring that delivery happens smoothly requires access to information on how the supplier manages and controls its key processes. All are essential for the seller to provide goods or services ordered at the right time, with the right quality, at the right price, delivered to the right place, and in the correct quantity.

The following is a summary of how each contributes to the objectives listed in the previous paragraph:

- Inventory: adequate inventory increases the supplier's chances of delivering the quantity ordered on time. However, excess stock inhibits the supplier from proposing a lower price because of the cost of stocking the surplus;
- Quality-efficient: the supply company's quality control maximizes the chances of delivery to meet the established quality standards. Contrarily, over-specifying quality requirements negatively affect a supplier's ability to have a competitive price;
- Operations: skillfully controlling operations will allow the supplier to meet the time, quantity, and quality criteria;
- Purchasing: well-managed purchases using modern concepts are essential to suppliers delivering materials and services with adequate quality and low cost;
- Marketing: good marketing processes help the supplier deliver within the deadlines and in the quantity ordered;
- EHS - Environment, Health, and Safety: the existence of systems and processes, such as a properly prepared safety record, raises the motivation of the supplier's employees. A motivated workforce allows you to achieve the set goals.

10.10.9 CSR - Corporate Social Responsibility

Shareholders open companies to make a profit, and this premise is not wrong since these people's capital will be at risk when they create a company.

The focus is assessing whether the supplier operates strictly with established ethical and legal practices and satisfies legal and ecological requirements. The central question is to achieve maximum profitability without compromising laws and environmental degradation.

Compliance evidence can incorporate policies and processes to implement the best actions in ethics, the market, and society.

10.10.10 Culture

It is legitimate to aspire that suppliers and customers share similar values. Every day, the relevance of the relationship model between the customer and supplier at the organizational level increases.

Purchasers continually evaluate business relationships because intense conflicts can lead to premature termination.

Terminating a commercial relationship causes setbacks, such as finding a new supplier. On the other hand, a strengthened commercial relationship promotes sustainable and long-term partnerships.

CHAPTER 11

SELECTION OF SUPPLIERS AND REQUEST FOR PROPOSALS

"We see our customers as guests to a party, and we are the hosts. It's our job every day to make every important aspect of the customer experience a little bit better".

Jeff Bezos[43]

A rigorous choice of suppliers to present proposals is necessary to obtain more advantageous commercial conditions.

In this sense, it is worth questioning the reasons for researching the commercial conditions of various companies before making a purchase. It would be simpler and faster to consult only one seller and authorize delivery.

Detailed and thorough research on several proposals aims to understand the general commercial conditions currently in the market and to plan the item's purchase requirements. Thus, the client company gains more security in achieving the goals set for the purchase process.

This information search will only be successful if the chosen suppliers represent the market.

Baily[44] explains this procedure: "The consultation with suppliers identifies a set of current and potential companies in the market, investigates the capacity of each one, analyzes the structural characteristics of the market and their behavior in prices ..."

Based on this premise, what is the best source of information for selecting suitable suppliers? There is no better database than the registration of a company's suppliers. This assertion is a function of the presumption that

---

[43] Jeffrey Preston "Jeff" 'Bezos is an entrepreneur known for founding Amazon, the most important and famous e-commerce company in the United States.

[44] BAILY, Peter; FARMER David; CROCKER Barry; JESSOP David. Procurement Principles and Management in the Digital Age. Twelfth edition. USA: Pearson, October 21, 2021

the register is correctly structured and permanently updated. In this case, a supplier register is valuable in choosing the right companies to consult in each situation.

Preconditions help select who will participate in the process. Consult who supplied the last time if the performance was satisfactory.

It is also favorable to rotate, replacing bidders who delivered the worst offers in the previous purchase with other companies not invited recently but registered. This action provides better market monitoring and increases the possibility of knowing its general conditions.

Concepts such as the ABC classification system help select items that deserve more detailed study regarding the choice of suppliers.

As an illustration, an A-rated item requires that all eligible suppliers receive an invitation to bid. This item is of high value, and any improvement in commercial conditions is worth a lot.

However, the material classified as C does not justify any special effort. List a few suppliers and ensure the existence of all the minimum necessary information to complete the purchase.

It is advisable to pay attention to the size of the providers. Despite an excellent service standard, a supplier may have insufficient structure to meet the order. Care is mandatory in this case, not avoiding consulting it during the process but considering the need for an eventual division of the quantity when finalizing the process.

Another prominent aspect that is more relevant to the registration process is complying with international quality standards. Many companies require documents from suppliers proving certification to these standards as a precondition for submitting proposals.

Within the scope of requesting and receiving offers, it is worth highlighting advances in information technology and providing electronic communication resources that reduce the time required to complete acquisitions.

The advent of networks such as the Internet has changed conventional communication between individuals and companies, introducing fast and efficient connection mechanisms.

One of the challenges for purchasing departments is understanding the best technique to use this range of technological tools effectively.

Interestingly, despite the advancement of technology and concepts, company leaders still require the purchaser to seek a minimum number of proposals, whether the disbursement of the item will be $100.00 or $1,000,000.00.

Modern management theories recommend focusing on ways of acting that can generate significant returns.

More important than the number of hours worked is the quality of work performed, which will make the company successful.

Returning to the concepts of the ABC classification, it makes sense to suggest a table with the minimum number of proposals to complete the purchasing process, as shown in Figure 11.1.

Item	Form of consultation	Form of presentation	Number of Proposals
A	Written	Written	5
B	Unwritten	Written	3
C	Unwritten	Unwritten	1

Figure 11.1.: Suggestion of guidelines for consulting suppliers

Reading the table, you must observe the following:

1. The "Item" column indicates the material class;
2. The column "Form of consultation" indicates the means to request the proposal from suppliers. The written form includes electronic mail and electronic messengers but not only these. The Unwritten one allows the voice call;
3. The column "Form of presentation" clarifies how the bidders will forward the proposals. The means of communication described in item '2' are valid;
4. The "Number of proposals" column suggests the minimum number needed to complete the process.

This table does not constitute a single proposition for the subject. Another suggestion is to highlight the need for differentiated treatments compatible with the importance of the material under analysis.

Once again, the objective is to question attempts to standardize procedures, ignoring the importance of each purchase by stipulating a merely bureaucratic routine.

Finally, it is necessary to set a deadline for the receipt of proposals to ensure compliance with the dates specified for the delivery of the material or service object of the request.

CHAPTER 12

ANALYSIS OF PROPOSALS

"Success is about executing what you do today with unquestionable, breathtaking excellence."

Tom Peters[45]

M any colleagues consider the analysis of proposals a bureaucratic action. They could not be more wrong. Upon receipt of proposals, an extensive evaluation of the conditions offered is mandatory. Any inattention when examining the basic parameters can lead to an inappropriate supplier.

It is worth noting that price, although especially important, should not be the main judgment criterion. Before starting the financial analysis, the purchaser must investigate whether all materials or services satisfy the applicant's quality requirements.

Fortuitously, a seller may offer unknown or untested material. In this case, the recommendation is to ask the end user to evaluate the new product and conclude whether it is a valid option. Sometimes the quality department must participate in the qualitative assessment.

After the quality analysis is over, it is not yet time to compare prices. First, confirming whether the suppliers' proposed delivery times are compatible with the company's requirements is essential. If there are proposals with deadlines longer than those requested, there are two alternatives to validate them if it is in the interest of the purchaser:

- Check with the applicant whether the proposed deadline, even after the intended delivery date, satisfies the company's needs;
- Negotiate a reduction in the term with suppliers, framing it within the expected time parameters[46].

---

[45] Thomas J. Peters, has a doctorate in management, worked at the White House and was a management consultant at McKinsey & Company. He is a business management guru.

[46] Of course, it only makes sense to negotiate an adjustment in the delivery period with the supplier if the other commercial parameters are advantageous.

If both options are unfeasible, the proposal does not meet the organization's needs, even if some commercial conditions are favorable.

Finally, it is time to evaluate the proposed cost. Baily[47] points out the relevance of price in the process: "Buying price is probably the factor most often associated with procurement responsibilities. The procurement function is important in judging the correct price for any purchase, and this aspect of the task is seen at its most dramatic in the commodity markets".

A common mistake in evaluating price is disregarding the financial component associated with the price × term factors. Companies with sophisticated management programs have formulas to calculate the present value of each proposal and rank them based on the financial factor.

For companies without this tool, performing the analysis using a financial calculator or spreadsheet program is an option. In the chapter on financial mathematics, there is a thorough examination of these issues.

Owing to their importance, the following factors should be part of the purchaser's scrutiny when comparing bids:

- Price adjustment clause
- Material description
- Supplier identification
- Taxes
- Other costs (packaging, freight)
- Deadline
- Payment term
- Proposed price
- Ordered quantity
- Validity

Less experienced professionals may have difficulty with the terminologies used for payment terms. The table in Figure 12.1. has a glossary with the meaning of the most common.

---

[47] BAILY, Peter; FARMER David; CROCKER Barry; JESSOP David. Procurement Principles and Management in the Digital Age. Twelfth edition. USA: Pearson, October 21, 2021

Abbreviation	Description
1MD	Monthly credit payment of an entire month's supply
2% 10 Net 30	Payment of the invoice is due within thirty calendar days, but payments within ten days can take a discount of 2%
21 MFI	The 21st of the month following the invoice month
2MD	Monthly credit payment of an entire month's supply plus an extra calendar month
30 days End of Month	Payment is due at the end of the month following the month of the invoice
60 days End of Month	Payment is due at the end of the second month following the month of the invoice
CBS	Cash Before Shipment
CIA	Cash In Advance
CND	Cash Next Delivery
COD	Cash On Delivery
CWO	Cash With Order
EOM	End Of Month. Payment is due at the end of the month of the invoice
Net 14 or 14 Days	Payment of the net amount outstanding on the invoice is due fourteen calendar days after the date of the invoice
Net 15	Payment of the net amount outstanding on the invoice is due fifteen calendar days after the date of the invoice
Net 30	Payment of the net amount outstanding on the invoice is due thirty calendar days after the date of the invoice
Net 60	Payment of the net amount outstanding on the invoice is due sixty calendar days after the date of the invoice
Net 7 or 7 Days	Payment of the net amount outstanding on the invoice is due seven calendar days after the date of the invoice
Net Monthly Account	Payment is due at the end of the month following the month of the invoice
Upon Receipt	Payment due immediately upon delivery of the Invoice

Figure 12.1.: Payment acronyms

The table in Figure 12.2. provides a glossary with the meaning of the most common terminologies for transport[48].

---

[48] In the annex there is a much more extensive and extremely useful glossary

Abbreviation	Description
CFR – Cost and Freight	Exclusive term for maritime transport. In this case, it is up to the seller to pay the costs and freight to transport the goods to the specified destination port. However, the risk of loss or damage or any additional costs arising from incidents occurring is the customer's responsibility.
CIF – Cost, Insurance, Freight	Exclusive term for ocean transport. The seller must pay the cost & freight necessary to transport the goods to the specified destination port. The seller must pay for marine insurance against the customer's risk of loss/damage during the carriage.
CPT – Carriage Paid To	The seller delivers the goods to the carrier and must pay the carriage necessary to bring the goods to the named destination. The customer will pay all costs incurred after the delivery of the goods. The customer is responsible for the risk of losses, breakdowns, and additional costs arising from incidents. The use of this term is independent of the means of transport (including multimodal).
CIP – Carriage and Insurance Paid	This term is the same as CPT, except the seller must pay for the insurance against the customer's risk of loss or damage to the goods during the carriage. The use of this term is independent of the means of transport.
DAP – Delivered At Place (specified place of destination)	The seller pays for shipping to the selected location, except for costs related to import clearance, and assumes all risk before the goods are ready to be unloaded by the customer.
DDP – Delivered Duty Paid	This term represents the maximum obligation for the seller. The seller will pay all costs and assume the risks of conducting customs formalities, including paying the export and import procedures, fees, duties, and taxes.
DPU - Delivered at Place Unloaded	The seller delivers until the means of transport is unloaded and assumes the risk to the agreed destination. The use of this term applies to any means of transportation.
EXW - Ex Works	The term represents the seller's minimum obligation since he only needs to ensure the goods are available to the customer. The customer must perform all tasks for export and import clearance. Transport and insurance are the customer's responsibility.
FAS - Free Alongside Ship	Exclusive term for ocean transport. The term indicates that the seller's responsibility ceases when the goods are alongside the vessel at the designated port of shipment. The seller must release the goods for export. The customer must bear all costs and risks of loss or damage to the goods from that moment.
FCA - Free Carrier	The term indicates that the seller delivers the goods released for export to the carrier indicated by the customer at the location specified. The seller pays for shipping to the selected location.
FOB - Free On Board	Expression exclusive to maritime transport indicates that the customer's responsibility for costs and risks begins when the goods are on the ship docked at the designated port of shipment. The seller must release the goods for export.

Figure 12.2.: Transport acronyms

CHAPTER 13

PURCHASE ORDER

"A verbal contract is not worth the ink that is signed."

Samuel Goldwyn[49]

The purchase order is a necessary document to confirm a purchase. Even if the supplier exhibits impeccable references, the customer must have legal instruments to ensure the material arrives as ordered, even when buying from usual suppliers. Purchase orders provide legal protection.

Most acquisitions proceed without significant problems. However, in a few cases, serious deadlocks can occur, even with traditional suppliers, and in these cases, a well-crafted order protects the customer's rights.

It is always opportune to reaffirm that the purchase order is a contract, given its bilateral relationship, and must contain the topics in Figure 13.1.

Acceptance of the document by the seller	Location and delivery time
Approval by the purchasing company	Selling company data
Deadline	Unit of measure of the material
Payment conditions	Date of issue
Price adjustment conditions	Complete material specification
Purchasing company data	Responsible for paying the freight
Request number	Quantity purchased
Total price	Taxes levied
Unit price	

Figure 13.1.: Indispensable data when making a purchase order

The orders must be available for consultation by various departments in the computerized management system, enabling the people involved with the material to know the status of the process and the delivery forecast. This information is also helpful for the finance and accounting departments, which have a relevant stake in the process.

---

[49] Samuel Goldwyn, stage name for Samuel Goldfish was a film producer and one of the founders of Paramount. He created Goldwyn, which, by merger, became Metro-Goldwyn-Mayer in 1924.

When there is a need to modify the purchase order, the change must be immediately detailed in a specific document and communicated to everyone.

Readers may interpret the placement of so much data when preparing the purchase order as an exaggeration. However, if a more severe supply problem exists, these data will protect the purchasing company from further losses.

CHAPTER 14

FOLLOW-UP

"It is better to act too quickly than to wait too long."

Jack Welch[50]

Follow-up is a process to monitor the delivery of materials and maximize the chances that the delivery will satisfy the conditions established in the purchase order to guarantee the fulfillment of the delivery deadline.

For an efficient operation of the purchasing area, follow-up is necessary since many suppliers do not deliver on time.

Although inconceivable, the delivery of several items would not occur or would take place with delays without active monitoring by the customer.

David Burt[51] explains the importance of the activity objectively: "The supply management department's responsibility for an order does not terminate with the making of a satisfactory contract. Supply management is responsible for an order through to receipt and approval of material for use. Even though a supplier intends to meet a required delivery date, plenty of problems can arise to prevent it from doing so. When there is a reasonable chance that the supplier may not stay on schedule, important orders with critical delivery dates should receive active follow-up attention. When such orders are placed, the procurement professional should determine specific dates ."

As experience demonstrates, conducting a well-structured follow-up puts pressure on suppliers. If there are multiple production orders, deliveries closely monitored by the customer will have priority.

---

[50] John Frances Welch Jr. was an American executive, started his career at General Electric Company and became the company's eighth Chairman and CEO. Author of several books and consultant to presidents of the largest American companies.

[51] BURT, David N; PETCAVAGE, Sheila; PINKERTON, Richard. Proactive Purchasing in the Supply Chain: The Key to World-Class Procurement. 1st edition. USA: McGraw Hill, December 6, 2011

Follow-up is more effective if there is one person or group of people dedicated exclusively to the task, if the structure of the Purchasing Department allows it.

The recommendation is reasonable because purchasers are often overworked and relegate tracking to the background or fail to run it!

The activity demands controls that detail the status of each order. In practice, it means comparing contracted deadlines with delivery dates, both for closed orders and forecasts for open orders, to provide the Purchasing Department with information on the progress of deliveries.

Another critical function of monitoring is to measure the performance of suppliers during each purchasing process.

Until now, the focus has been on administrative controls for tracking deliveries, with little influence on ensuring the receipt of materials. It is opportune to analyze how to keep track of deliveries, as there are several ways to do this:

a. Inspection performed at the manufacturing site: suitable for critical cases where delivery does not allow delays. Going to the factory helps detect any flaws in the product's manufacture in advance or verify compliance with the promised deadline. Using this information, purchasing professionals can analyze the need for additional action to ensure the receipt of materials within the contracted terms;

b. Telephone contact: contributes to streamlining deliveries and minimizing delivery delays. Sometimes, looking up the delivery date of an item with more than one supplier's employee makes it easier to identify contradictions in information;

c. Forwarding of formal messages: this proceeding is necessary if the information provided by the supplier is inaccurate or contradictory. It serves to notify the supplier and pushes it to take a definitive position. The best strategy is to forward correspondence to the top management of the selling company, who are often unaware of specific subordinates' attitudes.

The purchasing department can delegate follow-up to its professionals or people from another area, as suggested below:

• The task is an attribution of the purchaser, who executes it concurrently with other attributions;

- A purchasing assistant with an exclusive role in monitoring deliveries allows purchasers to be involved only in the event of a problem;
- Another department performs follow-up, usually the materials receiving area, which informs the other areas about the status of the order;
- An independent team of purchasers, who work exclusively on this task, is subordinate to the manager of the Purchasing Department.

CHAPTER 15

RECEPTION AND INSPECTION OF MATERIALS

There are two types of people in this world. Those who think they can and those who think they can't. They are both right.

Henry Ford[52]

Receiving and inspecting materials is one of the final steps of the purchasing process. Although there is a person designated for both tasks in the organization, asking for the delivery of material is the purchaser's responsibility. Even when another department receives the materials, the purchasing department remains in charge of the delivery.

Thus, when questioned by a requester about the supply of an item, it is not acceptable for the purchaser to argue that there is already an order with the supplier and that the question "is incumbent on the material receiving area." Such an act goes opposite to the actual function of a purchasing department.

Inspection is essential during delivery; however, comparing the order specifications with the received item is simple.

An essential condition to accept materials is that the person in charge has broad and continuous access to all purchase order data; otherwise, the activity becomes unfeasible. The incoming inspection is unrelated to the typical rigor of the material quality control function, which has specific procedures.

A characteristic of the process is to immediately report to the purchasing department the discrepancy between the order and the delivery, that is, who has the competence to decide whether to return the product or receive it conditionally.

---

[52] Henry Ford was an American entrepreneur and mechanical engineer, founder of the Ford Motor Company and author of the books My Industry Philosophy and My Life and My Work and the first entrepreneur to use the assembly line concept to produce automobiles in large quantities, less time, and less cost.

If it is impossible to solve a problem immediately, the right action is to return goods to prevent future problems. The supplier must receive official communication with the causes for rejecting the material.

When there is a great need for the product, and there are conditions for its use, even with the inaccuracies detected, the purchasing department may, exceptionally, authorize its entry after consulting the material requester. The recommendation is to negotiate discounts for the losses associated with discrepancies in these situations.

An important caveat is that the delivery of the material must comply with the conditions defined in the purchase order, and receipt with divergence can only occur in exceptional cases.

In the chapter on purchasing problems to achieve objectives, there was an emphasis on the inconsistency of purchasers performing activities in other areas. An example is the Purchasing Department, which verifies the invoice data issued by suppliers before making a payment.

Except for small companies, whose structure does not allow for another arrangement, this practice is unreasonable and meaningless because invoices must go directly from the receiving area to the financial sector for payment processing.

When there is a divergence between the invoice and purchase order, the purchasing area must intervene to resolve the pending issue. Any different action overlaps the functions between purchases and accounts payable.

15.1 Oversupply reception

Purchase orders are documents issued with legal value, with a few verbal exceptions or by unofficial means, whose use depends on the particular interest of the current purchase, exceptional market characteristics, or a specific company policy. They detail the quantity purchased, but this does not prevent deliveries with quantities different from those established.

Occasional differences between order and delivery arise for several reasons, such as the supplier's eventual difficulty in precisely delivering the requested quantity. The supply of metal plates or bars with the amount defined by weight and not in units illustrates this issue well.

There are also materials manufactured in processes in which it is difficult to define the exact amount to obtain, such as the injection of plastic parts.

Some occurrences are beyond the supplier's control, justifying the prudent decision to receive or reject excess quantities. Occasionally, slight variations in the quantity supplied are acceptable in the commercial sphere, whether above or below that ordered.

However, this does not oblige receiving additional quantities in all cases. Each purchase must follow a specific procedure.

Some companies agree to receive quantities larger than those ordered, setting a limit of 10% of the order volume for the excess. However, such conduct on large-value purchases means significant payment.

Other companies take the opposite position and veto the entry of surpluses, regardless of the excess volume. These companies even include this imposition in the general supply clauses associated with purchase orders.

Defining an ideal approach or the right attitude toward this nature is ineffective; it is impossible to establish a fair general rule for all cases. Each supply must be analyzed individually, considering all the details, and defining the appropriate solution for the circumstances.

Issues such as the inconvenience of attrition with the supplier, quantity in stock of the item, comparison of the cost of the material supplied with its cost in the market, whether it is the case of a product manufactured exclusively for the company, or whether it is a periodic purchase, should influence the decision.

A simple account helps to understand the concept: a particular company purchases a monthly volume of US$ 5,000,000.00. The Purchasing Department authorizes the receipt with a variation of up to 10%, whether a surplus or a smaller quantity.

To better expose the concept, hypothetically, half of the items in class "A" (read the chapter dealing with classification instruments for materials) are received with quantities 7% above those originally requested (presumably the quantities stipulated as being necessary).

Hypothetically, the "A" items represent approximately 70% of the total purchased, US$ 3,500,000.00, and half of the "A" items arrive with a value that is 7% higher. The impact on cash flow is as follows:

- US $ 1,750,000.00 = half of US $ 3,500,000.00
- Surplus = US $ 122,500.00 (7% of US $ 1,750,000.00).

Indeed, the outcome of this example is unacceptable. Purchasing departments should always act to prevent this situation. Therefore, all purchasing professionals must continually perform similar analyses to manage the company's cash effectively.

PART II

TECHNIQUES AND TACTICS FOR THE GOOD PERFORMANCE OF THE FUNCTION

CHAPTER 16

MATHEMATICAL AND FINANCIAL CONCEPTS APPLIED TO PURCHASES

Mathematics is the alphabet with which God has written the universe.

Galileo Galilei[53]

Why should a purchaser know financial calculations? In fact, anyone professionally involved with transactions that require payments should know the basics of finance.

Purchasers contract services and buy materials for organizations, but eventually, they do not acknowledge the variation in the sum disbursed in these transactions at different times.

The value of money comes from making it possible to obtain the desired product or service. It is a resource for getting something, not just in the present but also in the future. After all, why would anyone want to accumulate money in investments other than the possibility of using that amount for something relevant later?

The fundamental point is that the number of goods bought with a specific quantity of money on a given date differs from those purchased on a posterior date with the same amount.

The purchasing power of money changes over time, so there is a variation in the volume purchased at different times. This variation in purchasing power is not due solely to inflation.

Occasionally, at a future date, it may be possible to purchase more items with the same face value as the currency used the last time.

In conclusion, as the purchasing power of money varies over time, it is incorrect to compare values relating to different dates nominally. It would be

---

[53] Galileu Galilei was a Florentine physicist, mathematician, astronomer, and philosopher from the 16th/17th centuries.

103

something like comparing dollars with euros. Therein lies the relevance of financial mathematics to purchasers and others professionals.

How do we compare values and decide with confidence? If the problem is to compare defined amounts for different dates, the solution is to recalculate the equivalent value of each one for a single previously selected date as if they were all originally there. This action makes it possible to choose the most advantageous alternative.

At this point, the reader will probably think: "put this way, it's simple, but how do you go about transporting values in time correctly?"

Financial mathematics is a tool for carrying out the transport of values over time. This chapter will present these mechanisms in a didactic manner, allowing the readers to understand the concepts and execute the applications themselves.

TIP

In books, on the internet, or television, we often hear someone communicating the astonishing fall of an indicator, highlighting a reduction of two or three times in its value!

Not long ago, we heard the president of an environmental pollution control organization highlight that, with the measures implemented, he expected to reduce the emission of waste into the atmosphere by five times!

The most we can reduce a greater than zero quantity of this nature is one time, going from the current value to zero.

16.1 Fundamental concepts used in financial calculations

Executives are prepared to replicate successful ideas assimilated during their academic and professional lives. In this context, it is reasonable to assume that conditioning induces the application of previously successfully used procedures in similar situations. This preparation is typical in master's courses, MBA (Master in Business Administration).

In an MBA, executives study dozens of cases involving companies and markets in different conditions. These are usually real cases that occur in corporations that authorize schools to explore the strategies adopted in these circumstances.

Such analyses prepare professionals to decide in a specific way when faced with a similar context, capacitating them to react promptly to market variation.

Likewise, in the financial calculations within the scope of purchases, it is possible to prepare professionals to behave similarly to master's students. Therefore, in this book are essential concepts for carrying out financial calculations.

16.1.1 Interest

Money has the characteristics of a commodity. With some freedom of thought, it makes sense to characterize banks as commercial companies with the function of transacting money. Everything works like a retail establishment with a sole product in the banking system, money.

Colleagues in the financial sector may feel provoked and refute the statement, listing many sophisticated products offered by banks, but reduced to the most elementary form, they are all linked to the need to move customers' money.

From this point of view, it is reasonable to suppose that there is a "price" for money. Borrowers return the sum received to the bank, plus an extra amount interpreted as "rent" paid for the temporary money transfer. The designation assigned to this "rent" is interest.

On the other hand, whoever deposits in any investment will receive the money invested plus a certain amount at the end of the negotiated period. This surplus constitutes the interest from lending money to the bank for a period.

> Interest: the amount charged by the holder of the
> money to lend it to those who need it.

Given the above, it is acceptable to establish that the possession of money is transitory. Having money today does not exclude the possibility of not having it in the future.

16.1.2 Capital

The previous topic clarifies that those with money can lend it and receive interest. The designation for money available is capital.

In the dictionary, a search for the meaning of capital will result in money that someone uses to start a business or invest and make more money.

In the financial system, the term capital has a specific meaning for mathematical applications, correlated to the definitions above, and is:

> Capital: money available for lending to those who need it (the investor's point of view), or money required but not available, so it is essential to obtain it through a loan (the "borrower's" point of view).

A particular aspect is that the word "capital", in a sense used here, is associated with the operation's initial moment. This definition does not depend on whether someone gives money or asks for a loan.

16.1.3 Period

It is helpful to organize concepts logically to make them accessible to the readers. Having capital for a time interval allows you to earn interest. The total interest in a transaction depends on the investment time.

It is reasonable to conclude that the interest and time factors are directly proportional; the longer capital remains with third parties, the greater the interest earned. The designation for the time factor is the term "period".

> Period: time interval in which the capital is available for investment or loan, determining the financial result of the operation.

Determining interest is a period function; solving any financial mathematical problem without knowing this variable is impossible.

16.1.4 Future Value

Both those who invest and those who apply for a loan share the same concern: what is the value of the transaction at the end of the period?

Deciding to agree to a deal depends on the answer. When interest rates are high, the final value grows a lot in relation to capital. When interest rates are low, the difference between the balance and the initial amount is modest.

The Value resulting from the transaction, called "Future Value", has the following definition:

Future Value: the result of a loan or investment at the end of the period.

16.1.5 Correlation between variables

A necessary action is identifying the relationships between the variables in a problem. It is common for people to reason using association features. It is often unavoidable to remember someone when breathing in the scent of a perfume worn by a close person. Why does it happen?

The best answer seems to be that the brain's "memory" function also works through associations. For example, it relates the perfume's smell to the person you know who habitually uses it.

Applying the same associative principle makes understanding the mechanisms of Financial Mathematics easier. It is possible to see links between capital factors, interest, quantity, and time.

Everything starts with the following rule:

Future Value = Capital + Interests

This equation establishes the relationship between the following three parameters. Naturally, this expression simplifies understanding the points commented on and is intuitive.

Tip
There are plenty of people who think that deflation and discount are the same things. This is not correct. Deflation is a negative price change index, being the opposite of inflation. Deflation means that, in one month, the average price of the basic food basket used to calculate inflation was lower than the previous month's average.

Mistakenly, some people believe that deflation is positive, ignoring that it usually results from falling economic activity and/or rising unemployment.

In contrast, a discount means a reduction in value, as in the case of a commercial discount, with a decrease in the price of a product to induce the consumer to buy it more.

The calculation is also different. The measure of deflation uses formulas from financial mathematics, whereas the discount value results from multiplying the initial amount by the discount percentage

16.2 Some percentage information

Percentage fundamentals are present in numerous financial calculations performed daily at work. Although various readers are familiar with such concepts, omitting information on the subject from the text is not admissible.

The basis of the numerical system is decimal with characterization by different forms:

- Fraction: as observed in the school period, the representation of a fraction is:
  1/10 or $\frac{1}{10}$

The representation above identifies "one-tenth".

- Decimal representation: the decimal point separates the numbers:
  0,1

The terminology above also identifies one-tenth. There are two ways to describe the same greatness.

In the percentage representation, the system is similar, changing only to the centesimal configuration:

- 1/100 or 0,01 or 1%

The application of percentages is essential when comparing variations in base one hundred; that is, the number of hundredths that the measure varied.

16.2.1 Percentage applications

A person travels by car to a city 180 miles away from home. After driving for 81 miles, the driver must turn to an alternative road, as a landslide obstructs the main road.

The new itinerary adds 27 miles to the original route. What is the percentage of increase from the initial distance?

It is a classic case of applying percentages. A value is subject to variation. The objective is to characterize the magnitude of the variation. In this example:

Starting distance: 180 miles
Additional route: 27 miles
Percentage change = 27 / 180 = 0,15 = 15% (reads 15 percent)
There will be an increase in the original journey of fifteen percent.

The use of percentages is frequent in the calculation of variations. This concept applies to weight, time, surface, volume, population, and financial area changes.

16.2.2 Application examples

Example 16.1: The Ministry of Labor stated that the average salary in the country this year will fall to the previous one.

Last year, the median salary was $63,000, and for this year, the forecast is $61,740. What is the expected reduction in percentage terms?

Resolution:
Previous year's average salary: $ 63,000
Average salary this year: $ 61,740
Variation of the average wage: - $ 1,260

Percentage change: -1,260 / 63,000 = -2%

Example 16.2: The Human Resources Manager at Clean Services, Mr. Ramos, studied the company's staff and concluded that reducing the current team of 1,200 people by 3.75% is possible. How many employees will remain in the company after the reduction?

Resolution:

Current staff: 1,200

Expected reduction: 3.75%

Percentage of employees who will remain in the company:

100% - 3.75% = 96.25%

Staff after reduction:

1,200 x 96.25 / 100 = 1,150

TIP

Interpreting the results from applying percentage concepts as sufficient to decide on a particular issue is inadvisable. There are relative variations or percentages and absolute variations, the difference between the two quantities involved.

A minor percentage change is acceptable if the absolute difference is satisfactory in specific situations. Suppose a company whose profit of $11,000,000 in the previous year accounted for 10% of sales. This year, sales grew 18%, but the return on sales dropped to 9.25%. Profit measured as a percentage of sales decreased; however, in absolute terms, profit increased to $12,006,500

16.3 Most common financial symbols

The variables explained in the previous sections are indispensable for all financial calculations. Of course, using symbols to represent them is helpful as it simplifies the analysis of the problem. Below is a presentation of these symbols:

16.3.1 Capital, Principal, or Present Value

Capital, also called Present Value, with the meaning previously stated. As the expression implies, the value is associated with the current or most recent date, and its representation is PV.

The PV symbol is on most financial calculators, books, and articles.

$$\boxed{\text{Capital or Present Value} = \text{PV}}$$

In specific calculations, the term PV occasionally corresponds to a value not associated with the current date. This applies when the value is closer to the present moment than the others are.

Example 16.3: The Antares Airline is buying one million boarding passes. The unit price is $ 1.22. Delivery occurs within 30 days. The company that will print the boarding passes offers two payment options:

a. Single payment in 60 days, without increase;
b. Installments at 90, 120, 150, and 180 days with an increase of 4.25% on the total, which is the financial cost of the supplier to split the payment.

Which condition is more advantageous if the financial cost of Antares is 1.35% per month?

Comments: This example contains payments that occur at various times. The disbursement closest to the current date is alternative a, with a single installment expected to occur within 60 days. For calculation purposes, it is valid to use it as PV.

This chapter will explain how to solve this financial problem common in purchasing departments.

16.3.2 Future Value

The "FV" representation adopted in this case indicates Future Value.

$$\boxed{\text{Future Value} = \text{FV}}$$

Example 16.4: Francis Clothing Industry purchased 5,000 rolls of thread from a significant manufacturer at $2.18. Payment will happen on the date of delivery of the goods. The supplier agrees that payment occurs after 28 days of delivery. However, in this condition, the unit value will be R$ 2.35. If Francis's financial rate is 1.00% monthly, which of the two options is more advantageous?

Comments: The price for payment on the delivery date, $ 2.18, is the PV of the example. Here, too, the resolution will be ahead. As a result, the value of $ 2.35 will be the FV.

16.3.3 Interest rate

Any question involving financial mathematics is subject to the interest rate. It is impossible to perform the calculations and obtain the results without it.

The international notation for interest rate is the tiny "i", which originated from "interest."

$$\boxed{\text{Interest Rate} = i}$$

16.3.4 Period

The period is crucial in financial mathematics. All supply proposals establish a deadline for paying the amount offered; disbursements can occur against delivery in 28 days, 30 days, or any other period. The important thing is that it will always be necessary to set a payment deadline.

The symbol used to represent the period is the lowercase letter "n".

$$\boxed{\text{Period} = n}$$

The fact that the value of money changes over time implies a mandatory relationship between the interest rate and the period. A given interest rate always has an associated unit of time. For example:

- 5.00% per year

- 0.50% per month
- 0.02% per day

Example 16.5: Mr. Estefan is the vice president of Sun Shoes. He negotiates with the director of a supplier the percentage adjustment in the maintenance and cleaning service price of the company's facilities. Stefan accepts a 4.8% increase in service value, effective May 1st, and without any other adjustment within a minimum period of one year.

Mr. Meirelles, director of the service provider, intends to divide the 4.8% into equal monthly percentages, applicable on March 1st, April 1st, and May 1st.

What should be the monthly percentage for the total adjustment to remain at 4.8%?

Comments: The total readjustment percentage is 4.8%. The objective is calculating the monthly rate i to dilute the readjustment in three months. The solution is ahead.

16.3.5 Periodic payments

In addition to the above parameters, there is another: installment or periodic disbursement. This situation appears in example 16.3. It is possible to make a single payment in 60 days or divide this amount into four, paying them at intervals of 30 days.

The term periodic payments applies to a series of disbursements when it meets two requirements:

- All parcels have the same value;
- The interval between payments is constant.

Capital letters PMT are the symbol of periodic payments in financial mathematics.

$$\boxed{\text{Periodic Payments = PMT}}$$

> Tip
>
> Each symbol mentioned has a corresponding key on financial calculators. In the case of repetitive calculations, these machines save time. It is enough not to eliminate redundant values from the memory of the financial keys.
>
> When solving mathematical operations, enter the value corresponding to each parameter in the corresponding key.
>
> Regularly, in similar analyses, only one variable changes. In this case, insert the new number on the key corresponding to the indicator subject to change, keeping the others unchanged.
>
> For instance, if the objective is to calculate the future value for several alternatives in which the present value and interest rate are constant and only the period varies, change the period, keeping the other keys' values unchanged. For each new period entered, a different future value will result.

16.4 Cash flow diagram

Graphically representing specific problems facilitates understanding if such an option is viable. Aware of this condition, financial professionals have created a Cash Flow Diagram tool.

This instrument aims to graphically expose an organization's cash flow behavior over a fixed time horizon. It can only depict known and confirmed facts, such as payments for purchases made, and, alternatively, predict future cash inflows and outflows. For that reason, its designation is projected cash flow, which includes confirmed disbursements and forecasts.

The drawing of the cash flow diagram is simple. The first step is to draw a horizontal line to represent time and place cash inflows and outflows on the scheduled dates.

Arrows pointing up represent inflows (accounts receivable), whereas arrows pointing down indicate outflows (disbursements), as shown in Figure 16.1.

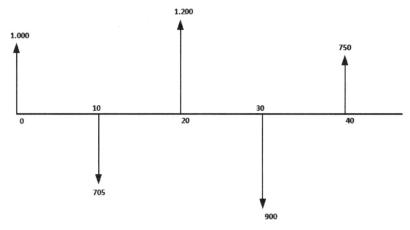

Figure 16.1.: Cash flow diagram

In addition to being an excellent tool to assist in decisions, it allows for many analyses, especially for comparing alternatives, which is a frequent application of cash flow diagrams.

Now is the appropriate time to review example 16.3. According to the text, the acquisition of boarding passes can occur in two ways:

1. Disbursement of $ 1,200,000.00 in 60 days; or
2. Payment in four installments of $ 317,962.50 within 90, 120, 150, and 180 days of delivery.

It is difficult to identify the most favorable condition using this information alone. It is helpful to represent the situation in a cash flow diagram. Figure 16.2. shows alternative 1, while Figure 16.3. shows alternative 2.

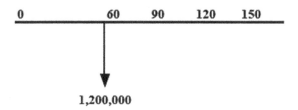

Figure 16.2.: Graphical representation of the single payment alternative

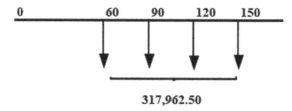

Figure 16.3.: Graphical representation of the installment payment alternative

With only the information in the figures, it is impossible to compare the options to choose the best one, as fundamental data is missing: the interest rate.

However, we can see how it is easier to understand the problem, which helps us solve it.

Example 16.6: The Organic and Fresh Supermarkets sales manager has drawn up the table below listing customer payment terms. Multiplying the coefficients by the cash purchase amount will result in the disbursement for the corresponding date:

N° of days	Coefficient	N° of days	Coefficient
14	1.0116	42	1.0437
21	1.0185	50	1.0548
28	1.0256		
35	1.0339		

A particular customer does not intend to pay in cash, considering using a bank loan modality with a monthly financial cost of 2.95%. This information makes it feasible to calculate the best alternative from the customer's perspective. Plotting the coefficients on a graph will aid understanding.

Comments: Obviously, the Value of immediate payment corresponds to the 1.0000 coefficient, as this condition has no financial cost. The other values are the same as in the table; the diagram is in Figure 16.4.

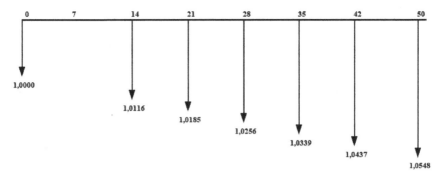

Figure 16.4.: Graphical representation of the coefficients applicable by the supermarket

Starting from the graph and using the interest rate the bank charges, it is simple to determine the best alternative. Details on how to make this account are later in this chapter.

It is essential to clarify that there are two manners to indicate dates on the horizontal axis:

- Start from the "0" (zero) date, corresponding to the initial event or today's date, and identify the subsequent days with sequential numbering, as done in the diagrams presented;
- Use the calendar to identify the dates of the events. In the supermarket example, the beginning is the date of purchase (suppose it is March 8th). Thus, the first coefficient corresponds to March 22nd, the second to March 29th, and the others follow the same order.

Tip

The interest rate and the period must be in the same time unit. To paraphrase, when the interest rate is a percentage per month, the period will be in monthly multiples.

In some cases, the two parameters are in different time units. If this is the case, converting the periods to the interest rate time unit will be easier and faster. The reverse operation is more complex, requiring financial concepts and time-consuming calculations.

16.5 Simple interest system

There are two systems for calculating interest, future value, and principal: simple interest and compound interest.

As the name suggests, the simple interest system is easier to understand, so its analysis comes first.

The essence of the simple interest system is to consider the initial capital exclusively to calculate the interest during the application period. The method definition is:

- **Simple interest**: its characteristic is to utilize only the initial capital (present value) to calculate the remuneration during the entire investment period.

Example 16.7: The Brigadier company invested $1,000,000.00, for four months, in the North American bank, with an interest rate of 1.2% per month, in the form of simple interest. What will be the investment balance at the end of the period?

Resolution: As the investment complies with the rules of the simple interest system, only the initial capital will be the basis for calculating income throughout the period. Figure 16.5. shows the evolution of the interest.

Starting capital	Period	Interest Rate	Interest	Balance at the end of the period
1,000,000.00	1° month	1,2%	12,000.00	1,012,000.00
1,000,000.00	2° month	1,2%	12,000.00	1,024,000.00
1,000,000.00	3° month	1,2%	12,000.00	1,036,000.00
1,000,000.00	4° month	1,2%	12,000.00	1,048,000.00

Figure 16.5.: Table for calculating interest

The table shows that the yield calculation always considers the value of $1,000,000.00 ($1,000,000.00 × 1.2% = $12,000). Although the balance increases at the end of each period, it is never part of the basis for calculating the value of interest, which is the main characteristic of the method.

Due to the methodology for calculating yields, there is no commercial use of the simple interest method in the business environment except in a variety of discount operations.

16.5.1 Calculation of the amount, known the principal, the interest rate, and the number of periods

For a "PV" capital available for investment for "n" periods, at an interest rate "i" per period, what is the resulting "FV" amount?

The calculation of the amount is simple, just using this formula:

$$FV = PV + PV \times i \times n$$
or
$$FV = PV \times (1 + i \times n)$$

To illustrate the application of the formula, we will use example 16.6:

PV = $ 1,000,000.00
i = 1.2% / month
n = 4 months
FV =?
Substituting the values in the formula results:
FV = $ 1,000,000.00 + ($ 1,000,000.00 x 0.012 x 4)
FV = $ 1,000,000.00 + $ 48,000.00
FV= $ 1,048,000.00

16.5.2 Calculation of capital, known the amount, the interest rate, and the number of periods

The capital calculation, when the other variables are available, occurs through the development of the formula presented in section 16.5.1, resulting in the following equation:

$$PV = FV / (1 + i \times n)$$

Example 16.8: White as Snow Ice Cream Industry expanded its facilities and financed the work with a loan from the National Bank of $3,900,000, with interest included and maturing in five years. Mr. Epstein, the company's finance manager, negotiates a rate of 6% per year. How much did White Snow receive from the bank when it contracted the debt?

Resolution: With the above equation, the solution is simple. Just list the known parameters and replace them with the values:

FV = $ 3,900,000.00
i = 6% /year
n = 5 years
PV =?
PV = $ 3,900,00.00 / (1 + 5 x 0.06)
PV = $ 3,900,00.00 / 1.30
PV = $ 3,000,00.00
White as Snow received $ 3,000,000.00 from the bank.

16.5.3 Calculation of the period, known the capital, the amount, and the interest rate

In action like the previous one, it is possible to calculate the period if the other parameters are known:

$$n = \frac{FV - PV}{PV \times i}$$

Example 16.9: Cabral stores make most purchases with a deadline to pay. For immediate payment, a particular item costs $ 10,000.00, and billing for future payment changes to $ 10,300.00. Calculate the period for an interest rate of 2.0% per month.

Resolution: Because the other factors are known, using the formula is possible:

PV = $ 10,000.00
FV = $ 10,300.00
i = 2.0 % / month
n= ?
n = (10,300 – 10,000) / (10,000 x 0,02)
n = 300 / 200
n = 1.50

Since the interest rate is a monthly percentage, the equation calculates the period in months. To convert to days, multiply 1.5 months by 30 (the average number of days per month); the result is 45 days.

16.5.4 Calculation of the interest rate, known the capital, the amount, and the period

The development of previous procedures makes it possible to calculate the interest rate in the simple interest modality:

$$i = \frac{FV - PV}{PV \times n}$$

Example 16.10: The Chief Financial Officer of Packaging Marvelous is studying a transaction for the prepayment of receivables proposed by the Economic Bank. He has $1,045,000.00 in invoices. Upon the transaction, the bank will retain the interest, and Marvelous will receive, in net amounts, $1,000,000.00. What is the bank's interest rate if bonds mature within 45 days? Calculation following the simple interest method.

Resolution:
PV = $ 1,000,000.00
FV = $ 1,045,000.00
n = 45 days or 1.5 months
i = ?
i = (1,045,000 – 1,000,000) / (1,000,000 x 1,5)
i = 45,000 / 1,500,000
i = 0.30 or 3% / month

Tip
It is often possible to pay in three installments, without adding interest or settling on a single occasion, on the date corresponding to the intermediate installment. This is like spending 30, 60, and 90 days installments of $300.00 or disbursing $900.00 in 60 days.

Many believe they are similar conditions. Although for a slight financial difference, especially when interest rates are low, the best condition is the single installment on the average date.

16.6 Compound interest system

The compound interest system is the most used in the financial and business markets. What is the basis of compound interest?

In the simple method, the initial capital is the basis for calculating interest over the entire cycle. In the compound method, the sum of the initial capital and interest from previous periods constitutes the basis for calculating the interest for the current period.

The definition of the compound interest system is as follows:

> Compound interest: in this method of calculation, during the entire application period, the basis for calculating the yield on a specific date will be the balance existing in it, that is, the initial capital plus interest from all previous periods.

Steiner[54] talks about it simply but efficiently: "... "compounding" the interest and assumes that all interim cash flows can be reinvested at the same original interest rate. "Simple" interest is when the interest is not reinvested."

To compare the variations between the results of each method, we use example 16.6, calculate the interest using the compound method and check the differences between the two systems:

Capital	Period	Rate	Interest	Balance
1,000,000.00	1° month	1,2%	12,000.00	1,012,000.00
1,012,000.00	2° month	1,2%	12,144.00	1,024,144.00
1,024,144.00	3° month	1,2%	12,289.73	1,036,433.73
1,036,433.73	4° month	1,2%	12,437.20	1,048,870.93

When comparing the results of the two methods, it is evident that both produced equal balances in the first period. From the second period onwards, interest and, consequently, the balance of the composite system is higher. At the end of the last period, between the two totals, there is a difference of $870.93.

The compound system is present in almost all types of financial transactions. It is worth mentioning bank credit operations, diverse kinds of investments, calculation of interest in acquisitions, determination of a value

---

[54] STEINER, Robert. Mastering Financial Calculations: A Step-by-Step Guide to the Mathematics of Financial Market Instruments. 2nd edition. USA: Prentice Hall, 2007

equivalent to an amount in previous periods (transfer of values from the future at an earlier date), and comparison of alternatives.

16.6.1 Calculation of the amount, known the principal, the interest rate, and the number of periods

As other variables are known, it is possible to calculate the Future Value of an investment. The formula that correlates the variables is as follows:

$$FV = PV \times (1 + i)^n$$

Example 16.11: Old Hill Mining Company is one of the largest importers in the country. The price of one of the leading production inputs is $1,235.00 per ton for cash payment. The exporter agrees to receive it within 180 days with the charging of interest and upon presentation of a bank guarantee.

If the interest rate negotiated is 0.65% per month, what is the payment amount on the due date?

Resolution: this is an application of the indicated equation. The parameters are:

PV = $ 1.235,00
i = 0,65% per month
n = 180 days = 6 months[55]
FV = to be determined
Substituting the values, the calculation will be:
FV = $ 1.235,00 x $(1 + 0,0065)^6$
FV = $ 1.235,00 x 1,03964
FV = $ 1.283,95

The resolution of this problem presupposes using a financial or scientific calculator to perform calculations involving potentiation operations.

---

[55] Note that the period and interest rate must be in the same unit of time. It is not enough to divide the rate by 30 to calculate it in daily terms. The calculations required for this are more sophisticated.

16.6.2 Calculation of the principal, knowing the amount, the interest rate, and the number of periods

A formula derived from the equation of the previous sub-item allows for the calculation of capital using the other parameters:

$$PV = \frac{FV}{(1 + i)^n}$$

Example 16.12: Mr. John, a purchasing supervisor at Globe Chandeliers, an eight-store chain, is studying the purchase of high-pressure floor-washing machines. The manufacturer of the desired model sent a technical brochure and commercial offer. Each washing machine costs $4,890.00, so eight units will cost $39,120.00. The suggested payment is 120 days after the delivery. Mr. John wants to recalculate the price for payment upon delivery of the machines at a rate of 1.2% per month.

Resolution: again, the calculation is easy using a financial formula:

FV = $ 39,120.00
i = 1,20 % / month
n = 120 days = 4 months
PV = ?
PV = $ 39,120 / (1 + 0,012) ^{4}
PV = $ 39,120 / 1.04887
PV = $ 37,297.28

16.6.3 Calculation of the period, known the capital, the amount, and the interest rate

Thus far, the equations are simple, requiring knowledge of potentiation. Calculating the period requires a more complex concept called logarithm.

This book does not detail the origin and definition of logarithms, highlighting that it is a particular mathematical resource. Financial and scientific calculators often have a key to calculating the Neperian logarithm, a specific type used here, without knowing the subject in depth.

Based on the other variables, the formula for obtaining the period is:

$$n = \frac{\ln (FV / PV)}{\ln (1 + i)}$$

Example 16.13: Gold Dairy requires bank guarantees from milk producers in its purchase contracts. The amount insured by the warranty depends on the contract value, execution date, and incidence of interest rates to monetarily update the amount payable at the end of the contract.

The annual interest rate was 8.2%. Calculate the contract duration if the value at the end of the contract is $178,016.00 for an initial value of $120,000.

Resolution: applying the formula will result in the following:

PV = $ 120,000.00
FV = $ 178,016.00
i = 8,2% / year
n = ?
n = ln (178,016 / 120,000) / ln (1 + 0.082)
n = 0.39438 / 0.0788
n = 5 Years

16.6.4 Calculation of the interest rate, known the capital, the amount, and the period

The calculation of the interest rate also depends on the other variables. From the previous equations results:

$$i = (FV / PV)^{1/n} - 1$$

Example 16.14: Mr. Anderson Gale, chief financial officer at Best Tools, a manufacturer of abrasive tools, has a cash balance of $2,500,000 to invest in for six months. He analyzes two alternatives:

1. Apply to a bond with a yield of 0.36% per month;
2. Apply for a certificate of deposit, which at the end of six months, will produce a net income of $ 62,134.00.

What is the most attractive alternative from the perspective of return on investment?

Resolution: There are two ways to resolve the issue:

a. Calculate the yield obtained on the bond after six months and compare it with the other alternative, or;
b. Calculate the interest rate corresponding to the application on a certificate of deposit and compare it with the bond percentage.

The choice is to use the second method, but the suggestion is for the reader to perform the procedure in "a" to exercise the concepts presented.

PV = $ 2,500,000.00
FV = $ 2,562,134.00 (PV plus informed yield)
n = 6 months
i = ?
$i = (2,562,134 / 2,500,000)^{1/6} - 1$
i = 1.0041 – 1
i = 0.0041 = 0.41% / month

This rate is higher than the bond rate; therefore, the best alternative is a certificate of deposit.

COMMENTS

The approach is tiring but necessary. Readers who are less accustomed to calculations will find this chapter tedious. Fortunately, financial calculators simplify the analysis of financial problems. Machines have features that simplify the calculations seen thus far.

Equations make it easy to understand the essential concepts in problem-solving. The primary condition for resolving a problem is to understand the context and possibilities of elucidation.

Tip

In many financial transaction analyses, the decision should not be based exclusively on calculations. Calculations consider only objective or measurable data.

However, decisions also depend on intangible aspects that, although impossible to measure, play an active role in the choice. Imagine, for example, outsourcing activities. Financial results exclude mandatory organizational changes to adapt to the new situation. Would the financial gains offset the changes? It is an assessment worthy of analysis.

16.7 Installment and periodic payments

The acronym PMT, for periodic payments, is in the financial symbols section without any analysis. When paying in installments, the prerequisites for applying the concept PMT are present if they are of similar value and have the same constant interval.

The graphical representation should have the form shown in Figure 16.6.:

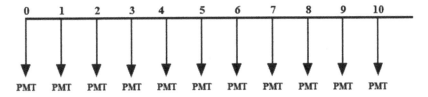

Figure 16.6.: Cash flow for periodic payments

In the flow shown in the table, on the dates identified by numbers 1, 2, 3, ..., the payment in the amount "PMT" occurs. The values are always the same, and the time interval between them is constant.

Despite the mention of "payments", used because it is close to the reality of purchasing professionals, the tool is equally helpful for cash entries if periodicity and constant value conditions occur. This principle applies when a company provides a service for which it receives a fixed monthly fee.

16.7.1 Determination of the PMT value, known the principal, the period, and the interest rate

It is time to present the formulas for calculating periodic payments following the procedure.

For a series of payments, like the one in Figure 16.6., how to calculate the value of each installment when the present value "PV", the interest rate "i", and the number of installments "n" are known? The following equation provides an answer:

$$PMT = \frac{PV \times i \times (1 + i)^n}{(1 + i)^n - 1}$$

For the term in italics and bold in the formula, some authors attribute the name "Capital Recovery Factor' using the letters CRF (i, n). So, the formula will look like this:

$$PMT = PV \times \mathbf{CRF(i,n)}$$

Example 16.15: The Steel Products Company is renewing its cleaning service contract to $2,540,000.00. The parties agree to a four-year term for the contract, and the previous total corresponds to the present value of monthly installments. The monthly interest rate is 1%. What is the amount for each payment?

Resolution: This is another application of the formula:

PV = $ 2,450,000.00
n = 48 months
i = 1% / month
FV = 0
PMT =?
PMT = [$ 2,540,000 x 0,01 x (1 + 0,01)^{48}] / [(1 + 0,01)^{48} – 1]
PMT = 2,540,000 x 0,01 x 1,61223 / (1,61223 – 1)
PMT = $ 66,887.68
Therefore, the monthly disbursement will be $ 66,887.68.

16.7.2 Determination of the principal, known the PMT, the period, and the interest rate

Reversing the previous analysis: how to determine the principal amount knowing the term, interest rate, and the amount of installments?

$$PV = PMT \times \frac{[(1 + i)^n - 1]}{i \times (1 + i)^n}$$

There is also a denomination for the term in italics and bold, *Uniform Series Present Worth Factor*, represented by **P / A**$_{i,n}$.

$$PV = PMT \times \textbf{P / A}_{i,n}$$

Example 16.16: Albert, the purchaser of the Fast Transport carrier, must buy office supplies. The supplier's proposal offers the option of splitting the payment into four monthly installments of $1,550.00, the first occurring 60 days after delivery.

As it is a small-value purchase, Albert prefers to pay the total within 30 days of delivery but at a discounted price. If Fast invests at an interest rate of 0.78% per month, what is the maximum acceptable amount for a single payment?

Resolution: This is an application of the formula seen.

PMT = $ 1,550.00
i = 0,78% / month
n = 4 months
PV =?
PV = 1,550 x [(1 + 0,0078)^4 – 1] / [(1 + 0,0078)^4 x 0,0078]
PV = 1,550 x (1,03157 – 1) / 1,03157 x 0,0078
PV = 1,550 x 3,9236
PV = 6,081.58
The maximum value that Mr. Adalberto can accept is $ 6,081.58.

16.7.3 Determination of the amount, known the PMT, the period, and the interest rate

In this item is the correlation between the amount and the installment payments.

$$FV = \underline{PMT \times \textit{[(1 + i)}^n - 1]}$$
$$\textit{i}$$

Like the two previous cases, there is a particular denomination for the factor that associates the amount with installments. The name of the term in italics and bold is *"Uniform Series Compound-Amount Factor"*, identified by $\mathbf{F / A_{i,n}}$.

We can represent the relationship by:

$$PV = PMT \times \mathbf{F / A_{i,n}}$$

Example 16.17: Rudolf Car Rental plans to replace the vehicles in the rental fleet with new ones. Mr. Mercedes, managing director, evaluates the Bank Trust's leasing proposal:

- Installment amount per vehicle: $695.00
- Number of installments: 24
- Residual value = zero

Mercedes is unsure if now, late in the first quarter, is the right time to renew the fleet of 40 cars, as they are only eight months old and have an average of 24,000 miles each.

He could wait for another six months, as the resale value would be little affected and the amount of the installments would remain invested. The company obtains a rate of 0.85% per month for the resources invested.

How much will Rudolf Car accumulate if it delays replacement for six months?

Resolution: using the formula will result in the following:

PMT = $ 695.00
n = 6 months

i = 0,85% / month
FV = ?
FV = 695.00 x [(1 + 0,0085)^6 – 1] / 0,0085
FV = 695.00 x 6,129
FV = $ 4,259.62

The obtained future value corresponds to one vehicle. For forty cars, the total cost is $ 170.384,80.

16.7.4 Determination of the PMT value, knowing the amount, the period, and the interest rate

How to calculate the Value of installments from the amount? The equation is:

$$PMT = \frac{FV \times i}{(1 + i)^n - 1}$$

There is a name for the term written in italics and bold: *Sinking-Fund Deposit Factor*, **A / F$_{i,n}$**. Thus, the equation is as follows:

$$PV = PMT \times A / F_{i,n}$$

Example 16.18: Mining Silicon negotiates the purchase of drilling equipment. The supplier requires an advance payment to start manufacturing the machines, which is a condition the customer accepts. The agreement divides this initial amount into 12 monthly installments of equal value.

The monthly interest rate is 0.5%. If the adjusted advance until the delivery date at the end of the 12 months corresponds to $2,250,000.00, what is the value of the installments?

Resolution: From the available information results:

FV = $ 2,250,000.00
n = 12 months
i = 0.50% / month
PMT =?

PMT = (2,250,000 x 0.005 / [(1 + 0.005)^{12} – 1]
PMT = 2,250,000 x 0.08107
PMT = $ 182,407.50
The monthly installments will be $ 182.407,50

Comments

When analyzing cash flow with installments, to apply the concept of periodic payments, the first step is to confirm that all installments have the same value and the intervals between them are equal. With the requirements confirmed, you can use the formulas.

Emphasis on assumptions is essential because there are other flows with different installments for which there are specifics financial formulas. This book does not discuss such models because they have insignificant purchase applications.

The information presented is sufficient to analyze the most common questions in the daily lives of purchasers.

Tip

Financial transactions, with cash inflows and outflows, use concepts related to compound interest, whether the movement occurs at the beginning or the end of each interval. However, payments or receipts at the end of a period are more frequent.

When there are multiple installments with the first allocated on the day "zero", and there is an interval between them of 30 days, the second occurring in 30 days, the third in 60 days, and so on, how to calculate the Present Value?

One possibility is calculating the PV corresponding to (n - 1) installments made on dates 30, 60, 90, and so on. To this PV, add the first installment, resulting in the entire value on the current date, the Total Present Value.

Another option is easier. Programming the calculator to consider payments occurring at the beginning of periods. A key with the inscription BEG (some brands may use different symbols) allows you to set the equipment to calculate in "BEGIN" mode, indicating that financial transactions occur at the beginning of the period. Enter "n" periods, the interest rate, and the installment amount to obtain the PV directly.

16.8 How to use financial calculators

Not all purchasers use financial machines to perform calculations involving displayed formulas, asking why they should use the calculator. There are two evident benefits:

- Agility: type the values on the keys corresponding to the parameters, and the time to obtain the answers will be much shorter than the equations require;
- The calculator eliminates the need to memorize the formulas, thereby minimizing errors. However, knowing the formula makes it easier to analyze the situation.

Naturally, reading the manuals that come with financial calculators makes the user take advantage of all the equipment's functionality. Frequent use provides greater familiarity with functions.

Bob Steiner[56] highlights how the brand stands out! He wrote: "Some of the calculations used in financial arithmetic are most easily performed using a specialist calculator. The ones most widely used in the markets are probably Hewlett-Packard calculators". Of course, the reader does not need to purchase an HP calculator.

16.8.1 The financial keys

There are several models of finance machines, most of which use the basic notation discussed here. Briefly, these are the most frequent keys with their respective function:

- **PV** - key associated with capital, main value, or present value;
- **FV** - key associated with the future value;
- **n** or **N** - key related to the number of periods or number of installments in periodic payments;

---

[56] STEINER, Robert. Mastering Financial Calculations: A Step-by-Step Guide to the Mathematics of Financial Market Instruments. 2nd edition. USA: Prentice Hall, 2007

- **PMT** - key associated with periodic payments;
- **i** or **I** or **I / yr** - key associated with the interest rate. The last jargon is because, in a few models, it is necessary to inform the frequency in annual terms.

There are other functions for sophisticated calculations in most financial calculators, but they do not fit in this scope, and therefore we will not study them.

16.8.2 Using the resources of calculating machines

Purchasing professionals familiar with technological advances often work with gadgets to streamline activities. Microcomputers, modern multifunctional, high-tech copiers, tablets, and smartphones stand out.

All these factors contribute to increased productivity. Despite this, the classic calculator is constantly on staff's desks. However, not everyone knows all the major features of calculators and how to use them.

In general, calculators follow an operating pattern; they seek to represent the order of mathematical operations in progress. The same is true for financial calculators.

16.8.2.1 Determining the Future Value

The daily practicality is useful. There is usually more than one way to perform a task; thus, it is necessary to identify the mode that will save time and sweat.

Once you know those equations that are difficult to retain in memory, it is an agreeable sensation to realize that, in practice, they are expendable.

Below is an example of using the calculator when determining the future value.

Example 16.19: Good Plant's construction company launched a real estate development with offices. Anyone interested in purchasing a unit can choose between immediately providing the down payment of $30,000.00 or dividing it into two installments, the first at the time of negotiation and the balance in one year.

The residual value is subject to an interest rate of 12% annually. What is the amount of debt in a year?

Resolution: Determining the Future Value of an installment is easy. On a financial calculator, the key sequence will be (to emulate the calculator keys, we will use square brackets):

[30000] 5 keys to enter the value
[/] key
[2] key
[=] key
15000 (display split value)
[PV] key
[1] key
[n] key
[12] 2 keys to enter the value
[i] key
[FV] key

Following the order of the keys, the calculator displays the result: **-16800**[57]

At this point, a question emerges: why is the result negative? It is negative because of the program run by the financial machines. The device's operating system constructs a fictitious cash flow to obtain the result. In this process, the positive value informed for PV corresponds to a cash inflow of this hypothetical flow.

In this logic, the machine determines the value of FV that cancels the cash flow, that is, all outputs compensate for the various inputs so that the balance is zero.

By the sequence of numbers entered on the keys, the PV corresponds to a cash entry; therefore, the FV must be an outflow, which explains the negative sign.

This consideration is crucial because virtually all calculators follow this concept. An uninformed reader might imagine an error in the result.

---

[57] Some calculator models require an extra key, to be pressed before the one corresponding to FV, to indicate to the equipment that no more values will be entered, and with this the result will appear on the display

16.8.2.2 Determining the Present Value or Capital

In this topic, it is also possible to simplify the procedures for calculating capital.

Example 16.20: The All-Life battery industry has a cash balance available for use. Mr. Robert, a purchaser, works with high-value purchases. The vendor's proposed price is $1,200,000 for payment within 45 days.

Considering All-Life invests at an effective financial rate of 1.286% per month, what is the maximum cash price financially equivalent to the forward value?

Resolution: The key sequence needed to solve the example is (to emulate the calculator keys, we use square brackets):

[1200000] 7 keys to enter the value
[FV] key
[1.5] 3 keys to enter the value
[n] key
[1.286] 5 keys to enter the value
[i] key
[PV] key

The calculator display will show the following result: **-1,177,194.58**

Therefore, the highest acceptable amount for cash payment will be $ 1,177,194.58.

16.8.2.3 Determining an operation's interest rate

The benefit of using a financial calculator is evident in this analysis. It simplifies the procedures for determining the interest. Using exercise 16.20 (to emulate the calculator keys, we will use square brackets):

[1200000] 7 keys to enter the value
[FV] key
[-] key negative sign
[1177194.58] 10 keys to enter the value
[PV] key
[1.5] 3 keys to enter the value

[n] key

[i] key

The result on display will be: ***1.286***

Professionals inexperienced in using financial calculations would perform the following operation:

$$\$ \ 1.200.000,00 \div \$ \ 1.177.218,60 = 1,019352$$

Therefore, for these people, the interest rate would be 1.9352% for 45 days or a month and a half. In this flawed logic, dividing 1.9352 by 1.5 would be the way to calculate the monthly rate, 1.2901% per month, above the correct percentage.

16.8.2.4 Determining the number of periods for an operation

Calculating the period is the least frequent method of financial application. Even so, there are situations in which this procedure is necessary. Examples are:

- Estimating how long an amount will remain in an investment to accumulate the total needed to acquire something or achieve a goal;
- Calculate the minimum time for return on capital invested in machine or equipment;
- Determine the number of intervals required to split a given percentage into a specific period.

There are other cases to list, but it would prolong the subject too much. Example 16.21 shows how simple it is to resolve this issue using a financial calculator.

Example 16.21: The Bank Satellite's Employee Retirement Fund has assets worth $3,500 million. Assuming there will be no future contributions or withdrawals, what is the minimum time for equity to double its value if applied at 0.76% per month?

Resolution: The key sequence is as follows (we use square brackets to emulate the calculator keys):

[-] key negative sign
[3500] 4 keys to enter the value
[PV] key
[7000] 4 keys to enter the value
[FV] key
[0.76] 4 keys to enter the value
[i] key
[n] key

The result will be 92.00, so it takes 92 months invested, without any movement, for equity to double in value.

16.8.3 Applications of the concept of "Installment payments"

The examples are simplifications; however, the situations do not differ in everyday tasks.

The composition of the cash flow diagram facilitates the analysis of everyday issues. The professional contemplates the situation and selects the most appropriate tools to achieve the desired results.

Determining the parameter requires exponential and logarithmic calculations, which are uncommon in daily life. The financial calculator speeds up this process. It is even more helpful in installment payments.

16.8.3.1 Determination of initial capital in applications with installment payments

In this case, the procedure is the same. There is only a new key to resolution, the **PMT**.

Example 16.22: Mr. Ferrarini, the purchasing supervisor for Alliance River Transport, reviews the purchase of parts to maintain cargo handling equipment. According to projections informed by the area of operations, he plans to prepare a supply contract valid for 12 months in the local currency.

He uses a financial rate of 0.81% per month for the analysis. The data presented estimates an ongoing monthly expense of $580,000.00. Based on the information, what will be the value of the contract?

Resolution: According to the text, the requirements for using the PMT concept are present: parcels of the same value and equal intervals between them. The result comes from the following sequence (to emulate the calculator keys, we will use square brackets):

[-] key negative sign
[580000] 6 keys to enter the value
[PMT] key
[12] 2 keys to enter the value.
[n] key
[0.81] 4 keys to enter the value
[i] key
[PV]
It results in $ 6,606,997.50. The value of the contract is $ 6,606,997.50

16.8.3.2 Determination of future Value in applications with installment payments

The procedures for calculating future Value are like those used in computing capital.

Example 16.23: Stores Electric Home Products is a large retail chain specializing in selling portable home appliances. It maintains an average safety stock of 3% of the monthly movement, currently approximately $3.5 million.

History shows an average loss of 15% of this stock owing to obsolescence or storage damage. What has been Electric's monetary loss in the last six months if the company borrows money at a rate of 1.25% per month?

Resolution: Initially, arithmetic operations are necessary to determine the value of monthly losses (to emulate the calculator keys, we use square brackets):

[3500000] 7 keys to enter the value
[x] multiplication key.
[3] 1 key to enter the value
[%] key
[=] key
The result will be 105.000,00
To continue, add the other mathematical operations:

[x] multiplication key.
[15] 2 keys to enter the value.
[=] key

The counting shows a monthly loss of $ 15,750.00, resulting from obsolescence and damage. It remains to calculate the amount for the last semester:

[-] key negative sign
[15750] 5 keys to enter the value
[PMT] key
[6] 1 key to enter the value
[n] key
[1.25] 4 keys to enter the value
[i] key
[FV] key
The result is: $ 97,502.80
Then, Electric's current policy results in a semiannual loss of $ 97,502.80.

16.8.3.3 Determination of the Value of installment payments, known the capital

In this part, the Present Value is known, and the intention is to calculate how much each installment will be.

Example 16.24: Grupo Menendez has the practice of making a provision for indirect purchases for the following year. The provision amount is $4,800,000 in present date currency. What is the corresponding monthly amount if the group finance rate is 0.78% monthly?

Resolution: Follow the key sequence (to emulate the calculator keys, we use square brackets):

[-] key negative sign
[4800000] 7 keys to enter the value
[PV] key
[12] 2 keys to enter the value.
[n] key
[0.78] 4 keys to enter the value

[i] key
[PMT] key
The result is 420,568.84.
Menendez group must provision $420,568.84 per month.

16.8.3.4 Determination of the Value of installment payments, knowing the Future Value

With the future value informed, the objective is to calculate a uniform series of payments based on available information.

Example 16.25: Eternal Weld is about to sign a contract with a company to provide medical insurance to its employees. Mr. Trinidad, Managing Director of Eternal Weld, must choose the plan with adequate coverage.

He established a year-end corrected cost of $3,800,000. What is the maximum monthly amount paid if the financial rate is 1% per month?

Resolution: This is a case of a simple solution using a calculator with financial resources. The sequence of operations is as follows (to emulate the calculator keys, we use square brackets):

[3800000] 7 keys to enter the value
[FV] key
[12] 2 keys to enter the value.
[n] key
[1] 1 key to enter the value
[i] key
[PMT] key

The maximum monthly disbursement will be $ 299,625.40.

As we entered the FV with a positive sign, the value 299,625.40 has a negative signal on the machine's display, but this does not invalidate the result. As previously shown, this is a consequence of the calculator-processing method.

> Tip
>
> Certain financial calculator models have, by default, the interest rate programmed for multiple periods of 12 months. Therefore, such models can interpret the Value entered for "n" (period) as the number of years when performing operations. However, for monthly capitalization, distorting the result.
>
> In these cases, it is possible to configure the machine for one period per year (in the memory related to the interest rate, with multiples of 1) to perform the calculations safely. Consult your calculator manual before using it.

16.9 Resolution of exercises

In this part, you will find the resolution of the pending exercises.

Example 16.3: The Antares Airline is buying one million boarding passes. The unit price is $ 1.22. Delivery occurs within 30 days. The company that will print the boarding passes offers two payment options:

a. Single payment in 60 days, without increase;
b. Installments at 90, 120, 150, and 180 days with an increase of 4.25% on the total, which is the financial cost of the supplier to split the payment.

Which condition is more advantageous if the financial cost of Antares is 1.35% per month?

To choose the best option, it is necessary to calculate the total value of each alternative for the same date. Since we have a single value in 60 days, it will be simpler to calculate the PV of option b, installment payments, for 60 days.

Resolution:

Alternative a: it is already set for payment in 60 days. The total for one million passes is $ 1,220,000.00.

Alternative b: According to the text, the requirements for using the PMT concept are present: parcels of the same value and equal intervals between them. Calculate the PV for payment in 60 days. Adding 4.25% finance cost to the total in 60 days will give $1,271,850.00. Dividing by 4 will give the value of each installment: $317,962.50

The PV comes from the following sequence (to emulate the calculator keys, we will use square brackets):

[-] key negative sign
[317962.5] 8 keys to enter the value
[PMT] key
[4] 1 key to enter the value
[n] key
[1.35] 4 keys to enter the value
[i] key
[PV]

The result will be $ 1,230,057.24. Therefore, <u>alternative a</u> is better since it has a lower value for 60 days

Example 16.4: Francis Clothing Industry purchased 5,000 rolls of thread from a significant manufacturer at $2.18. Payment will happen on the date of delivery of the goods. The supplier agrees that payment occurs after 28 days of delivery. However, in this condition, the unit value will be R$ 2.35. If Francis's financial rate is 1.00% monthly, which of the two options is more advantageous?

There is more than one way to solve it. The first is to calculate the PV of the two alternatives and choose the one with the lower value; the other is to calculate the interest rate charged by the supplier and compare it with that of Francis. We will use the second option.

Resolution:

The total value will be 5,000 x 2.18 = $ 10,900.00 (PV) for payment on the delivery date. If the option is to pay 28 days after delivery, it will be 5,000 x 2.35 = $ 11,750.00 (FV).

The interest rate "i" comes from the following sequence (to emulate the calculator keys, we will use square brackets):

[-] key negative sign
[10900] 5 keys to enter the value
[PV] key
[11750] 5 keys to enter the value

[FV] key
[0.9333] 6 key to enter the value of n (28 / 30)
[n] key
[i]

The result will be 8.355%. The supplier's interest rate is higher than the Francis rate, so paying on the delivery date is better.

Example 16.5: Mr. Estefan is the vice president of Sun Shoes. He negotiates with the director of a supplier the percentage adjustment in the maintenance and cleaning service price of the company's facilities. Stefan accepts a 4.8% increase in service value, effective May 1st, and without any other adjustment within a minimum period of one year.

Mr. Meirelles, director of the service provider, intends to divide the 4.8% into equal monthly percentages, applicable on March 1st, April 1st, and May 1st.

What should be the monthly percentage for the total adjustment to remain at 4.8%?

Resolution:

To solve it is necessary to assume a fictitious number for the amount currently paid, such as $1,000, which will be the PV. The adjustment of 4.8% will make the payment $1,048 (FV). The proposal divides the adjustment into 3 months; therefore, n = 3. Now calculate the interest rate i of this fictitious problem in terms of numbers.

The interest rate "i" results from the following sequence (to emulate the calculator keys, we will use square brackets):

[-] key negative sign
[1000] 4 keys to enter the value
[PV] key
[1048] 4 keys to enter the value
[FV] key
[3] key to enter the value of n
[n] key
[i]

The result will be 1.5751%. The following multiplication is sufficient to confirm the monthly adjustment percentage: 1.015751 x 1.015751 x 1.015751 = 1.048, demonstrating the solution.

Example 16.6: The Organic and Fresh Supermarkets sales manager has drawn up the table below listing customer payment terms. Multiplying the coefficients by the cash purchase amount will result in the disbursement for the corresponding date:

N° of days	Coefficient	N° of days	Coefficient
14	1.0116	42	1.0437
21	1.0185	50	1.0548
28	1.0256		
35	1.0339		

The customer does not intend to pay in cash, considering using a bank loan modality with a monthly financial cost of 2.95%.

Resolution:

To identify the best option, it is necessary to calculate all the coefficients for the purchase date (PV) and choose the one that results in the lowest value. Because it is repetitive, the calculation for one is here, and only the result is available for the others.

For the first coefficient, the financial calculator key sequence is as follows (to emulate the calculator keys, we will use square brackets):

[-] key negative sign
[1.0116] 6 keys to enter the value
[FV] key
[0.4667] 6 keys to enter the value of n (14/30)
[n] key
[2.95] 4 keys to enter the value of i
[i]
[PV] key

The result is 0.99797. The following table contains all the coefficients calculated for the purchase date (PV).

N° of days	PV	N° of days	PV
14	0.99797	42	1.00207
21	0.99798	50	1.00491
28	0.99814		
35	0.99942		

From the table, the conclusion is that paying in 14 days is better, although for a minimal difference.

CHAPTER 17

COMMERCIAL AND ECONOMIC CONCEPTS

Beware of little expenses. A small leak will sink a great ship.

Benjamin Franklin[58]

In this chapter, the approach focuses on the impacts of economic and commercial concepts on the market for products and services.

For a purchasing professional, it is beneficial to understand the fundamentals of these theories, even if only superficially, to apply the knowledge derived from this information in the analysis of acquisitions and suppliers.

The following detailed knowledge is valuable for purchasing management, particularly planning.

17.1 Profit Maximization and Supply Theory

The idea of profit maximization is essential to guide strategies that aim to raise profitability to the highest possible value, given internal limitations and market conditions.

If net profit results from the simplified account of revenue minus costs, it is up to the business administration to establish viable levels of prices and costs, which will lead to the greatest possible profit.

The classification of costs comprises two groups: fixed and variable. Fixed costs do not vary depending on the volume produced and are independent of it. Rents, insurance, and maintenance of facilities are examples of fixed costs.

Variable costs have changes directly related to production volume. Examples of variable costs are the raw materials and electricity consumed in manufacturing products.

---

[58] Benjamin Franklin (1706 —1790) was one of the leaders of the American Revolution, known for his quotes and experiences with electricity. He was also the first US ambassador to France.

The total cost and revenue change are directly proportional to the quantities produced and sold fluctuation. These concepts led to the development of marginal cost and revenue concepts, which make it possible to calculate the variation in cost or revenue for each manufactured unit.

A detailed analysis of how cost and price will change as production increases or decreases and how sales vary is the way to characterize these marginal parameters. The theory is simple; however, calculating the marginal revenue and cost of goods is laborious.

It is intuitive to assume that an increase in the selling price causes a drop in demand. However, this is not an independent condition, as variations in demand result from numerous factors, and isolating only one parameter is not feasible.

In this context, the microeconomics concepts related to supply and demand are indispensable. The Supply and Demand Theory model demonstrates how prices fluctuate with a balance between supply and demand variations.

In economics, the Supply and Demand Law exposes consumers' dominant purchasing behavior at specific times depending on quantities and prices. It is worth mentioning that prices tend towards stability in the equilibrium between supply and demand.

17.1.1 Microeconomics concepts

Microeconomics investigates the formation of prices in various markets. It studies the interactions between consumers and suppliers, price formation, and the sales potential of a product or service.

These conclusions result from detailed analyses such as consumer preferences and purchasing power, pricing criteria, and production chain organization to specify the most relevant.

The Supply and Demand Law exposes consumers' predominant behavior in purchasing goods and services at established times depending on the quantities and prices of the products.

17.2 Supply vs. demand

Prices tend to stabilize in an environment of balance between supply and demand in a given market.

The Supply theory evaluates the availability of a product in the market. Specific definitions are essential:

- Demand for a product or service is the desired volume by the consumers in a defined period. It indicates the upper limit the consumer may wish to purchase depending on the price and income.
- Consumer habits and preferences: a strong determinant of demand for a product is present in a group of people's will or consumption patterns. Therefore, they end up buying more items.
- The offer is the quantity of a given product or service that the producer wants to put on the market in a particular period, to sell to consumers interested.
- Price: if all other variables remain constant when the price of a product increases, the quantity demanded decreases.
- Complementary products: products that complement each other; that is, the consumption of one results from the consumption of the other, such as cars and fuel. A characteristic of the products in this group is that an increase in the price of one causes a decrease in the demand for the other.
- Substitute or competing products: consumers start to buy products from this group, causing an increase in demand to replace other merchandise whose prices have risen.
- Income: when consumers' revenues decrease, they have less money to pay for expenses, forcing them to spend less on specific goods. Normal good is the designation of a product whose demand declines because of a fall in people's income. On the other hand, an inferior good is a product whose demand increases when people's income decreases.

Timothy Taylor[59] offers excellent exposure to demand: "We defined demand as the amount of some product a consumer is willing and able to purchase at each price. That suggests at least two factors in addition to price that affect demand. Willingness to purchase indicates a desire based on what economists call tastes and preferences. If you neither need nor want something, you will not buy it.

---

[59] TAYLOR, Timothy; GREENLAW, Steven A; SHAPIRO David. Principles of Microeconomics. 2nd edition. USA: 12th Media Services, December 31, 2017

Being able to buy suggests that income is substantial. Professors usually afford better housing and transportation than students because they earn more income. The prices of related goods can also affect demand. If you need a new car, the price of Honda may affect your interest in Ford.

Finally, the size or composition of the population can affect the demand. The more children a family has, the greater is their need for clothing. The more driving-age children a family has, the greater their demand for car insurance and the less for diapers and baby formula. These factors matter for both individual and market demand as a whole."

Competition changes the market balance and interferes with the variables that influence transactions.

It is incorrect to interpret demand as an actual purchase, just as believing that the supply is the actual sale is wrong.

Demand expresses consumers' desire to buy, whereas supply reflects producers' sales aspirations. In practice, purchases are below demand, and sales are lower than the offer.

The fact that the satisfaction that a good provides to consumers influences its value is noteworthy (the foundation of the Theory of Utility of Value). According to this analysis, the relative prices result from a subjective conception of the value made by the consumer.

17.2.1 Demand vs. price

Market balance is a consequence of the influence of a range of factors, and below are the most relevant:

- The ability of companies to manufacture products with the desired technological advancement: history is full of successful products that became obsolete, replaced by more modern alternatives with the potential to win consumer preference;
- What people want or need: consumers decide their purchases based on their preferences and habits;
- Availability of products and services: the existence of a sufficient quantity of assorted products capable of satisfying the same need promotes competition and negatively influences prices since, to maintain or increase sales, producers, as a rule, must reduce prices

to remain competitive in the dispute for the customer's interest and decision. In this regard, are substitute products or services;

- Purchasing power: the consumption of a product depends on people who have the financial capacity to satisfy their desire to buy it. It is the characterization of purchasing power linked to the income factor.

Price is fundamental to customers' decision-making processes under various commercial conditions. Individual consumers are "rational" beings and stipulate the adequate amount of goods and services they intend to purchase based on income, prices, and preferences (this is the base for the "Restricted Maximized Utility" thesis, in which income constitutes the primary constraint on demand).

The economic analysis leads to the inevitable conclusion that demand is inversely proportional to the price of a good. If the price of a product increases, demand decreases, and vice versa.

Consequently, the concept of elasticity emerges, a formula to measure the intensity of variation in the quantity demanded by consumers of a given good as a function of price fluctuations.

Even more intuitively, price reduction makes any product more attractive than the alternatives offered by competitors.

Likewise, the lower the product's price, the more it increases consumers' interest in buying it. A reduction in price boosts consumers' purchasing power and increases demand if the other variables do not change.

It is important to emphasize that associating consumer preference and income with the price factor allows for the development of mathematical models that seek to predict the effect on the quantities demanded by consumers when the price varies.

If the price of a product increases, the immediate outcome is a reduction in collective purchasing power, called the income effect. As a result, the consumer searches for cheaper products as an alternative to goods whose prices have risen, generating the Replacement Effect Phenomenon.

In periods of rising income, the demand curve moves away from the origin, as shown in Figure 17.1. In conclusion, as long as the price remains stable, the quantity demanded will increase, as consumers will have more income to pay for the product they choose.

The higher the price consumers are willing to pay for merchandise, the more producers will be interested in providing it. Most importantly, higher prices stimulate production.

On the other hand, when the price is below the equilibrium value, there is a lack of supply of goods for the quantity demanded by the market due to the loss of interest of producers in manufacturing them. Consequently, the prices tend to rise.

It is possible to draw a graph of demand curves. In Figure 17.1, there is a demonstration with two demand curves showing the shift in the curve as consumer income changes.

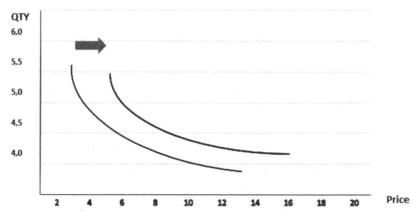

Figure 17.1.: Demand curve (quantity x price)

High prices stimulate production. The curve moves to the right as income increases. It explains why higher-income consumers agree to pay more for merchandise, encouraging more manufacturers to produce and supply the market, making more money.

When the price is below the equilibrium value, there is a shortage of goods for the quantity demanded by the market; consequently, the price rises.

Timothy Taylor[60] addresses this relationship: "A demand curve shows the relationship between quantity demanded and price in a given market on a graph. The law of demand states that a higher price typically leads to a lower amount demanded."

At times, the market reaches equilibrium. There is no excess or shortage in this situation, either in terms of demand or supply. Product and service consumer demand are practically the same as what producers want to sell.

---

[60] TAYLOR, Timothy; GREENLAW, Steven A; SHAPIRO David. Principles of Microeconomics. 2nd edition. USA: 12th Media Services, December 31, 2017

Price equilibrium occurs naturally, with producers disputing consumer preferences in competitive markets. Under these conditions, the following stand out:

- Perfect competition: a situation in which there are numerous producers and consumers, and no player has the power to influence the market's direction;
- Imperfect competition: at least one consumer or producer has the potential to drive the market and dictate the conditions for conducting business.

Supply and demand theory applies to purchases. A reduced supply suggests a monopoly (only one producer) or oligopoly (few producers), a situation in which the supplier sets the market price because customers have little influence (imperfect competition).

In this environment, researching and developing new suppliers stimulates competition, increases supply, and as a result, prices tend to fall.

The development of alternative products to replace those with increased prices has the same effect (the so-called substitution effect).

A further action for the purchaser is to adjust the volumes according to the market situation. For example, when he perceives that prices are favorable, he should suggest increasing the purchased quantity to the inventory management area.

Another possibility is to become a member of a purchasing group, an entity formed by a list of companies to consolidate purchases and, with the increase in quantity, strengthen the general negotiating power of the group's participants and influence market variables in this context of imperfect competition.

Finally, identifying unnecessary costs to eliminate from the price is a task to develop with suppliers. In the process, there may be a reduction in the number of suppliers in the chain, joint development of new products, and orientation of the leading suppliers according to the interests of those involved.

17.3 Macroeconomics and the main variables

Macroeconomics is a branch of economic science dedicated to studying, measuring, and observing regional or national economies in a broad context.

The elaboration of an accurate analysis, which facilitates the understanding of the behavior of the economy of a specific region, depends on the choice of macroeconomic variables.

The main variables are:

- the exchange rate;
- the inflation rate;
- the interest rate;
- the level of employment.

These variables are interrelated, meaning any change in one impacts the others.

Timothy Taylor[61] examines the variables and their implications: "We can determine an economy's macroeconomic health by examining many goals: growth in the standard of living, low unemployment, and low inflation, to name the most important."

When the economic situation is in conditions interpreted as unfavorable, interventions are necessary to bring the economy back to satisfactory standards.

For example, if inflation rises to values considered far above-established targets and harmful to economic activity, a relevant action would be to raise the interest rate. With the cost of money rising, inflation tends to decrease.

17.3.1 Inflation

The term inflation refers to the continuous and general increase in the prices of goods and services in an economy, expressing a decrease in the purchasing power of money.

The inflation rate, commonly referred to as the inflation index, usually expressed as a percentage, is the result of a calculation using various price indicators and reveals the variation in prices of a predefined basket of products and services.

---

[61] TAYLOR, Timothy; GREENLAW, Steven A; SHAPIRO David. Principles of Microeconomics. 2nd edition. USA: 12th Media Services, December 31, 2017

In economic theory, there are definitions for three types of inflation:

- Demand;
- Costs;
- Inertial.

Demand inflation results from an increase in the population's purchasing power, exceeding the economy's ability to provide goods and services (a situation in which demand grows more than supply).

Compared with the availability of goods and services, this excess demand leads to a struggle among consumers to satisfy their needs and allows producers to raise prices. In this case, the price increase may continue to a level that forces customer demand to decline, and a balance between supply and demand occurs.

Cost inflation is associated with production structure. In this situation, demand changes little, but the costs of essential inputs increase, resulting in a consequent pass-through to product prices.

One cause of cost inflation is the action of monopoly companies or oligopolies that raise their prices by managing market conditions above the increase in production costs.

Finally, inertial inflation arises because of the psychological impact of inflationary trends from the previous periods. When demand or cost inflation persists for lengthy periods at high rates, economic agents adapt to the inflationary process and systematically increase prices to avoid future losses. This action perpetuates inflation.

17.3.2 Employment

The second macroeconomic variable measures the number of people employed within the economically active population (the number of people in the labor market).

Employment level measurement uses an indicator representing non-agricultural payrolls in the United States. It determines the number of people employed and paid in the United States. Includes the entire workforce except those in the primary sector (the economy segment that produces raw materials, such as agriculture, livestock, fisheries, and mining).

This index is part of a report on the employment situation, representing approximately 80% of the jobs included in the calculation of the Gross Domestic Product (GDP) of the United States.

The unemployment rate is another essential piece of information. It measures the percentage of unemployed people who searched for a job 30 days before the survey concerning the total workforce of the working age.

A percentage higher than that estimated by the market may indicate weakness in the US labor market, negatively impacting the US dollar.

Household consumption is directly proportional to a population's level of employment and income. In situations of falling consumption, which is a limiting factor for growth, there is a reduction in GDP (Gross Domestic Product) and an increase in unemployment.

17.3.3 Exchange rate

The exchange rate is the numerical relationship between the currencies of two countries. This parameter indicates the amount of domestic currency needed to buy a unit of a specific foreign currency. It expresses the exchange relations between the two countries. For example, 1.00 US Dollars = "X" GBP. Bob Steiner[62] defined: "An effective exchange rate is a measure of the change in a country's exchange rate against a basket of other currencies important to that country's trade."

It is one of the most important macroeconomic variables, mainly because it affects a country's commercial and financial relations with others. Currency fluctuations interfere with imports and exports.

Devaluation of the national currency raises the exchange rate and makes the country use more currency units in imports, making goods imported abroad more expensive. This effect discourages imports.

The exchange devaluation action induces other countries to increase their purchases of goods, which will be cheaper in their currencies. This situation encourages exports from countries whose currencies suffered devaluations. Nonetheless, this benefit is often insufficient to offset the losses resulting from a decrease in the value of the national currency.

---

[62] STEINER, Robert. Mastering Financial Calculations: A Step-by-Step Guide to the Mathematics of Financial Market Instruments. 2nd edition. USA: Prentice Hall 2007

On the other hand, an increase in the value of the national currency against other currencies boosts imports by increasing people's purchasing power, as the prices of products from abroad will be lower.

The same currency appreciation action decreases exports, as domestic products become more expensive in foreign currency, and discourages purchases by other countries.

Finally, the trade balance concept expresses the relationship between imports and exports of goods and services between countries. When a country's exports outweigh its imports, the effect is the emergence of a trade surplus; the balance is positive, and more money comes in than goes out. When imports are higher than exports, trade deficits also appear in value, indicating that the country spent more than it received.

The trade balance will be more favorable when the country exports more than imports in monetary terms.

17.3.4 Interest rate

Central banks command base interest rates, such as the Federal Reserve (Fed) of the United States and the European Central Bank (ECB) responsible for the Eurozone's single currency.

Competence in interest rate management is essential, as it interferes with increasing or reducing credit for individuals and companies and affects other macroeconomic variables.

In times of a sharp fall in interest rates, the population has more credit at their disposal, they can consume more, and one consequence is pressure on demand. This movement increases inflation rates.

When interest rates rise, the immediate effect is curbing consumption and investment and reducing inflation.

All governments need tools to contain price increases, and the economy's base interest rate is the most effective.

Central banks intervene in the financial market by negotiating government bonds, which leads to the average rate of operations reaching the intended objective. When it is essential to raise the target for the interest rate, the Central Bank influences the operations of the financial market and, therefore, achieves the desired objective.

James K. Hawkins

The increase in interest rates influences employment because when they are high, the effect is to reduce consumption, causing a decline in sales. This situation forces companies to lay off idle employees.

In times of recession and falling inflation, central banks reduce interest rates to increase consumption and encourage higher employment.

CHAPTER 18

NEGOTIATION

We cannot negotiate with people who say what's mine is mine, and what's yours is negotiable.

John F. Kennedy[63]

Negotiation is one of the essential characteristics of human beings. Most of the time, people negotiate without realizing this.

Asking for a discount on the car repair budget at the garage, setting an allowance with the children, or requesting a salary increase are ordinary everyday acts. They all have in common the fact that negotiations are present.

Roger Fisher[64] has the same approach: "Like it or not, you are a negotiator. Negotiation is a fact of life. You discuss a raise with your boss. You try to agree with a stranger on a price for his house. Two lawyers try to settle a lawsuit arising from a car accident".

People endeavor to achieve what they need or what gives them pleasure, and occasionally there is a conflict with what other people want or need. In such situations, reaching an agreement that satisfactorily reconciles the interests and necessities of those involved is imperative. Otherwise, the process would be fruitless.

The best alternative to resolving this problem is negotiating and looking for ways to overcome these differences.

Without intending to fill readers' heads with theories on the subject, it is helpful to scrutinize the expressions most frequently used in various definitions of negotiation. Below are examples:

• Bargaining power;

---

[63] John Fitzgerald Kennedy (May 29, 1917 – November 22, 1963), often referred to by his initials JFK, was an American politician who served as the 35th president of the United States from 1961 until his assassination in 1963.

[64] FISHER, Roger; URY, William L, PATTON Bruce. Getting to Yes: Negotiating Agreement Without Giving in. 3rd Revised ed. USA: Penguin Books, May 3, 2011

- Choosing the best alternative from a collective point of view;
- Get Agreements;
- Global proposals overlap individual ones;
- Make concessions;
- Perform a resource exchange;
- Parties must speak and listen;
- The result must satisfy, even partially, the interests and needs of everyone;
- Understand that some parties control the features others want.

In a negotiation, such expressions play a fundamental role, so it is useful to incorporate them into the vocabulary. The effort to understand the needs and interests of others is an essential factor in successfully reaching an agreement.

When people decide to buy a car, they want it for locomotion, transporting objects or people, to stick to a few possibilities.

A car salesperson who cannot identify what the customer wants will face difficulties in making a sale. What is the use of exalting the virtues of economy and mechanical simplicity for someone interested in a powerful car with excellent performance?

18.1 The importance of subjective factors

Although the effort to collect data and information about the subject of conversations and the intention to focus on measurable variables, essential aspects that are difficult to quantify deserve attention. They integrate subjective components worthy of consideration, inducing people to perceive the same situation differently. It is not prudent to disregard the influence of subjective factors on a negotiation's result.

Sometimes, a negotiator returns home disappointed because he judges the negotiation outcome as unsatisfactory. Curiously, other negotiators would be pleased to get the same results, considering them suitable.

The reason for the difference in interpretation is the influence of subjective elements. By assumption, the purchaser's best bid for an item is $20,000. He intends to obtain a 5% discount, which he considers satisfactory.

At the beginning of the conversation with the seller, he asks for a 7% discount, slightly above what he wants, as he assumes there will be a counterproposal from the seller, and after a discussion, it will reach 5%.

To the purchaser's surprise, the seller, with a smile, immediately agrees to grant the 7% discount. It seems to be an unequivocal demonstration of satisfaction with a better-than-expected result.

Disappointment with the deal will be the purchaser's feeling, even getting a price below what he wanted. Frustration stems from the seller's prompt acceptance and visible signs of satisfaction.

Conversely, the purchaser would not consider the result unfavorable if he knew that the seller was at risk of dismissal and needed to sell desperately. For this reason, he gave up part of the commission to grant the 7% discount to get the deal. Nevertheless, perceiving subjective factors involved in the transaction is often tricky.

18.2 Possible Results in the Negotiations

One aspect to highlight in commercial purchases is the cyclical characteristic. Owing to this recurrence, a purchaser's behavior in a current deal will affect future negotiations with the same supplier.

What is the benefit of obtaining a positive result from momentary inequality of forces if the supplier tries to reverse the situation in subsequent negotiations? There are no advantages to this procedure.

This understanding makes it possible to distinguish the possible negotiation outcomes.

18.2.1 Lose-Lose

This is the most unwanted result, as everyone has losses with the business done, which may eventually not even materialize.

The lose-lose result has a variety of characteristics:

- Adoption of defensive positions that demonstrate insecurity to third parties;
- Indications that participants have poor information about the business, opponent, and market;
- Lack of prior planning on both sides;
- Negotiators demonstrate low flexibility, making it difficult to change positions;

- Negotiators focus too much on the other party's weaknesses;
- Reduced attention to the other's speech;
- The needs of others do not require further attention. Each participant is exclusively concerned with their goals;
- The perception that compromise is evidence of weakness.

Roger Fisher[65] details the characteristics of negotiators revealing why there is this type of result: "The hard negotiator sees any situation as a contest of wills in which the side that takes the more extreme positions and holds out longer fares better. They want to win, yet often produce an equally hard response that exhausts the negotiator and their resources and harms the relationship with the other side".

18.2.2 Win-Lose or Lose-Win

At first glance, it is an excellent result for those who "win", but it will be bad for everyone in the long run.

Many people cannot control their desire to obtain all benefits, even if it harms the other side.

The win-lose result has the following characteristics:

- Considers the needs of others unimportant;
- Focus on people and not on the issues under discussion;
- Interpreting the act of compromise as a demonstration of weakness;
- Lack of long-term vision;
- Non-compliance with assumed commitments;
- The one-sided focus on the problem;
- There is a desire to "win" at any cost;
- There is no recollection of what the other party said.

18.2.3 Win-Win

This is the most beneficial result of negotiation. If there is an effort on the part of the participants to guarantee a maximum collective gain, this

---

[65] FISHER, Roger; URY, William L, PATTON Bruce. Getting to Yes: Negotiating Agreement Without Giving in. 3rd Revised ed. USA: Penguin Books, May 3, 2011

result tends to consolidate. It is noteworthy that those involved do not need to benefit equally. Occasionally, one side may be more favored, but only because of the particularities of the process.

The win-win outcome should be the goal of every negotiator at every opportunity to reach an agreement, as it is the one that brings more gains to the participants.

The win-win result has the following characteristics:

- Dedication to well-designed planning;
- An effort to memorize the main points of others' speech;
- Participants take a long-term view;
- Significant flexibility of those involved in the process;
- There is a commitment to keeping promises made;
- Transmission of trust to the other party;
- Use of qualified Information;
- Valuing the needs of others.

18.3 The assumptions of the negotiations

The basis for negotiating is the dedication to developing the best possible deal under these circumstances. Fisher[66] elaborates a good exposition on the question: "A wise agreement can be defined as one that meets the legitimate interests of each side to the extent possible, resolves conflicting interests fairly, is durable, and takes community interests into account."

Based on these premises, there are three essential parameters in a negotiation that deserve active management, leading to the best result:

- Time,
- Information and,
- Power.

When one negotiator is better positioned in these aspects, he is more likely to benefit from the process.

---

[66] FISHER, Roger; URY, William L, PATTON Bruce. Getting to Yes: Negotiating Agreement Without Giving in. 3rd Revised ed. USA: Penguin Books, May 3, 2011

18.3.1 About the time

Haste is a precursor to a bad deal. It is challenging to negotiate well when there is an urgency to finish the discussion. In a negotiation, having more time for the process increases the chances of success.

Requesters often approach purchasers, usually at the beginning of the working day, demanding the delivery of specific material to "still today; otherwise, the operation will stop."

All purchasing professionals have experienced these situations. In these cases, there is a clear disadvantage for the purchaser vis-à-vis the supplier, and the more predictable consequences are higher costs, poorer quality, and delayed delivery.

In this scenario, having time is essential, so it is unacceptable for a purchasing professional to delay an acquisition until the last minute, creating an urgency for himself.

Collaborating with users to clarify the consequences of emergency requests is indispensable, as discussed in a previous chapter.

18.3.2 Information

Information is power; whoever has the most qualified information will have more chances of achieving a good result in a negotiation. Therefore, the following are crucial:

- Know in detail the characteristics of the business itself;
- Be familiar with the dynamics of the market in which the company operates;
- Have a history of the supplier's performance over time;
- Know the behavior of people involved in previous negotiations.

Collecting information is an essential part of negotiation planning, influencing the outcome.

18.3.3 Regarding power

Understanding the bargaining power of each participant in an ongoing negotiation is essential. Conditions such as product quality, the urgency to sell or buy, price, and the existence of exclusivity influence a commercial negotiation.

Addressing the power issue means knowing the strengths of the supplier and purchaser, as specified below:

- Possible strengths of the supplier
  - Accepts to sell with extended payment terms;
  - Always meet the quality set by the customer;
  - Ensures immediate technical assistance;
  - Excellent delivery track record;
  - Have exclusivity in the manufacture/sale of material or service provision;
  - It demonstrates flexibility in terms of quantity (it can deliver large or small amounts according to the client's needs);
  - It has certifications in quality programs;
  - It has registered trademarks or patents;
  - It is competitive in price;
  - Provide a guarantee superior to that of the competition.
- Possible forces of the purchaser
  - Acquisitions made regularly;
  - Demonstrates punctuality in payments;
  - Developing a new supplier is viable;
  - Existence of diversity in the sales market;
  - It is possible to develop substitute material within a reasonable time;
  - Makes high-value purchases;
  - Order large quantities;
  - Power to influence other purchasers.
  - Shows ability to manufacture the material or perform the service;

Every ongoing business requires interaction between the customer and supplier, each exposing its strengths and trying to hide its weaknesses. Those who can better control these factors will obtain more favorable outcomes.

In the sphere of power, the most frequent doubts of purchasing professionals are:

- How to negotiate with exclusive suppliers?
- How to deal with cartels?

Initially, it is worth distinguishing an oligopoly from a cartel's meaning. These associations are different.

A characteristic of an oligopoly is that it concentrates on a few companies with the capacity to supply a particular product to a specific market.

On the other hand, a cartel is an illegal union between companies intending to dictate market rules, combine prices, distribute areas of activity, and divide quantities among members.

Exclusiveness cases are the most challenging situations in the purchasing department, as the customer is at a disadvantage compared to the supplier, who is fully aware of its unique condition.

The purchaser has few options when negotiating with exclusive suppliers. However, he can put some tricks into practice:

- Price: focusing the negotiation on price is complicated, as the exclusive supplier rarely reduces the value. There are more chances of success if the attempt is to try to extend the payment term without a financial cost, which is another form of gain;
- Centralization of purchases: if branches of the company consume the same material, centralizing the acquisition increases the quantity and makes the negotiation relevant to the supplier;
- Administering the quantity: in items with an exclusive supplier, ordering significant amounts with deliveries scheduled in a contract induces the supplier to think about the total volume, arousing their interest, as opposed to what would happen with smaller quantities;
- Emergencies: emergencies are always unfavorable, and with exclusive suppliers, there is a worsening of the situation because, if there is something unforeseen, the possibility of a shortage of material due to a lack of options increases. Increasing stock can be a way to avoid emergencies, not to mention the importance of well-thought-out planning to make these situations rare;
- Import, development of new suppliers, and investment in alternative materials: the supplier must constantly be pressured by the possibility

of the purchaser, in a brief period, to import the material, develop another supplier, or approve a substitute material. These actions strongly impact the seller, mainly because any possibility would compromise the supplier's dominance in the market since the fact would come to other consumers' knowledge. A more complex alternative would be for the client company to manufacture materials. Finally, even if none of the options is viable, the purchaser must make the supplier believe otherwise;

- Formation of purchasing groups (oligopsony): companies that consume the same product get together and buy large volumes. Grouped companies need not be in the same sector. For example, a company that supplies hotel trays can team up with a catering company. However, it is more common for companies in the same sector to group their orders. Successful purchaser clusters include hospitals, hotels, and small pharmacies.

Dealing with cartels is even more arduous because of collusion between member companies. The purchaser has few alternatives for action, highlighting the development of new suppliers and/or materials or the import of the product. In specific cases, it is even possible to pit a supplier against another cartel member and thus gain an advantage, but this is certainly not easy.

The same suggestions for negotiating with exclusive suppliers apply in the case of cartels.

18.4 Basic rules for effective negotiation

It is common for some negotiations to prove unproductive, often because of a lack of guidelines that make the process more productive and avoid conflicts or frustrate the creation of unrealistic expectations about the conclusion of the agreement.

Occasionally, a more detailed examination is sufficient to reach a satisfactory agreement to generate the necessary conditions. The following suggestions are helpful.

18.4.1 Be well prepared

Prioritizing the analysis of the main points is excellent for obtaining a good result in the negotiation, such as planning tactics for each process step before meeting with the other negotiator.

William Ury[67] addressed the importance of preparing in advance to negotiate: "Before every meeting, prepare. After every meeting, assess your progress, adapt your strategy, and prepare again. The secret of effective negotiation is that simple: prepare, prepare, prepare".

Competently planning the conduct of a negotiation is a prerequisite for efficient execution and, by extension, obtaining the expected results. Thus, the purchasing department must be in tune with the schedule of internal customers to develop their work to satisfy their needs and avoid shortages.

It is always good to remember that the seller works with a small range of materials, being a knowledgeable specialist in the market and its peculiarities. However, the purchaser acquires countless items and knows each one superficially. The disparity between them is significant and adverse for purchasing professionals.

One of the alternatives to reduce inequality is working hard to plan the various aspects of negotiation and collecting as much qualified information as possible.

18.4.2 Be a good listener

Literature on the subject is emphatic in pointing out the person's ability to be a good listener as a precondition for negotiating well. People who focus on the interlocutor are more likely to get good deals because they understand and retain the transmitted content.

Au contraire, those who tend to talk too much and ignore other people's information are more disadvantaged than good listeners.

---

[67] URY, William L. Getting Past No: Negotiating in Difficult Situations, Revised edition. USA: Bantam Dell, April 17, 2007

The ability to communicate is essential. Frazelle[68] highlights this issue well: "The inability to communicate naturally breeds frustration, blocks trust, and creates barriers to progress and creativity."

Encouraging others to share what they want to achieve helps formulate proposals that meet the needs of those involved. Recommendations to improve the condition of a good listener are as follows:

- Allow others to express themselves without interruption;
- Avoid distractions during the speaker's speech, even if it seems irrelevant;
- Conceal eventual discomfort if the interlocutor manifests antagonistic positions to yours;
- Develop the ability to retain the content of the conversation;
- Ignore environmental interference and keep the attention on the business under discussion;
- Understand between the lines, as not everything is said exclusively with words.

---

[68] FRAZELLE, Edward H. Supply Chain Strategy: Unleash the Power of Business Integration to Maximize Financial, Service, and Operations Performance. 2nd edition. USA: McGraw-Hill, October 27, 2017

18.4.3 Make concessions little by little

> Charles is a large pharmaceutical laboratory purchaser acquiring imported raw materials for a newly developed product.
>
> After receiving only two proposals, Charles chose to negotiate with the Royal seller, who offered a shorter delivery time. The other commercial conditions are equivalent to those of the competitor.
>
> Charles was confident that he could reduce the vendor price from $10.20 to $9.60 per unit, which he and his manager set as the maximum.
>
> Francis, the seller, aware of the reason for the meeting, previously met with the company's board of directors and received authorization to reduce the price to $9.30 to get the sale.
>
> Early in the conversation, Charles suggested reducing it to $9.50 as a business condition. Francis replied that he could come up with $9.60.
>
> Obtaining the target price, Charles agreed to the offer and placed the order at $9.60 per unit.
>
> Questions
>
> a) Did Charles get the best deal possible for his company?
> b) If the answer is no, what could he have done differently?

Even with the price cut from $10.20 to $9.60, the target value set, meaning a 5.88% discount, he did not obtain the best deal for the company.

With better handling of the process, the chances of reducing the price by 8.82% (from $10.20 to $9.30) would be more significant.

Charles proposed a value without first investigating the seller's minimum price. It is worth mentioning that knowing the seller's minimum price during negotiations is not feasible, but getting close is.

If Charles managed the concessions better, offering them piecemeal, he would obtain a price of less than $9.60.

The purchaser must try to convince the seller that he will buy the merchandise if there is a price reduction.

As an action, it should seek to minimize the seller's expectations, always remembering that making a counteroffer is not an option precisely because it does not know the opponent's limits.

To avoid losing credibility, a negotiator can never mention a meager price outside market standards to avoid retreating in the future and accepting higher values.

Figure 18.1. shows an example of the parties' positions, boundaries, and, most importantly, identifying the range in which agreements are possible. The seller initially proposed a value of 100, while his minimum price was 70 (information unknown to the purchaser).

If asked to provide a value, the purchaser would start from 60 and could pay up to 80 (information unknown by the seller).

Under the conditions mentioned above, it is possible to conclude the deal between 70 and 80, the "feasibility margin of negotiation."

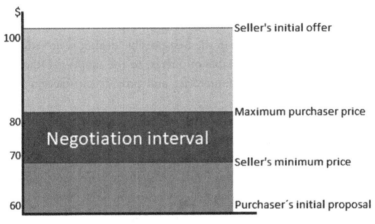

Figure 18.1.: Potential gap for agreement

18.4.4 Never accept the first offer

This situation is like that in the previous topic. If moderation in concessions is the rule, then accepting the supplier's first offer is inadvisable.

Anyone accepting an initial offer demonstrates anxiety about closing a deal, which will produce unfavorable results. This negotiator ignores the principle that those who sell ask for a lot, whereas those who buy offer little.

This attitude affects not only prices but also other conditions offered. Accepting the initial proposal frustrates the other negotiator, and he considers having gotten a bad deal.

In this process, it is essential to encourage the seller's sense of success, but when the purchaser quickly accepts the proposed first option, the effect is the opposite.

Under these conditions, the seller interprets the customer's haste to accept the offer as a sign that earning more would be possible, leaving the deal frustrated.

18.4.5 Recognize the importance of seller satisfaction

Because acquisitions are periodic, purchasers should not ignore the possibility of renegotiating with the same seller in the future.

Aware of this situation, ensuring that the supplier feels satisfied with the deal is essential to strengthening their relationship.

As the objective is to obtain the best possible deal, it is not advisable to consider price as the only variable of interest to the supplier. Other aspects can favor acceptance of a counteroffer and provide satisfaction with the agreement.

Examples of negotiable terms with the potential to stimulate the closing of the deal are as follows:

- The supplier resorted to bank loans. If the purchaser finds out, he can suggest paying upon delivery of the material at a good discount but lower than the interest the bank charges;
- The customer wants to split deliveries, but the supplier initially disagrees. The purchaser suggests the possibility of a slight increase in quantity, and the agreement becomes in the seller's interest;
- The client company has famous brands and is a leader in its market segment. A new supplier is usually interested in receiving an order from that company to use as a reference in other businesses, favoring negotiation for the purchaser if he/she knows how to use this condition.

18.4.6 Do not compromise the objectives of negotiation due to personal differences

In certain situations, for any reason, the purchasing professional may not have a good relationship with the seller. This circumstance must not interfere with the purchasers' decisions. It is a mistake to allow personal issues to hinder departmental performance.

When meeting an untactful seller, the purchaser must maintain self-control and isolate the person from business issues. William Ury[69] mentions the importance of the approach: "...soft on the people, hard on the problem. Instead of attacking each other, you jointly attack the problem".

It is essential to develop an excellent professional relationship with supplier representatives in any situation, even when there is a diversity of beliefs or any other nature.

Goodwill in treatment is essential to increase the chances of success in a negotiation. Never allow the process to turn into a battle of egos!

18.4.7 Avoid presenting the first offer

One classic mistake when negotiating is initiating conversations by offering something to others. When a purchaser acts this way, the supplier can guess how much he is willing to pay, and the deal tends to materialize at a higher price.

As a rule, the negotiator who makes an offer first is at a disadvantage by revealing his/her intent without knowing what the other participant intends to achieve.

The following story encourages reflection for those still skeptical of the statement's veracity.

Leo Baekeland sold the rights to his invention, Velox Photographic Printing Paper, to Eastman Kodak for $1 million in 1899. The innovation resulted in the sale of the first successful photographic paper.

Baekeland planned to start the conversation by asking for $50,000 but was willing to accept $25,000 to close the deal.

---

[69] URY, William L. Getting Past No: Negotiating in Difficult Situations. Revised edition. USA: Bantam Dell, April 17, 2007

Fortunately for him, Eastman representatives presented the proposal first![70]"

18.4.8 Refuse to split the difference

Lucy is a purchaser at Madison University and is negotiating with Robert, a salesperson for the Demartists Furniture Industry, to buy a thousand university chairs. Lucy wants to make a deal with the Demartists to preserve standardization since the other university units use the chair of that company.

Robert proposed $50.00 for each chair, but Lucy proposed paying $40.00.

Faced with the impasse and after a prolonged period of fruitless conversations, the seller suggests halving the difference between his offer and Lucy's proposal, $10, and closing the deal for $45 each.

Lucy thought and considered splitting the difference a fair solution for both and accepted the seller's offer.

Questions:
1. Was Lucy right to agree to split the difference?
2. If negative, what attitude should Lucy have taken?

When there is a price impasse, it is common for someone to suggest splitting the difference between the values to close the deal. The premise is to calculate the difference between the values, divide by two, add to the smallest, and close the deal with the total obtained.

It seems an impartial rule, but, in percentage terms, the result is not fair for those who argued for the lowest value.

Regarding the purchase of Madison University, Lucy should refuse to split the difference. The seller reduced his offer by 10%, while the purchaser increased the value by 12.5%. In percentage terms, the customer was at a disadvantage.

When the seller offers to split the difference, he makes a new offer. Those who are buying should continue to negotiate to aim at values below this new level.

---

[70] ZENZ, Gary J. Purchasing and the Management of Materials. 7th edition. USA: Wiley, January 14, 1994

Alternatively, as per the seller's suggestion to split the difference, Lucy could have proposed a similar procedure, but in percentage terms, which would reduce the price by 11.1111% to $44.44.

18.4.9 Identify the reasons for the impasse

Occasionally, fruitless discussions consume hours because those involved fail to identify the core of the disagreement, a curious situation as the meeting between the parties aims to resolve the issue.

This type of debate is more common when it involves internal problems, pitting purchasers against users who describe the intended materials or services differently than desired and leading to errors.

Often, someone requests the hiring of security guards when the objective is to improve security; another asks for the purchase of reprographic machines when the real need is for printing services, whereas a third party demands the purchase of a vehicle when the need is for transport service.

In these situations, it is up to the purchasing department to demonstrate, in a reasoned manner, that the best solution from the company's point of view differs from the applicant's initial idea. Arguments must occur without generating wear and tear between the parties involved.

18.4.10 Try to avoid the time to negotiate being too short

SITUATION A

James is the managing director of a pharmaceutical company branch and plans to lease a new location as the business expands.

He inspected a place in the city's center, which he liked, and now he will meet with the owner to analyze whether it is feasible to close the deal.

James considers the office suitable for business but is in no hurry to close the deal. He set a maximum rental value of $6,000, as he found that the site's expenses would increase to $1,500.00 starting the following month.

James plans to look elsewhere if he cannot complete the deal for $6,000 or less.

SITUATION B

Oliver owns commercial property in the city center that has been unoccupied for six months.

Talking to the building manager, he found that in the next month, the expenses would go from R$ 1,300.00 to R$ 1,500.00.

Oliver faces financial difficulties and cannot pay the new amount. He urgently needs to rent the property and is optimistic about the venture's success, as a laboratory director has shown great interest in renting the office.

If Oliver does not find a tenant quickly, he risks paying another month of expenses and will need to get a loan as he does not have the necessary amount.

The week before, Oliver intended to receive $8,000 monthly to rent the property.

Question: Knowing the two situations, for what value would it be possible to do business?

Oliver needs to quickly rent the property, which has been unoccupied for six months, as expenses will increase in the next month.

James, on the other hand, is in a comfortable situation. Even considering the property adequate, he is in no hurry to close the deal and has set a rent limit of $6,000.

In the challenging context where he finds himself, Oliver must act to minimize his losses, and the solution is to forego higher rent.

This should reflect on the long time it takes to advertise the place without getting a tenant. In this context, the best thing for Oliver would be to accept a lower rent than he has stipulated. If so, he could do business with James for $6,000. Naturally, Oliver ignores James's intended value, but if he is skillful at negotiating, he will get the deal close to that value.

Looking coldly, closing the deal will be an advantage for Oliver, even if he accepts a lower value than initially intended.

As for the case details, time should be an ally, never an enemy. Those who have more time to negotiate have more chances of success.

Therefore, anyone should refuse to participate in last-minute negotiations whenever possible because the damage is almost inevitable. If possible, the purchaser should transfer time pressure to the seller.

18.4.11 Insinuate that there are limits as a form of pressure

Purchasers must use their skills to obtain the best deal. He may suggest that he has limits on concluding an agreement and use the argument to put pressure on the seller.

For example, the purchaser might mention the existence of a financial limit, something like "...I am allowed to pay up to $12,500.00 for this material; the cost department will re-evaluate any proposal with a higher value."

Sellers understand the disadvantages of subjecting the purchasing process to other areas. Therefore, the business will exit under these conditions if the purchaser's proposition is minimally acceptable to the seller. It is possible to cancel acquisitions during a reanalysis.

This argument does not prevent acceptance of a higher value if the supplier cannot reach a lower price. You can always argue that you have tried and obtained validation from the cost department for the seller's minimum value.

18.4.12 Put yourself in the seller's shoes

Empathy is the ability to understand another person's feelings in the present situation and try to put oneself in their shoes. This way of acting helps reaches an agreement.

Each negotiation involves at least two sides. On many occasions, "switching sides" with the other person helps to understand their point of view and identify any inflexibility that limits the chances of success.

It is not easy to understand the process from another 's point of view, but the attempt helps to develop new business options.

David Burt[71] highlights the importance of paying attention to the other person's feelings: "Maintain a climate of mutual benefit, trust, rapport, and a win-win outcome."

---

[71] BURT, David N; PETCAVAGE, Sheila; PINKERTON, Richard. Proactive Purchasing in the Supply Chain: The Key to World-Class Procurement. 1st edition. USA: McGraw Hill, December 6, 2011

18.4.13 Don't take advantage of each other's weaknesses

When they see the opportunity to do a profitable business, various professionals do not hesitate to take advantage of any weakness on the other side.

This negotiator only sees the opportunity to obtain a quick and profitable deal and disregards long-term effects.

An experienced negotiator understands that this strategy is inadequate and outdated. Focusing on an opponent's strengths when creating a business plan is always preferable.

Trying to impose your position because of the other party's difficulties usually produces a lose-lose result. After all, no one likes to see any aspect of themselves or their products undervalued.

Such an attitude usually generates resentment that will complicate future negotiations.

18.4.14 Avoid personal relationships with the seller

> Johnny has been a salesperson for Distoll, a carton maker and packaging supplier to the PHT Electronics Industry, a Boston-based company, for years. So far, all Distoll packaging delivered have met performance standards for quality and on-time delivery.
>
> After years of supplying, Johnny established a friendship with Matthew, a PHT purchaser, with whom he plays tennis weekly. In the view of both, proximity did not interfere with professional performance when they needed to negotiate.
>
> A few months ago, PHT asked Distoll for a proposal to purchase packaging for the next six months, with scheduled deliveries every 30 days.
>
> Distoll's proposal, sent by e-mail, highlights that there will be price adjustments from the second delivery based on the variation in pulp price in the international market.
>
> Matthew forgot to insert the readjustment clause in the order prepared for that purchase. Johnny noticed the error and questioned his friend about the omission of the readjustment clause.
>
> Matthew realized the error and asked Johnny to wait a few days to correct it. He explained that there was an analogous situation a week ago, and he did not want to communicate with his superiors about the new error in such a brief time.

Not wanting to impair his friend, Johnny agreed to wait a week for the correction and accepted the order without the clause.

Ten days later, Matthew went to work at a PHT branch in another state. When the second batch of packages arrived, the new purchaser did not accept the corrected price, as the order had no readjustment clause.

Matthew was far away and did not have a good relationship with the new purchaser, so the matter created great weariness for everyone involved, caused losses for Distoll, and left Johnny in an uncomfortable situation at the company.

Question: Was the two professionals' conduct correct when dealing with the problem?

Although the situation described is common in the purchaser/seller relationship, the lack of professionalism is evident since they could never behave in the way mentioned in the text.

The purchaser's failure less than a week ago does not justify the delay in correcting an omission as the recent one. He took advantage of the seller's friendship when he asked him to wait a bit to include readjustment.

In turn, the seller was also unprofessional, as rejecting the order without the clause was the only acceptable attitude. It is a classic case of personal and professional issues mingling and causing unwanted consequences.

Purchasing and sales professionals can occasionally relate outside of the work environment. This relationship often leads to partnerships between companies; however, it never justifies the lack of professionalism when deciding.

18.4.15 Elaborate alternatives during the process

The roadmap initially planned to negotiate is often not optimal. Occasionally, an alternative solution may be better.

As Kleemann[72] points out: "However, a full picture of how to approach the negotiation is only possible if also awareness for the objectives of the designated provider is raised. Not surprisingly, they are opposed to the customer's goals. On the other hand, identifying potential conflicts (cost reduction vs. profit maximization) is a crucial advantage of strategic planning negotiations. This

[72] KLEEMANN, Florian C. Outsourcing of Manufacturing Processes: Negotiating with a Single Sourcing Supplier. 1st edition. Germany: GRIN Verlag, March 5, 2012

way, it can be recognized that goals appearing to be conflictive could be resolved if the underlying intentions are identified and used to align interests, rather than entering into conflictive disputes."

The purchaser should devise ways to reconcile interests to reach an understanding. Once again, the importance of being flexible when negotiating!

Liam is a Commercial Bank purchaser and must buy 1,000 panels (screens) for placement at branch entrances. Among the products that meet the required quality standard, the Quespion Industry of Panels offered the lowest price.

The requisition specifies that delivery must occur within 40 days, but Quespion cannot supply the total amount within that period.

Initially, Liam is considering splitting the supply between the four companies that submitted a proposal, but the acquisition value will rise by 13%.

Dissatisfied with the situation, Liam decides to go deeper into the matter. The purchaser contacts the requester and finds that receiving 200 panels in 40 days meets the needs. The balance may arrive 60 days later.

With the added information, Liam questions the Quespion salesperson, who, in contact with production, confirms that he will meet the proposed schedule, although the deadline is short.

As a precaution, Liam resumes contact with the applicant and asks if a slight delay in delivering the balance would be manageable. Given the renovation schedule, he discovers that a slight delay will not harm.

After the usual arrangements, Liam issues the order for Quespion.

The purchaser looked for alternatives to enable the acquisition with the supplier at a lower cost since the only restriction was the delivery time.

If he considered the first delivery date the only possible, he would make a terrible deal, paying 13% more. During the negotiation, options emerged, and talking internally and externally made it possible to satisfy everyone's needs.

Not being content with a poor solution and developing alternatives are essential to doing better business.

18.4.16 Do not make commitments that you are not sure you can fulfill.

For a negotiator, a lack of credibility is the worst weakness. He will face difficulties in future negotiations. This issue is critical for purchasers, who must conduct internal and external negotiations daily.

Promising and not fulfilling is a severe conduct deficiency resulting from the desire to address everything and satisfy everyone without distinction, a characteristic of many professionals.

Before committing, the purchaser must check the feasibility of his proposal.

For example, suppose a human resources manager asks the purchaser for personalized folders and graphics for a training session attended by all the managers and directors.

It forwards the request well in advance and goes after all steps to avoid errors. The busy purchaser does not perform the follow-up but guarantees that the material will be available on the stipulated date.

However, the materials were unavailable during the training due to the supplier's failure. In such a situation, assuming that the purchaser's credibility in future relationships with these human resources professionals will be extremely low is reasonable.

18.5 Other negotiation topics

Now here are practical considerations for dealing with internal suppliers and customers.

18.5.1 Bluff

Marian is a garment purchaser and completes the acquisition of 12,000 meters of fabric necessary for the company's production.

She received proposals whose unit prices are below. The other commercial conditions are identical for all suppliers:

1. Cotton & Cotton $ 24.00
2. Fisteli and Sons $ 28.00

3. Seimric $ 29.50
4. Murtelle $ 31.00

Analyzing the proposals, Marian was surprised by the difference between the price of the best offer and the others. After a quick investigation, she discovered that Cotton & Cotton had too much stock and lowered prices.

Marian believed she would reduce the fabric price and called the seller to negotiate. Once the meeting started, Marian said she wanted to close with Cotton, but another company had a bid lower, $22.00, and to hold the order, the seller would need to match the price at least.

Mr. Walter, the Cotton representative, did not hesitate and replied: "$24.00 is our lowest price. You can order material from another supplier, as we cannot improve our offer by a penny".

Marian was surprised by Mr. Walter's position and soon ended the meeting. The next day, without any explanation, she ordered the material from Cotton for $24.00 a meter of fabric.

Questions:

1. In the situation described, was Marian's approach adequate?
2. If not, how could Marian have discussed the matter with the seller?
3. Was placing the order without explanation the correct step to close the case?
4. If not, how could Marian have acted?

Before delving into the subject, it is worth mentioning that there is bluffing in negotiations, and occasionally it produces positive results.

Knowing how and when to use a bluff is essential, as the purchaser will have to deal with the same seller in the future.

Marian's approach was wrong. Impositions like Marian's become traps when a supplier refuses. Since Marian knew about Cotton's excess inventory, she could subtly address the price cut issue by improving some factors in her counteroffer.

Placing the order without explanation was a second mistake. Sending the order without any argument makes it difficult for the seller to trust her in the future. One way to minimize discomfort would be to change purchase parameters to justify its maintenance with the supplier.

For example, Marian could suggest a different payment term when negotiating without focusing on the proposed price. This would be a new purchase condition, preventing the supplier from considering the purchaser unreliable.

18.5.2 What is there to negotiate besides price?

The purchaser's negotiation plan includes several criteria. Price is usually the most negotiated parameter, but in addition to that, purchasers must remain aware of the following factors:

- Technical Assistance and Warranty: for many professionals, it is unnecessary to negotiate this issue, which is a severe failure, as suppliers often agree to extend technical assistance and warranty time to get a good order;
- Payment Terms: negotiating the payment term for purchases, especially those of great value, can result in a gain like a price discount. Extending the payment period positively contributes to an organization's cash flow. Suppliers also value payment terms for sales. A frequently asked question is why vendors suggest 21, 28, or 35 days of payment. The answer is simple: they are all multiples of seven, so there is no way for the payment date to occur on weekends and to stay until the next business day. Reducing the deadline for receiving sales generates a financial gain. The same reasoning is valid in the purchasing area, which aims to extend the payment term without changing the original value of the proposal;
- Scheduled deliveries: among the possibilities of negotiation related to delivery times, in long-term planning, scheduled deliveries stand out as they allow the minimization of excesses or shortages of stocks and influence the costs of orders;
- Freight: numerous customers have a fleet that is not always fully committed to their needs. If this is the case, excluding the freight cost from negotiations is valid, and the customer is responsible for transporting goods. Before deciding, it is necessary to determine the transport costs and compare them with those of the supplier;
- Delivery time: the analysis of the delivery date must occur from different points of view, not only the urgency in the arrival of the material or the definition of the delivery day but also aiming to obtain profit. For example, if the customer only needs the material on

the 15th, delivery should not occur on the 11th, as payment will take place four days before unnecessarily, harming cash flow. This action seems unimportant, but the value wasted in these situations will be great in the countless acquisitions made annually;

- Quality: negotiating quality assumes the material is adequate for user needs. There are often products with features that are not useful to the customer without adding value; therefore, negotiating to reduce the price is essential;

- Quantities: The purchasers must negotiate the volumes according to their needs. There are suppliers who, for specific materials, establish minimum quantities, often above those desired by the customer, imposing on them the task of reducing these limits, making use of negotiation;

- Price readjustment: various negotiable criteria exist for price readjustment. The existence of price readjustments is an item on the negotiating agenda. Additionally, the setting of the readjustment index must occur through an agreement between the parties upon analysis by the client of the proposal in question, verification of other more appropriate indicators, and the frequency of incidence;

- Training: many equipment and systems require training; if this is the case, purchasers must negotiate not to pay extra.

As mentioned, there are issues to negotiate beyond price. The list, however, does not end here, and it is up to the reader to evaluate other aspects worthy of attention in subsequent negotiations.

18.5.3 Care for supplier performance when negotiating

The usual practice, especially in successful companies, is to assess the previous performance of suppliers in preparation for ongoing negotiations, that is, to identify the positive and negative aspects of the supplier in previous orders. This action serves to guide the purchaser when deciding on a new purchase.

Evaluating and prioritizing the main characteristics of each supplier, favoring global assessment, is crucial. Below are examples:

- Punctuality: deliveries strictly respect the stipulated dates;

- Pricing: pricing is part of the agreement. When the supplier demonstrates flexibility, it is positive;
- Quality: the materials delivered have the appearance, dimensions, packaging, and service that accurately follow the specifications;
- Technology: investment in research and development and focus on obtaining innovations.

The purchaser can evaluate the supplier using performance indicators related to the items mentioned above, thus stipulating the minimum score to keep the supplier active.

Companies scoring below the minimum should not participate in consultations until they show evidence of better performance.

Knowing the customer has evaluation systems will encourage suppliers to improve their performance, generating favorable purchasing conditions and significant gains.

18.5.4 Use a cost spreadsheet in negotiations

Many purchasers do not see the advantages of asking the supplier for a cost sheet for analysis. This perception comes from the idea that the index is useless, assuming data is manipulated to favor the seller.

The usefulness of the cost spreadsheet is noticeable in the long term, and it is possible to compare multiple spreadsheets presented and notice any inconsistencies.

The base of the worksheet is that any variation in the closing price results from individual variations in the values of the parameters that compose it.

Although not complex, there are professionals who misinterpret the cost sheets. A typical problem is that a supplier can entirely apply a raw material or component to increase the total costs. Purchasers must promptly reject this conduct. The correct thing is to readjust proportionally to the share of the item in the total cost.

The price comes from the composition of various costs, each with a partial influence. The proportion of each in the price formation must remain until a revision justifies the update.

Suppliers try to correct the price by applying total variation to suit them. This practice occurs, for example, when there is a substantial fluctuation in the national currency. To better understand this, the following is an example:

James K. Hawkins

In the manufacture of a product, the raw material comes from abroad. In the price composition for the customer, the material represents 50%, and the balance is labor, maintenance, and other local costs.

If imported materials suffer a 10% increase in costs at any given time, increasing the product's final price by 10% is incorrect. If the raw material represents 50% of the total, the right thing would be to readjust the product's price by 5%; that is, a 10% change in prices multiplied by 50%, which is the influence of the material on the final value.

CHAPTER 19

DECIDING TO MANUFACTURE OR CHOOSING TO BUY

"Whether you think you can or can't - you're right."

Henry Ford[73]

The question of which condition is more advantageous between manufacturing a component in-house or purchasing it in the market is not recent. Choosing between manufacturing or buying certain materials has been a part of a company's routine for years. Books on supply management written more than four decades ago contain abundant material on this subject.

At the end of the last century, companies focused on keeping all activities in-house, with bloated and inflexible structures, justifying this preference with security arguments.

Recently, the idea that companies should focus exclusively on their core business and transfer secondary activities to third parties is growing.

In addition, the average useful life of products decreases annually, reducing dependence on the manufacturer, which must be flexible to change quickly and adapt to the market's new reality.

It is also worth emphasizing that some items are manufactured internally without external competition. The consequences are loss of competitiveness, low productivity, and excessive cost.

On the other hand, manufacturing components in-house allows a company to reduce its dependence on the supplier market, especially when there are no reliable purchase options.

---

[73] Henry Ford, a mechanical engineer, was an American entrepreneur, founder of the Ford Motor Company and author of the books My Philosophy of Industry and My Life and Work-An Autobiography of Henry Ford. He was the first entrepreneur to use the assembly line concept to produce automobiles in massive quantities, less time, and less cost.

Although there are no foolproof methods to decide whether it is better to manufacture or buy the materials, it is possible to list aspects to analyze to be confident in the decision.

The subject is not a secondary matter in organizations, and decisions cannot solely consider the financial projections of the two forms of action. Both include dynamic parameters, and the selection process must consider the peculiarities of the relationship between customers and suppliers.

The essential points to analyze are below:

- Changes in legislation relating to the product or market in question;
- Concentrate energy and effort on the business, transferring secondary activities to the market;
- Frequent price variation;
- Government policies;
- Incidence of taxes and fees;
- National and international market trends;
- Production capacity of the supplier market;
- Reaction against abusive practices of monopolies or cartels;
- Safety in the prevention of industrial espionage;
- Short, medium, and long-term needs;
- The strategic importance of the material or service.

Despite the pertinence of the above arguments, there is a predisposition to focus on the core business, concentrating efforts on performance in the market. This tendency exists even when internal manufacturing costs are lower than supplier prices.

Factors that influence the decision to manufacture materials in-house[74]:

- Distrust with suppliers;
- Commitment to integrating the operation of the company's industrial plants;
- Desire to exercise direct control over production and quality;
- Fill the productive capacity of a plant to absorb fixed costs;
- Lower cost than the supplier market;

---

[74] Text adapted from the book LEE, Lamar; DOBLER, Donald W; BURT, David N. Purchasing and Supply Management. USA: McGraw-Hill, August 1, 1997

- Prevalence of the need to ensure project confidentiality;
- Willingness to maintain the stability of the workforce (in times of falling sales).

Factors that contribute to the decision to buy materials in the supplier market:

- Items with small volumes;
- Limited production resources;
- Lower cost than manufacturing in-house;
- Positive effects of purchases on inventory management;
- Possibility of maintaining indirect control over management;
- Strategy to have multiple sources of supply;
- Use of research work and specialized knowledge of suppliers;
- Willingness to preserve the stability of the workforce (in periods of increased sales).

As previously pointed out, if a company decides solely based on cost, the risk of making incorrect decisions regarding manufacturing or purchasing materials increases! This is undeniable. However, ignoring that cost is an essential factor in the decision is also a miscalculation.

In the option of manufacturing in-house, consider the following conditions:

- Costs of capital involved;
- Costs resulting from shutdown caused by quality and other related problems;
- Direct costs involved in manufacturing;
- Fixed manufacturing costs;
- Lifting storage costs;
- Operation management costs.

In the option to buy:

- Costs arising from quality or associated service;
- Costs of purchasing the items;
- Receipt and inspection costs;
- Transportation costs.

In the same vein, the thought of Baily, Farmer, Jessop, and Jones[75] list relevant factors to guide the decision between making or buying:

If the acquisition of the material is from an external source:

- Is there any excess production capacity in the company itself? If positive, would such excess capacity be available during the required planning period?
- Is there a supply of raw materials at economical price? If so, will the material be available at economical prices for the planning period?
- Is there any tooling work involved? If so, what is the cost? What is the lifespan? How will the delivery be? What is the condition of the equipment?
- Is there satisfaction with the current supplier in terms of cost?
- Therefore, is there a patent and the eventual need to pay royalties?
- Is there a commitment from the current supplier to develop an improved version of the item?
- Has the current supplier failed to quality, the amount, or delivery time, with the transfer of the cost increase to the sales price?
- Is there a chance to affect the quality?
- Does the production department ensure it meets quality standards in internal manufacturing? Is there excess specification? Is it possible to have problems with supplier-quality systems? If so, how severe are the quality flaws?
- Are other costs increasing? If so, what are the reasons for this? Is there any confidence that they will not suffer a similar impact?
- Is there any item coming in from abroad now? How does this affect the cost?
- Is there an import tax? If so, what is the tax rate? What is the import tax (if any) on raw materials and components?

If the material is manufactured in-house:

- Does the interest of an external supplier concerning the quantities involved exist?
- If the option is to buy, will this bring advantage in the availability of raw materials or components?

---

[75] BAILY, Peter; FARMER, David. Purchasing Principles and Techniques. 3rd edition. USA: Pitman Publishing, May 1, 1977

- Is there a good chance that the item is part of an integrated, multistep manufacturing process? Can external production be satisfactorily coordinated with the internal production schedule?
- Is making the production of the part feasible externally a real possibility? If so, is it possible to collaborate with an external supplier?
- Is there evidence of the accuracy of all drawings?
- Is reliable information available to indicate the expected usage time of the product to a potential supplier?
- Is the actual cost of the supply alternative to in-house manufacturing (for example, transportation and material handling costs) known? Is the information available today and in the future?
- Is there an obligation to preserve any confidential production technique?
- Is there a forecast of the future scenario in the item market during the respective planning period?
- Suppose the option for external production of a particular part occurs. Will it be possible to allocate all the capacity of the equipment involved in its manufacture to other internal production processes?
- Is there an idea of how a potential supplier can recommend alternatives to reduce product costs?

Regardless of the decision, the participation of the purchasing department in the review process is indispensable for success. It is unacceptable for companies to decide on issues of this magnitude without involving the purchasing area, as mistakes increase significantly.

PART III

TOPICS OF STRUCTURE AND STRATEGY

CHAPTER 20

VISIT OF SELLERS

"Focus is to say no."

Steve Jobs[76]

The connection between purchasing and sales professionals is a fact. One satisfies the needs of the other, the reason for frequent contacts, which generates business.

Sellers visit purchasers several times annually because of the convergence of interests in this relationship. Recent advances in communication technology have reduced the frequency of visits by salespeople.

Fewer meetings favor the purchaser and seller, who can manage their time more productively.

Despite innovative forms of communication, visits still look indispensable; however, it is necessary to question the real need and schedule them only if there is no alternative.

It is inadmissible for sellers to visit purchase departments without a specific matter to deal with. Visits for "seeing how things are going" are unacceptable, and purchasers should avoid them.

Purchasers barely realize the number of unnecessary visits sellers make. Calculate the number of seller visits in the last quarter and the time spent and compare with the time invested in analyzing offers. Thus, it is possible to determine the percentage of time contributing to closing deals and the percentage of time wasted.

In simplistic reasoning on the subject:

1. If a purchaser receives ten sellers, he has not requested to be present but just went to "see how things are going."
2. If each dialogue lasts fifteen minutes, which is not that long.

---

[76] Steven Paul Jobs was an inventor and entrepreneur famous as co-founder and CEO of Apple and for revolutionizing six industries: personal computers, animated films, music, phones, tablets, and digital publications.

3. The purchaser wasted two and a half hours per day talking about nothing.

It is common for purchasers to ignore how often they work overtime just because of the excess of visits.

Establishing clear rules authorizing salespeople to visit only in essential cases increases the productivity of purchasing professionals. However, this action deserves re-doubled attention to maintain a good commercial relationship.

Organizing an agenda that defines visiting days and times reduces the flow of suppliers and is valid for salespeople and customers. Suppliers adapt to come only when the matter is relevant.

When the seller's presence is essential, scheduling the visit at a specific time is helpful to ensure privacy and focus on meetings between parties.

CHAPTER 21

ETHICAL PRINCIPLES IN PURCHASING

We call ethics the range of things people do when everyone is watching. The range of things that people do when nobody is looking is called character.

Oscar Wilde[77]

"**P**urchasing is one of the basic functions common to all organizations. It is the process of acquiring goods, services, and equipment from another organization legally and ethically." This affirmation, from David Burt[78], stands out for associating ethics with the purchasing function in an indissoluble way!

Regardless of what they see, hear, or read, most people want human relationships to respect ethical principles, and business is no different.

Thus, relevant questions emerge for the discussion of the theme:

- Does a purchaser misbehave by taking advantage of his position in the company to make personal acquisitions on better terms than he would if he had bought from other sources?
- How does the customer benefit from the proximity between purchasing and sales professionals?
- Can the purchaser's friendliness with the seller be beneficial in an urgent situation?
- Is it fair to inform the price of a supplier to other competitors?
- Is it inappropriate for the purchasing professional to play golf with the seller?

---

[77] Oscar Fingal O'Flahertie Wills Wilde, or simply Oscar Wilde was an influential Irish writer, poet, and playwright, who became one of London's most popular playwrights in 1890. Today he is remembered for his epigrams, plays and books.

[78] BURT, David N; PETCAVAGE, Sheila; PINKERTON, Richard. Proactive Purchasing in the Supply Chain: The Key to World-Class Procurement. 1st edition. USA: McGraw Hill, December 6, 2011

- Is it inconvenient to participate in happy hour with vendors?
- Is it acceptable to bluff as a negotiating technique?
- Is it unethical for the purchaser to accept gifts?
- Can the purchaser maintain his distance from the seller's person even though both are in constant contact for extended periods?
- What is an ethical (or unethical) attitude in the business environment?

Is it difficult to answer the listed questions? Indeed, there are similar doubts regarding the potential to be a company concern due to the immateriality inherent to ethics.

Understanding what can be considered ethical or unethical in business depends on factors associated with the social origin, culture, and beliefs embedded in the organization, without disregarding the principles that the shareholders of that institution follow.

This sensitive issue can cause disturbances in an organization. Discovering a fraud scandal and monetary loss erodes a company's image with the internal public, customers, suppliers, and shareholders.

International organizations classify countries according to their ethical standards, giving them grades for their behavior in various areas.

In conclusion, there is an effort to prevent unworthy subjects and encourage companies to adhere to ethical commitments in conducting their business.

They operate with a competitive advantage because of their low probability of being associated with any fraud.

According to Peter Drucker[79]: "The more successful the manager of the future is, the greater his honesty."

However, in this context, it is opportune to mention a comment by Herbert Lowe Stukart[80]:

- ".... research comparing performance with ethics, carried out by the Exxon Education Foundation over two years, leads to the conclusion that ethics increases productivity and reduces labor problems,

---

[79] Peter Drucker, Austrian, has worked in several areas, such as journalism, writing, consulting, and management. With 39 books published and translated into more than 30 languages, he pioneered modern management studies and was recognized as the "father of management".

[80] STUKART, Herbert Lowe. Ethics and Corruption. 1st edition. Brazil: Nobel, January 1, 2003

reinforces the company, enabling it to grow and progress. A solid ethical foundation helps managers to cope better with abrupt external changes. Excellent companies are, above all, ethical."

There is a particular belief that honest people do not need guidance to be ethical and disloyal people will never change their behavior.

However, companies that clearly define ethical rules reduce their chances of undesirable behavior by instructing their professionals (not just purchasers) on how to treat and relate to sellers.

Communication is essential when implementing or changing a code of conduct in supplier relationships. Purchasers and other professionals who contact sellers (accounts payable, treasury, engineering, maintenance, production) must have access to instructions as soon as possible.

Disclosing the code to suppliers guides them in collaborating with the customer company's employees.

Having a code of conduct favorably influences the company's relationship with members of the purchasing area, clarifying doubts about permitted and prohibited actions, preventing the occurrence of unwanted practices, even small slips, but with the potential to evolve into significant fraud.

It is common for suppliers to test the character of the purchasing professional with small actions, which, over time, can turn into severe losses for everyone.

The text of the Principles and Standards of Ethical Conduct in Supply Management, prepared by the Institute for Supply Management (USA), is instructive in clarifying some points:

Principles and Standards of ethical conduct in supply management

1. Support the continuity of social practices.
2. Manage supply management activities in compliance with national and international legislation, following customs and practices, organizational policies, and standard principles of ethical conduct.
3. Know and comply with the terms and configurations of legislation applicable to supply management.
4. Contribute to enhancing the status of the supply professional.
5. Demonstrate loyalty to your employers by following the instructions they determine and using appropriately the authority conferred on you.

6. Develop and preserve professional competence.
7. Avoid compromising or unethical practices in relationships, actions, and communication.
8. Make mutually inappropriate agreements impossible.
9. Never request or accept cash, loans, preferential discounts, gifts, entertainment, favors, or services from current or potential suppliers capable of influencing the decisions.
10. Maintain a formal relationship with suppliers, acting with courtesy and impartiality.
11. Never have a personal business or perform professional activities that conflict with your employer's interests.
12. Manage confidential information carefully, considering ethical and legal precepts and government regulations.

CHAPTER 22

PERFORMANCE EVALUATION OF THE PURCHASING AREA, ITS PROFESSIONALS, AND SUPPLIERS

All good performance starts with clear goals.

Ken Blanchard[81]

Throughout the book, the emphasis is on the contribution of the purchasing department to the organization's operation; from this point of view, maintaining detailed data on the area's performance is essential.

Unfortunately, the reality is quite different. Few companies have instruments to evaluate the performance of an area.

Surprisingly, this is present when the market has a wide range of business management programs with mechanisms capable of collecting and controlling data and meeting frequent demands for corporate information.

From the perspective of modern management, the recommendation is to measure the performance of purchasers, department, and suppliers. There is no complexity in the implementation of assessment systems. They are simple to compile and consult.

Due to the importance of the subject, it is always opportune to pay attention to Frazelle's[82] alert: "Supply chain performance metrics are often at odds with one another and frequently exacerbate the very problems they are designed to solve."

---

[81] Kenneth Hartley Blanchard is an American business consultant, speaker and writer, author of "Leading at a Higher Level" and co-author of "The one-minute manager", among other works.

[82] FRAZELLE, Edward H. Supply Chain Strategy: Unleash the Power of Business Integration to Maximize Financial, Service, and Operations Performance. 2nd edition. USA: McGraw-Hill, October 27, 2017

22.1 What to evaluate

Companies have unique needs; therefore, they must choose the aspects they deem worthy of a more accurate assessment. Regarding this difficulty, Cecere[83] affirms: "Each leader wants to draw a road map, and they want to know where they are on their journey. There is a demand for excellence, but it's amazing how leaders often fail to determine what's good. There is a lack of clarity. The alignment of metrics to improve corporate performance is easier said than done. There is a struggle to align the functional silos."

It is worth analyzing in advance what deserves measurement to escape this trap. The concepts examined in the Purchasing Department Objectives chapter contribute to facilitating this task:

- Purchase goods and services of the desired quality at the appropriate time and at the lowest possible cost.

In this condition, the topics listed below stand out:

- Time
- Cost
- Quality/quantity

These are the starting points for choosing the most valuable parameters to compose a purchase evaluation system and understand the performance of employees, suppliers, and materials.

Following are suggestions on what to evaluate:

a) The Purchasing Department itself:
   - Cost per order;
   - The average number of proposals per acquisition;
   - Number of exclusive suppliers;
   - Time to complete requests;
   - Emergency purchase volume.
b) Suppliers:
   - Assistance provided by suppliers;
   - Punctuality in deliveries;

---

[83] CECERE, Lora M. Supply Chain Metrics that Matter. 1st edition. USA: Wiley, December 8, 2014

- Quality of materials received;
- Compliance with the established commercial conditions;
- Staff turnover of outsourced companies.

c) The economic and financial performance of the department:
- Financial cycle;
- How much do acquisitions absorb from the company's revenue?
- Value of purchases based on the number of items purchased;
- The total value of purchases.

d) Purchasing efficiency concerning the material storage and administration policy:
- Evolution of consumption;
- Inventory turnover;
- Obsolescence;
- Receiving excess quantities of materials;
- Internal requisitions with zero stock;
- Stock value.

e) Purchasers:
- Technical evaluation;
- Personal evaluation.

Purchasing professionals are often indecisive when choosing metrics and quantifying targets. These are doubts with no immediate or straightforward solution. In the market, what produces good results in one company is ineffective in others.

When analyzing the most appropriate meters, a company's professionals must consider its nature, market, and objectives.

Detecting the metrics to detail in the global performance evaluation is equally important. A commercial company may focus on "stock turnover," while an industry, producer of durable goods, may interpret quality as a parameter of greater interest.

Developing a performance evaluation plan should take advantage of material classification systems such as ABC. The study of materials cannot disregard individual contributions.

22.2 The entire purchasing department

There are various indicators to evaluate a purchasing department. Logically, each contributes to achieving the established goals; some are more impactful, whereas others have little influence on the results.

Cecere[84] competently explains the relevance of choosing what to measure: "The first step of the journey is to define operation excellence. The second is to identify the right metrics. The metrics chosen need to reflect all the elements of the complex system. It is not easy. Putting together the metrics framework requires a clear definition of strategy."

When structuring an efficient merit analysis system, one recommendation is to explore themes in the broader context of the purchasing area.

22.2.1 Cost per order

It is classic in purchasing areas, calculating the amount spent to accomplish a purchase, considering the department's fixed costs and other expenses.

In measuring the cost per order, all expenses incurred by the purchasing department in the selected period (usually one month) must be identified and summed. Obtaining the indicator comes from dividing this total by the number of orders issued during the reviewed period.

The result is the cost per order, as shown in the formula below:

$$\text{Cost per Order} = \frac{\text{Total Department Expenses}}{\text{Number of Orders Issued}} \text{ [85]}$$

22.2.2 Request fulfillment time

The total time to fulfill a request, commonly called lead time, is part of a company's inventory management mathematical model. This is why measuring it frequently and correctly is essential, in line with the organization's and the market's established standards.

---

[84] CECERE, Lora M. Supply Chain Metrics that Matter. 1st edition. USA: Wiley, December 8, 2014

[85] Salaries, charges, communications, publications, courses, consumables, travel, administrative costs etc.

Monitoring the replacement time of a material is one of the main methods of ensuring excellent purchase performance. The availability of an item when needed and in the expected quantity is part of an organization's objectives.

The calculation of the handling time begins when the purchase requisition is issued and ends when the material is available to internal users.

Regarding this measurement, the expressive variation in the company results is noteworthy. One organization may interpret a given period as long and undesirable, while another may consider the same period convenient.

Companies with multiple purchasers must calculate the department's overall time and the average time each purchaser takes to complete a purchase.

In addition to calculating the length of service, it is essential to establish goals for the criterion.

There are two measures related to the length of service:

- Order Placement Time: The time elapsed from the issuance of the material requisition to the delivery of the order to the supplier. It allows evaluating its influence on the total service time. If it is excessive, it is necessary to reduce it.
- Time for material to be available: it is the period from the issuance of the requisition of the material to the effective release of the item for use. Defining the delivery time of the material as the end of the measurement is incorrect, as quality control can reject the goods. The process finishes when the material is available for consumption. In the case of suppliers with "assured quality", the performance measurement must use the date of receipt of the material as the end of the process.

The following example illustrates the simplicity of the Service Time assessment procedure. List the date of issuance of the requisition of material, issuance of the purchase order, and date of release of the material for use, as registered in Figure 22.1.:

Requisition	Issuance of requisition	Issuance of order	Time to issue the order	Approval date of the material	Service Time
RH/002	January 4th	January 7th	3	January 14th	10
FI/004	January 4th	January 9th	5	January 22nd	18
VE/001	January 4th	January 7th	3	January 9th	5
VE/002	January 4th	January 11th	7	January 18th	14

Figure 22.1.: Timetable for issuing orders and meeting needs

205

After listing the necessary parameters, it is possible to calculate the indexes:

- Order Placement Time: calculated by the arithmetic average of the number of days elapsed between the moment of issuing the material requisition until the placement of the order with the supplier. In the case of the table, it is 4.5 days;
- Ready-to-Use Material Placement Time: arithmetic average of days after the delivery of materials and release for use, always from the issuance of material requests in the studied period. In the case of the table, it is 11.75 days

22.2.3 Number of exclusive suppliers

Any procurement professional is aware of the impossibility of working efficiently without having alternatives when needed or even as a business strategy. Purchasers face more difficulty performing the tasks if the exclusivity indices are significant.

Companies should pursue a low rate of exclusive suppliers. This task is difficult; the results will come in the long run. Setting goals for this type of activity is challenging for the same reason.

Calculating the percentage of items purchased from exclusive suppliers to total acquisitions consists of dividing the number of purchases under this condition by the total items ordered in the period studied and multiplying the result by 100.

Items identified as "A" in the ABC Classification of Materials deserve specific analysis, with a more ambitious goal of reducing the percentage of exclusive suppliers than others.

22.2.4 Average number of proposals per acquisition

Defining an adequate number of proposals for a specific type of purchasing depends on its importance. It is illogical to consult multiple suppliers for small-value purchases, as the procedure is expensive.

On the other hand, it is unreasonable to realize an expensive purchase with only one or two proposals when there are more qualified suppliers.

The number of proposals should vary according to the importance of the items in the material classification used. When viable, purchase processes for products in classes "A" and "B" of the ABC classification must have more proposals than those categorized as "C".

22.2.5 Emergency Purchases

Emergency purchases are among the main problems for purchasers due to the inconvenience they cause and because they negatively affect the department's results. Consequently, every purchasing department must maintain permanent control over the number of such cases.

Monitoring uses the percentage of urgent purchases in relation to the total acquisitions concluded in the period.

The objective is to reduce this percentage without significantly interfering with the Purchasing Department's routines.

22.3. The suppliers

Given the significant reliance of Purchasing Departments on suppliers, it is essential to review their performance. There are meters available for this purpose.

The number of vendor-related metrics is vast and using them all is impractical. About this impossibility, Cecere[86] resonates with Marty Kisliuk, prior director of supply chain at FMC, to expose: "If you don't measure the right things, you will not get better. However, if you measure them, it does not mean that you will get better. There is always tension. If you are not struggling with metrics, you probably are not using them. When I think about the metrics that matter, I start my thinking with business strategy."

I ask myself, "What is it? And how will we measure the success of this strategy?" I don't think any leadership team can deal with more than five to seven metrics simultaneously. There is an issue of focus and selective strategy. It varies by industry. The metrics that matter are going to be the ones that you can take action on."

Each organization must identify the most suitable ones. Here are suggestions for valuable indicators.

[86] CECERE, Lora M. Supply Chain Metrics that Matter. 1st edition. USA: Wiley, December 8, 2014

22.3.1 Assistance Provided by Suppliers

Although price stands out in importance, other parameters deserve attention. Delivery time, quality of the products offered, and the service suppliers provide are especially important for excellent performance in the purchasing area.

By assistance, we refer to the availability and interest of suppliers in the customer, not only during the purchase process but especially after delivery of the material.

Keeping suppliers who are kind but disappear when there is a problem is irrational. Not to mention those sellers who brag about being partners and ignore the customer after the purchase.

Purchasing professionals recall positive or negative situations from relationships without using a methodological approach with various suppliers.

Whether the information is positive or negative, knowing how to interpret it should be the objective of any evaluation procedure. Monitoring can be challenging owing to subjectivity, but this is not an impediment.

In addition to being viable, implementing the practice has excellent value, especially in deciding on a purchase if more than one supplier offers equivalent commercial conditions.

Tabulating the data when building this tool is simple. With an exclusive focus on the service provided, department staff assigns positive or negative marks to the *key suppliers*.

Note the emphasis on the term "key suppliers" to highlight that work should focus on those most important on the list of suppliers.

To better understand the subject, below are possibilities:

- Commitment, which the seller demonstrates by promptly showing up when asked to discuss any matter (the speed of closing the deal is not a "positive point," as every supplier is present and concerned on this occasion);
- Flexibility in negotiations;
- Cooperation when responding to a request for technical assistance;
- Exchange of defective merchandise without bureaucracy.

It is crucial to consider the entire organization as a "supplier." If the seller offers a good service, but the other professionals in the company behave unsatisfactorily, the supplier does not deserve a positive evaluation.

In this regard, the initial action consists of selecting the leading suppliers to list the situations experienced, both favorable and undesired.

The analysis requires special attention to avoid exclusively selecting negative situations that remain in memory.

As a suggestion, a scale ranging from -5 to +5 is practical for evaluating each occurrence. While the (-) sign applies to unwanted situations caused by the supplier, the (+) signal refers to positive situations. Although an assessment based on subjective instruments is not recommended, it is necessary for this purpose, and the caveat does not invalidate the conclusions.

An example of the subject is in Figure 22.2.:

Supplier	Jan	Feb	Mar	Apr	May	Jun	Grade
A	-	-	-	2	4	-	6
B	2	-	-	-	3	-	5
C	-	-	-	-	-	1	1
D	1	1	-	2	-	-	4
E	-	-	-	-	2	-1	1
F	-	-	-	-3	1	2	0
G	-1	-	2	-	-	-	1
H	1	1	3	-	-	2	7
I	-1	-2	-	-4	-	-	-7
J	-	-	-	-	3	-	3
K	1	1	-	-	-	-	2
L	-	1	-2	-	2	1	2
M	-	-	-2	-	-	-	-2
N	-	-	2	-	-	-1	1
O	-	-	2	2	-	-	4
P	-3	-	-	-	-	-	-3
Q	-2	-	-	-	2	-	0
R	1	-	-	-	-	-	1
S	-	-	-	-	1	1	2
T	-	-	2	3	-	-	5

Figure 22.2.: Table representing the evaluation of assistance provided by suppliers

Suppliers I, M, and P have an evaluation that advises against receiving new orders. Their ratings are poor! Do not select any of the three if another proponent has equivalent technical and commercial conditions.

Even when the total score is positive, the reasons for any negative evaluations deserve investigation. The severity of the failure that causes the low rating may justify the supplier's exclusion from new purchases to avoid future problems.

Finally, a history must contain at least six months of data, and the recommendation is to adopt more extended periods.

22.3.2. Delivery control and punctuality

The act of scheduling and planning purchases is essential for effective operations in business organizations.

Whenever the materials management area requests material delivery on a specific date, regardless of the existing management system or any other department, the purchasing department is responsible for ensuring the item arrives on time.

There are two reasons for focusing on the expected delivery date of the materials: physical nature and financial. Well-organized companies maintain strict control over deliveries to obtain gains by optimizing the existing physical space for storing materials while maximizing cash flow management.

Achieving these two objectives requires permanently controlling deliveries and calculating the rate of receipt of materials within the contracted period.

Although the intention is to reach 100%, it is not acceptable to ignore that deliveries made well before the dates set by the customer are also undesirable, mainly because of their impact on the company's cash.

There are two methods to compute the accuracy of deliveries. The first indicates the percentage of materials received on time, as shown in Figure 22.3.:

Month	Delivery	On-time	Percentage in the term
JAN	712	691	97,05%
FEB	602	587	97,51%
MAR	684	651	95,18%
APR	712	694	97,47%
MAY	680	633	93,09%
JUN	719	691	96,11%
JUL	895	864	96,54%
AUG	613	587	95,76%
SEP	598	570	95,32%
OCT	485	461	95,05%
NOV	554	532	96,03%
DEC	618	604	97,73%

Figure 22.3.: Delivery punctuality analysis model

210

Another way to control deliveries is to assign grades based on when the delivery takes place. Consider the expected delivery date in the order as ideal, which should be the purchaser's target and deserve the maximum score.

For example, the maximum score (100) will occur if the material arrives on time. Each day of late delivery reduces the assessment by two points. Each day of premature delivery decreases by one point (from the customer's point of view, lateness used to be more harmful than early delivery).

When the purchaser asks the seller to anticipate or postpone the delivery, it is essential to register the new condition, thus not negatively influencing the supplier evaluation.

This type of control makes it possible to monitor the leading suppliers' performance. The table in Figure 22.4. shows details of the method:

Code of material	Supplier	Delivery preview	Delivery done	Grade	Index
ZN222	P	28/out	28/out	0	100
PT004	P	15/out	15/out	0	100
AT198	R	24/out	22/out	-2	98
YY320	I	20/out	24/out	-8	92
AB774	S	18/out	21/out	-6	94
TA305	A	25/out	30/out	-10	90
PI552	A	24/out	24/out	0	100
SX200	B	14/out	25/out	-22	78
BZ170	B	14/out	18/out	-8	92
TN009	N	17/out	14/out	-3	97
AS114	C	19/out	14/out	-5	95
ZZ119	C	16/out	16/out	0	100
AY715	I	19/out	19/out	0	100
AN110	M	25/out	26/out	-2	98
PC190	M	27/out	24/out	-3	97
PN714	N	24/out	24/out	0	100
SS200	H	23/out	20/out	-3	97
ZA215	G	22/out	26/out	-8	92
CG312	B	19/out	20/out	-2	98
DD462	F	16/out	16/out	0	100
SI794	I	25/out	25/out	0	100
TA212	O	20/out	19/out	-1	99
LE302	M	29/out	20/out	-9	91
CO994	O	14/out	13/out	-1	99
TR783	R	17/out	19/out	-4	96
TA388	T	20/out	20/out	0	100
CI654	T	12/out	18/out	-12	88
RE963	I	18/out	18/out	0	100
IB448	A	30/out	30/out	0	100

RE963	B	18/out	30/out	-24	76
IB448	B	14/out	14/out	0	100
RE983	C	19/out	19/out	0	100
DI339	S	22/out	19/out	-3	97
SC449	H	24/out	26/out	-4	96
SO991	T	22/out	22/out	0	100
QQ774	M	19/out	19/out	0	100

Figure 22.4.: Part 1 of the table

Code of material	Supplier	Delivery preview	Delivery done	Grade	Index
MN212	R	19/out	19/out	0	100
OS704	H	29/out	20/out	-9	91
TA092	M	20/out	20/out	0	100
CI104	G	25/out	26/out	-2	98
TZ004	B	14/out	25/out	-22	78
SW006	B	17/out	14/out	-3	97
PN044	D	19/out	14/out	-5	95
SC221	F	19/out	19/out	0	100
FF214	D	25/out	26/out	-2	98
FC021	H	27/out	24/out	-3	97
NJ215	H	23/out	20/out	-3	97
AB772	M	22/out	26/out	-8	92
FI337	F	16/out	16/out	0	100
PK912	F	25/out	25/out	0	100
TI772	N	20/out	19/out	-1	99
ZZ221	N	29/out	20/out	-9	91
FA044	O	17/out	19/out	-4	96
TY150	O	20/out	20/out	0	100
FM090	P	12/out	18/out	-12	88
FJ077	Z	18/out	18/out	0	100
SW500	Z	30/out	30/out	0	100
SA710	R	18/out	30/out	-24	76
SP025	Z	14/out	14/out	0	100
TT012	A	22/out	19/out	-3	97
SK419	A	24/out	26/out	-4	96
TM221	X	22/out	22/out	0	100
FF121	X	28/out	28/out	0	100
SA335	R	15/out	15/out	0	100
TK332	L	24/out	22/out	-2	98
FF035	L	20/out	24/out	-8	92
AI700	J	18/out	21/out	-6	94
DD337	J	14/out	25/out	-22	78
GY992	A	14/out	18/out	-8	92
PT804	A	17/out	14/out	-3	97
PM077	D	19/out	14/out	-5	95
TZ100	C	16/out	16/out	0	100

SA902	M	24/out	24/out	0	100
CN800	S	23/out	20/out	-3	97
CA799	A	22/out	26/out	-8	92
CP615	M	16/out	16/out	0	100

Figure 22.4.: Part 2 of the table

The scores of suppliers with deliveries in the period would correspond to the arithmetic average of the points obtained for each supply, as shown in Figure 22.5.:

Supplier	Grade
F	100,00
Z	100,00
X	100,00
C	98,75
O	98,50
I	98,00
M	97,25
N	96,75
P	96,00
T	96,00
D	96,00
S	96,00

-------------------------------> Índice Médio

H	95,60
A	95,50
G	95,00
L	95,00
R	94,00
B	88,43
J	87,33

Figure 22.5.: Grades calculated from supplier averages

Examining supplier indices shows that companies H, A, G, L, R, B, and J performed below the average computed by the purchasing department, highlighting that companies B and J have poor results and do not justify participating in future purchasing processes.

The department's average index monitors the team's evolution, and each supplier's score provides subsidies for future purchase decisions.

A recommended action when implementing meters is to communicate the rules and results to suppliers; otherwise, the positive effects will be negligible.

More detailed analyses are helpful concerning items critical to the company's operation, emphasizing the control of deliveries and punctuality.

Customers with a rigid delivery control system tend to exclude poorly rated suppliers from future purchases.

22.3.3. Quality of materials received

Each item destined for production in industries deserves special attention from the purchasing department to meet the specifications defined in the material requisitions. On the other hand, a commercial company must ensure that products purchased for sale meet consumer preferences.

Nevertheless, it is worth highlighting the relevance of implementing strict targets to measure the quality of materials supplied. When a material has a lower quality than specified, returning it to the supplier is the best option, except in cases of extreme need for the item, if it is possible to use it. Therefore, the receipt may occur, but documenting the failure in the supplier's registration is necessary.

David Burt [87] details how the quality of products manufactured in an industry will reflect the materials' characteristics: "Some 75 percent of many manufacturers' quality problems can be traced back to defects in purchased materials."

Here, the core is to evaluate the suppliers, individually and as a whole, regarding the quality of the materials and to judge the performance of the Purchasing Department for this attribute.

How to process data influence accuracy, and selecting the best analysis option is essential to avoid distortions in interpreting the results.

In this context, when establishing quality tolerance standards, it is essential to consider the nature of the material, adapting the evaluation rules to the application of the item. Imposing the same rigidity of analysis applied to a raw material on papers used in copiers makes no sense!

Below are proposals to measure the Quality of materials delivered by suppliers.

[87] BURT, David N; PETCAVAGE, Sheila; PINKERTON, Richard. Proactive Purchasing in the Supply Chain: The Key to World-Class Procurement. 1st edition. USA: McGraw Hill, December 6, 2011

22.3.3.1. By deliveries

Control is simple: list the number of deliveries made, regardless of the number of materials in each.

The procedure must consider each product individually; the model finds four deliveries if four varied materials arrive from the same supplier. For example:

Solar Spring Factory delivered:

- 500 units of spring type 1;
- 100 units of spring type 2;
- 150 units of spring type 0;
- 500 units of spring type 8.

The calculation will be based on the following:

- number of deliveries: 4
- approval: 3
- approval with restriction: 0
- disapproval: 1

After listing the deliveries made in the period under review, identify those with quality problems and calculate the corresponding percentage, as shown in Figure 22.6..

Month (1)	Quantity of deliveries (2)	Received without restrictions (3)	% (4)	Received with restrictions (5)	% (6)	Disapproved (7)	% (8)
JAN	2.500	2.355	94,2	120	4,8	25	1,0
FEV	3.100	2.930	94,5	130	4,2	40	1,3
MAR	2.870	2.775	96,7	65	2,3	30	1,0
ABR	2.300	2.210	96,1	85	3,7	5	0,2
MAI	2.440	2.275	93,2	110	4,5	55	2,3
JUN	2.600	2.470	95,0	100	3,8	30	1,2
JUL	2.650	2.570	97,0	65	2,5	15	0,6
AGO	2.950	2.865	97,1	60	2,0	25	0,9
SET	3.120	2.980	95,5	115	3,7	25	0,8
OUT	2.770	2.610	94,2	110	4,0	50	1,8
NOV	2.600	2.485	95,6	110	4,2	5	0,2
DEZ	2.300	2.215	96,3	80	3,5	5	0,2

Figure 22.6.: Table containing the quality analysis of deliveries

1 – reference month;

2 – total number of deliveries made in the month;

3 – number of deliveries made without quality restrictions;

4 – percentage of deliveries without quality restrictions = (3 / 2) x 100;

5 – number of deliveries accepted, but with quality restrictions;

6 – the percentage of deliveries accepted, but with quality restrictions =
(5 / 2) x 100;

7 – number of deliveries with materials disapproved for Quality;

8 - the percentage of deliveries with materials disapproved for quality
(7 / 2) x 100.

Defining the goal for the criterion will guide the purchaser's action and determine whether the performance is good or needs adjustments.

22.3.3.2 By Value

Execution is as simple as in the previous case; just list the total value of items received and group those with quality problems, resulting in the desired percentages.

Owing to the disparity in the values in this measurement, meticulousness in validating the analysis is essential to avoid wrong conclusions. A single item with a significant value that does not meet the quality criteria compromises the results.

Below is a measurement model:

Month	Deliveries Value $	Total Approval $	%	Approval with Restriction $	%	Fail $	%
JAN	2.200.000,00	2.010.000,00	91,40	110.000,00	5,00	80.000,00	3,60
FEV	1.710.000,00	1.570.000,00	91,80	130.000,00	7,60	10.000,00	0,60
MAR	2.150.000,00	1.930.000,00	89,80	180.000,00	8,40	40.000,00	1,90

Figure 22.7.: Value-based quality assessment model

22.3.4 Employee turnover from outsourced companies

The purchasing department is responsible for choosing and contractually binding companies to provide services to the organization. The possibilities include options, such as cleaning, surveillance, transport, maintenance, and restaurant services.

Staff turnover is one of the options for analyzing service providers' performance. This indicator allows for strict control in large contingents of people required to execute contracted activities.

It is possible to measure the staff turnover rate with this formula:

$$PTI = (A + D) \times 100 / [(NB + NE) / 2]$$

In the formula, the letters symbolize:

- PTI – Personnel Turnover Index;
- A – Number of Admissions in the Study Period;
- D – Number of Dismissals in the Study Period;
- NB – Number of Employees at the Beginning of the Study Period (allocated to the service);
- NE – Number of Employees at the End of the Study Period (assigned to the service).

Contracted companies' constant replacement of employees is counterproductive to good service performance. Therefore, the Personnel Turnover Index must be low. The example in Figure 22.8. demonstrates how to perform such an analysis:

Supplier	Admissions third quarter	Dismissal third quarter	Number of employees in 1/7	Number of employees in 30/9	PTI
Cleaner Y	6	6	32	32	37,50
Security W	1	0	7	8	13,30
Maintenance Z	14	10	28	32	80,00
Messengers R	1	1	15	15	13,30
Carrying X	0	0	12	12	0,00

Figure 22.8.: Model for calculating the turnover of service providers' staff

The table study demonstrates the urgency of adopting energetic measures with Cleaner Y and Maintenance Z, as they have high personnel turnover rates; therefore, failures in the quality and progress of contracted services are likely.

22.4 The department's economic-financial performance

Having the correct information is an element of competitive advantage in ever-evolving markets. Financial conditions play an essential role in an organization's performance; consequently, knowing suppliers' economic situation is indispensable when deciding on a purchase.

A company must satisfy specific requirements to deliver to customers according to previously defined parameters.

22.4.1 Economic-financial performance

Financial indicators are relevant in purchasing performance. Rigorous elaboration is indispensable.

One alternative is to define the target based on the lowest proposed price during the purchase process. The purchaser must negotiate a discount on this price. This parameter is known as Cost Reduction or Cost Prevention.

The author believes the methodology favors the purchaser and does not constitute an efficient measure of economic-financial performance. Purchasers should pursue price reductions for the proposals received; however, the evaluation form here considers the current acquisition exclusively.

Measuring financial performance requires more effective tools; consequently, methodologies that study performance over time tend to be more efficient.

The analysis results should consider both the "pros" and the "cons" or, paraphrasing, highlight the savings and losses in cases where values exceeded the target in the period under review.

This system has variations, up or down, resulting from comparing the acquisition price with the target amount previously determined by reliable criteria.

There are formulas for calculating the target price depending on the structure and needs of the organization. For materials with periodic replenishment, the base price can be the weighted average of the last three purchases, for example.

A simple computerized management system can calculate the base price. Eventually, companies without an adequate structure to conduct such monitoring can use the last price paid for the material as a reference.

Below is a method to define the target price using the weighted average of the last three purchases:

- Last price: multiply by 3
- Penultimate price: multiply by 2
- Antepenultimate price: keep as is

This procedure gives more weight to the latest acquisition, the one most likely to reflect the current market situation.

To facilitate understanding, see an example of the method for a hypothetical raw material in Figure 22.9.:

Date	Previous prices (us$)	Weighting	Weighted price (us$)
April 15th	14,00	1	14,00 x 1 = 14,00
June 16th	14,75	2	14,75 x 2 = 29,50
September 5th	14,94	3	14,94 x 3 = 44,82
WEIGHTED AVERAGE			88,32 ÷ 6 = 14,72

Figure 22.9.: How to calculate weighted average prices

Dividing the sum of the three weighted prices by 6 gives the weighted average sought, $14.72.

In the following simulation (Figure 22.10.), the intention is to show how to monitor the economic and financial performance of the purchasing area through the weighted average (using the same weights as in the previous example) corresponding to the last three acquisitions.

Item	First purchase	Second purchase	Third purchase	Average Weighted	Current price	Current amount	Current total (5 x 6)	Total basis (4 x 6)	Result (7 – 8)
	USD	USD	USD						
Column	1	2	3	4	5	6	7	8	9
YB040	1.20	1.00	1.05	1.06	1.05	5,000	5,250	5,300	-50
SI540	0.69	0.87	0.77	0.79	0.78	4,200	3,276	3,318	-42
SW100	9.00	9.80	9.40	9.47	9.34	15,000	140,100	142,050	-1,950
PP450	35.80	34.40	32.00	33.43	33.85	36,000	1,218,600	1,203,480	15,120
BH114	1.33	1.32	1.12	1.22	1.20	95,000	114,000	115,900	-1,900
JK905	0.12	0.18	0.12	0.14	0.14	112,000	15,680	15,680	0
LP212	2.00	2.50	2.70	2.52	2.48	1,500	3,720	3,780	-60
GT545	3.45	4.12	4.50	4.20	4.14	65,000	269,100	273,000	-3,900
FV433	12.30	11.20	13.40	12.48	12.31	120,000	1,477,200	1,497,600	-20,400
ER568	345.00	320.00	365.00	346.67	351.00	1,000	351,000	346,670	4,330
QW456	121.00	111.00	134.00	124.17	125.72	3,000	377,160	372,510	4,650
VC478	23.00	19.00	32.00	26.17	26.50	55,000	1,457,500	1,439,350	18,150
XS715	338.00	367.00	345.00	351.17	355.56	2,300	817,788	807,691	10,097
ZS230	0.21	0.30	0.41	0.34	0.34	150,000	51,000	51,000	0
QQ200	12.00	12.40	13.00	12.63	12.45	28,500	354,825	359,955	-5,130
WB148	144.00	156.00	143.00	147.50	149.34	2,300	343,482	339,250	4,232
MK541	231.00	213.00	243.00	231.00	233.89	4,000	935,560	924,000	11,560
JM232	144.00	123.00	115.00	122.50	124.03	2,000	248,060	245,000	3,060
HH599	2.31	2.46	2.54	2.48	2.45	85,000	208,250	210,800	-2,550
LO248	332.00	314.00	325.00	322.50	326.53	2,300	751,019	741,750	9,269
LM563	121.00	134.00	131.00	130.33	131.96	5,000	659,800	651,650	8,150
Total									52,636

Figure 22.10.: Comparative table of current acquisition with the weighted average of the last three purchases

After compilation, there is no gain detected. The Purchasing Department spent 0.54% more than the target.

For the same example, but comparing only the value of the last acquisition, we have the table shown in Figure 22.11. (Values in USD):

Item	Last purchase unit	Current price	Current amount	Current total (5 x 6)	Total basis (4 x 6)	Result (7-8)
COLUMN	3	5	6	7	8	9
YB040	1,05	1,05	5,000	5,250	5,250	0
SI540	0,77	0,78	4,200	3,276	3,234	42
SW100	9,40	9,34	15,000	140,100	141,000	-900
PP450	32,00	33,85	36,000	1,218,600	1,152,000	66,600
BH114	1,12	1,20	95,000	1140	106,400	7,600
JK905	0,12	0,14	112,000	15,680	13,440	2,240
LP212	2,70	2,48	1,500	3,720	4,050	-330
GT545	4,50	4,14	65,000	269,100	292,500	-23,400
FV433	13,40	12,31	120,000	1,477,200	1,608,000	-130,800
ER568	365,00	351,00	1,000	3510	365,000	-14,000
QW456	134,00	125,72	3,000	377,160	402,000	-24,840
VC478	32,00	26,50	55,000	1,457,500	1,760,000	-302,500
XS715	345,00	355,56	2,300	817,788	793,500	24,288
ZS230	0,41	0,34	150,000	510	61,500	-10,500
QQ200	13,00	12,45	28,500	354,825	370,500	-15,675
WB148	143,00	149,34	2,300	343,482	328,900	14,582
MK541	243,00	233,89	4,000	935,560	972,000	-36,440
JM232	115,00	124,03	2,000	248,060	230,000	18,060
HH599	2,54	2,45	85,000	208,250	215,900	-7,650
LO248	325,00	326,53	2,300	751,019	747,500	3,519
LM563	131,00	131,96	5,000	659,800	655,000	4,800
					TOTAL =	-425,304

Figure 22.11.: Comparative chart between the current acquisition and the last purchase

There was a savings of 4.16% (current total with the accumulated of the last purchase).

It is essential to understand that different methodologies produce divergent results.

After identifying the base price using any method, it is necessary to tabulate the economic-financial performance of each month, as shown in Figure 22.12.

Month	Total basis USD	Total purchases USD	Gain USD	% Gain
JAN	14,335,300	14,274,220	-61,080	-0.43%
FEB	17,293,508	16,751,031	-542,477	-3.14%
MAR	11,720,301	11,514,301	-206,000	-1.76%
APR	16,350,700	15,950,000	-400,700	-2.45%
MAY	14,230,314	14,044,000	-186,314	-1.31%
JUN	15,520,202	15,440,312	-79,890	-0.51%
JUL	11,244,000	10,870,207	-373,793	-3.32%
AUG	17,809,205	17,701,500	-107,705	-0.60%
SEP	11,894,700	12,073,120	178,420	1.50%
OCT	14,945,300	14,512,830	-432,470	-2.89%
NOV	14,319,312	14,036,032	-283,280	-1.98%
DEC	12,521,370	11,997,399	-523,971	-4.18%

Figure 22.12.: Tabulation of monthly earnings of the purchasing department

When setting the base price, the weighted average of the last three purchases (occasionally four or five if reliable data are available) is preferable because it better represents the performance.

Another essential action is monitoring the performance when buying items classified as "A" into the ABC classification in an isolated evaluation.

Analytics, such as views, allow paying bonuses to purchasers as an incentive mechanism to seek increasingly significant reductions in the prices of purchased materials.

22.4.2 Value of Acquisitions

Another valuable piece of information is the total value of the purchases made by the purchasing department in a given period, which is a mandatory and permanent calculation.

These data are simple to verify, even for companies that do not have a performance evaluation system implemented in the purchasing area.

The total purchase value comes from the sum of each purchase made during the period. There are companies that, when questioned, need to make the calculations, as they do not have tabulated data for an immediate consultation. This situation is unacceptable because it is easy to obtain.

22.4.3 Average amount paid for purchased items

More than a performance metric, it is information. Although the parameter calculation is simple, the interpretation is not always helpful. The contribution of each item is heterogeneous and high-value purchases distort the analysis.

Setting goals is unnecessary. This procedure divides the total value of purchases from the previous topic by the number of items purchased in the same period. The result of this division is the average purchase amount per item, as shown in the table in Figure 22.13.

Month	Acquisitions value USD	Number of items	Value/items USD
JAN	930,000	1,150	808.70
FEB	970,000	1,560	621.79
MAR	866,000	1,440	601.39

Figure 22.13.: Table with the calculation of the average purchase price per item

22.4.4 Relationship between the value of acquisitions and the company's revenue

This meter characterizes the percentage of revenue spent on the "suppliers" account. The decrease in the "suppliers" report, due to the excellent work of purchasing, materials, and other areas, will increase the "profit." Every well-run company should plan the procurement of supplies to minimize this percentage.

David Burt[88] emphasizes the strong influence of supply on the profitability of organizations: "Supply management has an overwhelming impact on the firm's bottom line. It directly affects the two forces that drive the bottom line: sales and costs."

Increasing the "profit" account without considering the gains from purchases requires investments and expenses without guaranteeing positive results.

---

[88] BURT, David N; PETCAVAGE, Sheila; PINKERTON, Richard. Proactive Purchasing in the Supply Chain: The Key to World-Class Procurement. 1st edition. USA: McGraw Hill, December 6, 2011

The elaboration and consequent permanent analysis of this indicator are simple. In this case, dividing the total amount spent on purchases by the total net income - after taxes and returns - is sufficient.

The benefits of analyzing results in the medium and long term are significant, and the definition of goals depends on the type of market in which the company operates.

This meter tends to be more relevant for commercial and industrial companies and less impactful for service providers.

In Figure 22.14., there is an example of the percentage of the monthly value of acquisitions in relation to the company's gross revenue:

Month	Acquisitions value USD	Gross revenue USD	Percentage
JAN	930,000	2,906,250	32.00%
FEV	970,000	3,689,655	26.29%
MAR	866,000	3,018,750	28.69%

Figure 22.14.: Percentage of revenue used in acquisitions

22.4.5. Financial cycle

The operation of the purchasing areas impacts the financial cycles of companies. Monitoring the consequences implies knowing whether the company can finance its operations. The financial cycle indicator aims to produce evidence of this condition.

Calculating the financial cycle requires knowledge of three indexes of the company's activities: Average Sales Receipt Period, Average storage period, and Average Payment Term to Suppliers.

• Average Receipt Term for Sales Made (ART):

$$ART = \frac{\$S1 \times CTR1 + \$S2 \times CTR2 + \ldots \$Sn \times CTRn}{Revenues}$$

ART = Average Receipt Term for Sales Made;
S = Value of the sale made by the company;

CTR = Current term of receipt for the sale made [89];

Example: Company Y made the sales shown in Figure 22.15.:

Sale	Value USD	CTR (days)	S x CTR
S1	45,000	25	1,125,000
S2	56,000	23	1,288,000
S3	112,000	36	4,032,000
S4	171,000	45	7,695,000
S5	22,000	16	352,000
S6	25,000	30	750,000
S7	83,000	32	2,656,000
S8	74,000	17	1,258,000
S9	104,000	19	1,976,000
S10	48,000	23	1,104,000
TOTAL	740,000		22,236,000

Figure 22.15.: Table for calculating the Average Receipt Period for Sales Made

To calculate the ART, divide $22,236,000.00 by $740,000.00. The result will be 30.05 days of the average receipt period!

• Average Storage Period (ASP):

$$ASP = \frac{(Average\ stock)}{Cost\ of\ goods\ sold} \times 90$$

The data is as follows:

Average stock = starting stock added to ending stock divided by two;
Cost of Products Sold = refers to the total value of products the company sold during the period under analysis;
Ninety days is the period for the calculation of purchases and sales.
For company Y in the example, the information from the balance sheet was:

Initial stock: $61,430.00
Final stock: $34,120.00

---

[89] Considered a real term because it is the one in which the actual receipt took place and not the one contracted, subject to non-compliance.

Cost of Goods Sold: $207,200.00
By the formula, you will get an ASP of 20.75 days

- Average Payment Term to Suppliers (APT):

$$APT = \frac{\$P1 \times CPT1 + \$P2 \times CPT2 + \ldots \$Pn \times CPTn}{\text{Purchase Amount in the Period}}$$

APT = Average Payment Term;
P = value of the purchase made by the company;
CPT = current payment term for the purchase made[90].
Example: Company Y made the purchases shown in Figure 22.16:

Purchase	Value (P)	CPT (days)	P x CPT
P1	12,000	38	456,000
P2	8,000	45	360,000
P3	11,000	28	308,000
P4	9,000	31	279,000
P5	6,000	27	162,000
P6	14,000	37	518,000
P7	20,000	40	800,000
P8	4,000	42	168,000
P9	15,000	33	495,000
P10	10,000	38	380,000
Total	109,000		3,926,000

Figure 22.16.: Table for calculating the Average Payment Term to Suppliers

To calculate APT, we divide $3,926,000 by $109,000. The result will be 36.02 days of average payment terms to suppliers!
Using data obtained from Company Y:

ART = 30,05;
ASP = 20,75;
APT = 36,02.

It is possible to calculate the company's financial cycle using the following formula:

[90] The deadline is real, relative to the effective payment. The Purchase Order date may not happen in practice.

$$\text{FINANCIAL CYCLE} = \text{ART} + \text{ASP} - \text{APT}$$

Replacing Company Y's data will result in the following:
Financial Cycle = 36,02 - (30,05 + 20,75) = - 14,78

The value shows that company Y finances its operations in 14.78 days; that is, while it stocks and receives from its customers in 50.8 days, it makes purchases with an average term of 36.02 days to pay. Depending on this "financing" cost, it works poorly and needs to change its *status*.

22.5 Purchasing efficiency compared to stocking and materials management policy

The material management department is the internal customer that most requests services from the purchasing sector. An organization's inventories require periodic replacement, strongly influencing the financial situation. The good financial health of a company depends on efficiently managing inventories, minimizing the likelihood of material shortages, and not allowing significant expenditure of financial resources.

Frazelle[91] addressed the issue laterally, mentioning a specific situation, but with a focus capable of serving a wide range of companies: "The answer was to eliminate or minimize the need for physical warehousing by (1) developing a supply chain service policy, (2) determining the amount of inventory required to support that service policy, (3) optimizing and coordinating manufacturing schedules, and (4) optimizing the transportation operations." This part of the book examines mechanisms that indicate how the purchasing area participates in this process and contributes to maximizing the results.

22.5.1 Inventory Turnover

Although material planning activities are external to the purchasing area, purchasers can contribute to excellent inventory turnover management.

---

[91] FRAZELLE, Edward H. Supply Chain Strategy: Unleash the Power of Business Integration to Maximize Financial, Service, and Operations Performance. 2nd edition. USA: McGraw-Hill, October 27, 2017

As a rule, keeping inventories low while supplying production means less capital investment.

Inventory turnover calculation uses the following formula:

Inventory Turnover = material output / average inventory[92]

The term must be the same when applying the formula for the material output and the average stock.

Companies with high inventory turnover, in addition to gains from better use of invested capital, profit from low storage expenses (space, personnel, insurance)

Each company must maintain a sufficient inventory to minimize material unavailability and simultaneously avoid consuming a substantial portion of capital.

Permanent monitoring is necessary to avoid excessive increases in inventory turns and material shortages, paralyzing the company's operation or production.

22.5.2 Reception of surplus materials

As already mentioned, sometimes suppliers deliver larger quantities than ordered. Continuing this practice is detrimental to clients in economic and financial terms.

Due to the seriousness of the problem, evaluating a purchasing department's performance cannot exclude analyses linked to the receipt of surpluses.

The objective is to determine the monthly value of materials received above the quantity requested in the purchase order and to identify how much this represents in relation to the total ordered. Figure 22.17. details this indicator.

Month	Value of materials ordered	"Receipt surplus"	%
JAN	1,150,000	22,000	1,91%
FEB	1,300,000	15,000	1,69%
MAR	1,400,000	19,000	1,57%

Figure 22.17.: Calculation of the value of excess
quantities to the contracted volume

---

[92] The theme "inventory turnover" was the object of previous analysis, from a strictly financial point of view, during a study of the financial cycle of companies.

The ideal index is zero, hardly achievable; the closer you are to it, the better the performance.

22.5.3 Stock value

Monitoring inventory value is a good benchmark for purchasing and supply areas. Less informed professionals do not realize the relevance of this indicator, which, when analyzed in the general context, helps detect system failures.

How can a stock's value rise without a plausible explanation for months? Identifying the cause may reveal inefficiencies, justifying an analysis of the particularities of the company's operation and the economic moment experienced by the country.

To compute this parameter, it is sufficient to periodically measure the value of the stocked materials and analyze whether it is within the preset limits or presents unwanted or inexplicable variations.

22.5.4 Obsolescence

Numerous factors can make stored materials obsolete. Poorly designed and executed planning contributes to this occurrence.

Obsolescence wastes money, so reducing it to lower levels is necessary.

In the case of this performance meter, the set of goals would be "zero", although realistically speaking, this condition is impossible to achieve.

Therefore, efforts should focus on acting vigorously to minimize the volume of goods lost.

Two measures come from this item: the absolute value of obsolescence and the percentage it represents in relation to the total value of the inventory.

22.5.5 Internal material requisitions with zero stock

In the modern and efficient management of materials administration areas, implementing the necessary and sufficient conditions to keep inventories low and, in exceptional cases, operating with suppliers' stock, with the order's delivery at the time of use, is a sine qua non condition.

However, it is worth mentioning that this context is not frequent because of the impossibility of proceeding this way with the entire range of materials consumed by a company.

Therefore, a firm must maintain a small stock of materials but always in sufficient quantities to meet the essential demands for its regular operation.

Nothing discredits a materials manager more than an internal customer ordering a critical item from the warehouse and discovering it is out of stock.

Therefore, it is mandatory to have an indicator to measure the rate of internal requests received and not fulfilled because there was no material in the stock. This type of specific follow-up is vital for items indispensable to the operation whose "zero" supply can cause relevant inconveniences.

In this monitoring process, the intended rates change depending on the value and essentiality of the material.

For critical items, out-of-stock is unacceptable under any circumstances. The rate of unfulfilled requests must be "zero." As for the others, setting such a rigid goal is unnecessary because the cost of keeping all items sufficiently stored to meet all requests is prohibitive.

22.5.6 Consumption evolution

Like other undervalued indicators, many consider monitoring the evolution of consumption unimportant. These professionals could not be more wrong.

It is a meter that indicates trends according to the profile of oscillations, which can require challenging decisions from managers. For materials intended for operation, both in industrial and commercial companies, consumption should increase when sales grow.

The same logic may not apply to materials for administrative use, cleaning, conservation, and maintenance. Higher sales do not imply increased bond paper and pens consumption, for example.

As a result, it is advisable to compare consumption evolution data with other indicators, such as production and sales volume.

The parameter calculation takes place by measuring the values of the materials withdrawn from the warehouse in a particular period. Despite not being one hundred percent accurate, as nothing prevents a user from asking for more than he needs for immediate use, the information will be close to the real thing.

22.6 The purchasers

Thus far, this approach has centered on the materials and associated values. Now it is the time to study the work of those responsible for maintaining an organization supplied with the materials and services necessary for its full functioning.

The performance evaluation of professionals subordinate to the purchasing department focuses on the technical and personnel aspects.

22.6.1 Technical evaluation

Following the previous procedure, the technical evaluation of purchasing professionals occurs based on complete and objective data.

An ideal model evaluates individual results based on a previously defined goal. It also compares the performance of each procurement professional with the others, as suggested in the table in Figure 22.18. The comparison is only reasonable in organizations with at least two purchasers.

Assessment	Target	Sector average	Performance of purchasers						
			John	Peter	Joseph	Mary	Carl	Lucy	Louis
Time to issue an order	5	5.5	4.0	7.2	5.3	6.2	4.8	5.5	5.3
Time to receive material	8	9.1	7.4	11	10.3	9.3	8.1	8.4	9.2
Exclusivity (*)	0	0.021	0.027	0.029	0.031	0.017	0.019	0.021	0
No. of Proposals	4	4.1	4.4	4.1	3.8	5.2	3.6	3.5	3.9
Emergencies	0.07	0.11	0.12	0.11	0.12	0.1	0.14	0.08	0.11
Delivery punctuality	1	0.95	0.98	0.95	0.96	0.99	0.94	0.93	0.93
Return/Quality	0	0.027	0.021	0.034	0.025	0.03	0.042	0.014	0.022
Receipt with restrictions	0	0.022	0.018	0.022	0.031	0.014	0.022	0.031	0.017
Economic-Financial	-0.03	-03	-0.013	09	0.021	-01	-0.022	-0.012	-02
Acquisitions (x 1000) $	----	80	75	90	84	100.0	70	65	75
Number of items	----	530	450	519	510	634	710	435	455
Surpluses	0	0.01	0.015	0.031	0	0	0.025	0	0
obsolescence	0	04	0.012	0	0	0.013	0	0	0
Zero stock	0.02	0.021	0.012	0.022	0.025	0.02	0.024	0.03	0.014

(*) Excludes cases of long-term contracts previously signed with suppliers.

Figure 22.18.: Performance comparison of a company's purchasers

Different conclusions come from the analysis of a comparative table like this one. The purchasers who are most committed to the company's objectives stand out. There is also the identification of those with only average performance.

Finally, those who performed less than other department members also appear. For them, it is necessary to undergo training to improve their work procedures.

It is not reasonable to disregard the degree of complexity of each purchase. It is unfair to compare the time needed to acquire large, custom-made equipment with the time required to replace office supplies with immediate delivery.

22.6.2 Personal evaluation

Most suggestions for assessing purchasing performance favor the use of measurable data. The suppression of subjective connotations is intentional because of the possibility of misleading the interpretation of the evaluation process.

Limiting the focus to the objective aspect maximizes security when making decisions and facilitates course correction in the work of the purchasing department.

However, the focus on people requires adaptations in the analysis criteria. Evaluating procurement professionals involves a degree of subjectivity.

It is up to managers and supervisors to lead people to achieve the goals set by the company. Despite that, exercising leadership uniformly with all subordinates is a mistake. People have distinctive characteristics even if they perform similar tasks, and the approach must consider individual particularities.

As differences stem from the nature of people and the experiences accumulated over their lives, it is appropriate to conclude that individuals have a specific action potential. If managers ignore this situation, their work will be negative.

It is the leader's role to explore the potential of each subordinate, assigning them activities that they can perform satisfactorily, in line with their competencies. Here is the starting point for leaders to evaluate employee performance.

Performance evaluation consists of comparing the work developed and the result obtained by the professional with the expected behavior and the objectives set for the tasks. Within the purchasing area, the assessment must consider the requirements stipulated by the company regarding the purchaser's position.

The main requirements are:

- Availability: the diversity of the purchaser's activities requires permanent availability and readiness to act when necessary. Availability is a prerequisite of the role;
- Confidentiality: a purchaser can access confidential company and supplier data, often involving large sums of money. Therefore, he must be discreet;
- Emotional stability: a purchaser is subject to demands and pressures. Keeping cool when analyzing a situation and defining actions is essential for professional success;
- Initiative: manuals do not detail all activities. Occasionally, there are no guidelines for the task. This condition requires providing the service in the best way, respecting ethical requirements, and aiming to obtain the results expected by the company;
- Methodology and organization: ensure that the execution of the process steps follows the rules established for the tasks under its responsibility;
- Personal presentation: posture compatible with the position held and compliance with the organization's standards;
- Quality of work: minimizing the chances of error and achieving established goals;
- Sociability: frequent exposure to contacts with suppliers, internal customers, peers, superiors, and subordinates requires a high degree of cordiality;
- Teamwork: professional success depends on knowing how to work on a team. The team concept applies to professionals in the purchasing department and to colleagues with whom the purchaser interacts;
- Understanding service requirements: awareness of responsibilities, ambition for development, and persistence in obtaining helpful information, whether in books, on the Internet, with colleagues, or any other means capable of contributing.

Even with subjectivity, it is possible to compare purchasing employees in personal terms by assigning grades from one to five (one being insufficient and five being ideal), as shown in the example in Figure 22.19.

Question	John	Peter	Joseph	Mary	Carl	Lucy	Louis
Personal presentation	3,0	4,0	4,0	3,0	5,0	4,0	3,0
Understanding of the service	5,0	4,0	5,0	4,0	5,0	4,0	4,0
Circumspection	4,0	4,0	4,0	5,0	4,0	4,0	4,0
Availability	5,0	4,0	5,0	4,0	5,0	4,0	4,0
Emotional stability	3,0	4,0	4,0	4,0	5,0	3,0	4,0
Initiative	5,0	4,0	5,0	4,0	4,0	5,0	5,0
Methodology and organization	5,0	4,0	3,0	4,0	5,0	4,0	4,0
Quality of work	5,0	4,0	3,0	3,0	5,0	4,0	4,0
Sociability	3,0	4,0	4,0	3,0	5,0	4,0	3,0
Teamwork	4,0	4,0	4,0	4,0	4,0	4,0	4,0

Figure 22.19.: Purchaser's rating table

The evaluation tables, as exemplified, help purchasing managers understand subordinates' deficiencies and strengths. The correction of imperfections results from guidance and training and prevents further losses. Dismissing an employee who does not meet a company's demands may be necessary.

It is also worth noting that diverse companies have pitfalls when designing purchaser assessment mechanisms. Frazelle competently addressed this situation[93]: "How are most purchasers measured? Most purchasers are measured based on how low the price they can pay to a vendor for the product is. How do you get a low price? Large purchase quantities creating lots of inventories are the norm. (Is it any wonder it's called a lot size?)."

The above statement concludes that poorly defined goals can lead to results opposite those desired.

22.7 Data compilation

Compiling data without performing interpretive analysis is useless. Data isolated from a context without additional information can lead professionals to misinterpret the subject and make unwanted decisions.

---

[93] FRAZELLE, Edward H. Supply Chain Strategy, Second Edition: Unleash the Power of Business Integration to Maximize Financial, Service, and Operations Performance

Barely comparing, it would be like a doctor trying to diagnose a patient's illness, knowing solely that he has a fever of 103° F. The patient may have an infection or dysfunction; only clinical and/or laboratory tests can diagnose the disease.

The same occurs in any business activity, and it could not be different in the purchasing department. Only a collection of information provides a reliable picture of what is happening in the area.

In addition, to calculate the data needed to evaluate procurement performance, compiling and organizing such results is essential for global analysis.

The tables in Figures 22.20. and 22.21. provide suggestions. It is valid to disregard parameters unavailable in a particular company and add others not commented on here but existing in the organization where the reader works.

Rated item	Target	Performed in the month	Performed x Target	Performed in the previous month	Performed in the second previous month
Cost per order $	18.5	19.87	(-)	21.00	21.20
Order time (days)	5.00	5.50	(-)	5.70	5.70
Time to receive the material (days)	8.00	9.10	(-)	9.50	9.60
Exclusivity	0.0%	2.1%	(-)	1.8%	1.9%
No. of Proposals per acquisition	4.0	4.1	(+)	3.2	3.1
Emergencies	7.0%	11.0%	(-)	11.5%	12.2%
Delivery punctuality	100.0%	95.0%	(-)	92.0%	90.3%
Poor quality returns	0.0%	2.7%	(-)	3.0%	3.0%
Receipt with restrictions	0.0%	2.2%	(-)	2.8%	3.2%
Economic performance	-3.0%	-1.3%	(-)	-0.5%	-0.3%
Acquisition / Revenue	30.0%	36.5%	(-)	35.0%	35.4%
Inventory Turnover	2.7	2.1	(-)	2.0	1.8
Surpluses	0.0%	1.0%	(-)	1.2%	1.8%
Obsolescence	0.0%	0.4%	(-)	0.8%	1.6%
Zero stock	5.0%	8.5%	(-)	9.2%	9.5%

Figure 22.20.: Indicator compilation model

Assessment	Performed in the month	Performed in the previous month	Performed in the second previous month
Value of Acquisitions $	685,000	930,000	1,021,000
Number of Purchased Items	1,420	1,310	1,205
Stock Value $	850,000	915,000	684,000
Consumption $	1,100,000	995,000	1,210,000

Figure 22.21.: Indicator compilation model

Analyzing the data in isolation can lead the professional to make errors. The evaluation of the information reveals that the department's performance falls short of the pre-established goals. However, the monthly evolution shows improvements over time.

In this section, we study a variety of parameters and measures; logically, using all of them in companies is not feasible. In this case, it is essential to know how to select the most representative is necessary. The exhibition by Cecere[94] is worth remembering: "The second step is metrics definition. This decision needs to be based on business strategy. It needs to be conscious and include a set of deliberate choices. The challenge is the selection of a few meaningful metrics that represent all the elements of the complex system. Most companies measure too many things and are unclear on which metrics matter. Gaining clarity is a part of the journey."

---

[94] CECERE, Lora M. Supply Chain Metrics that Matter. 1st edition. USA: Wiley, December 8, 2014

CHAPTER 23

INTERNATIONAL PURCHASES

It's not enough to change the players. We gotta change the game!

Barack Obama[95]

In a world of perpetual progression, modernizing procedures related to the execution of daily tasks and creating new ones are fundamental to remaining in the market.

Achieving prominence in this scenario requires chasing new supplier options without getting stuck in old practices because they were efficient.

Searching for business alternatives beyond the country's borders fits perfectly into this scenario.

Every purchasing professional must research ways to supply the company efficiently. Understanding the benefits of sourcing from local suppliers or importing is valuable for purchasing planning.

In Figure 23.1., there is a comparison between the two options:

Parameter	National Purchases	Importation
Quality	Distinct levels	Scope favors higher standard
Delivery	Faster	Usually takes longer
Cost	Competitive for certain items	Competitive for certain items

Figure 23.1.: Comparison between importing and buying locally

The table expresses a generalization, as each acquisition requires a specific assessment to choose between two possibilities.

Importing goods is more common, although contracting services is also an alternative. For both, the advantages of imports are:

---

[95] Barack Hussein Obama II, American lawyer, and politician, was the 44th president of the United States from 2009 to 2017, being the first African American to hold the position.

- Expands the list of suppliers: business opportunities exist in Europe, Asia, Central America, Latin America, North America, and Africa. With many regions, countless supply sources stand out. A visible benefit of importing is that it provides a vast range of companies;
- Having more supply alternatives bring about options for purchasing products that meet the needs of users with favorable financial conditions. The customer has a high-performance range from the most specific items to the latest generation of products. The purchaser must detail requirements and identify the most suitable option;
- Access to transformative technologies: copious technological innovations have come from abroad. Waiting for local companies to develop under these new conditions wastes time. Going straight to the source is a differentiator that drives sales and generates value compared with its competitors.

There are other benefits besides those listed; however, there are risks. Disadvantages are:

- Delays in arrival: sea transport is widespread, and delays are possible. Although previously known, this contingency does not always reduce gains or produce losses. However, it is essential to evaluate its effects;
- Schedule the purchase well in advance: derivation from the previous sub-item; import programs require long preparation owing to the extended delivery period and risks of non-compliance with the expected arrival dates. Counting terms in days for local purchases and imports in fortnights or even months is customary. Planning the start of purchase is indispensable for successful imports;
- Supplier validation: auditing a supplier established in another country is more complex, but this does not justify failing to apply the stipulated requirements for domestic suppliers to an exporter before finalizing an import. It is possible to hire international companies capable of performing this process to avoid problems, naturally reserving this measure in the most critical cases.

23.1 Costs and taxes

There are taxes like those levied on local purchases. There are other exclusives that U.S. Customs and Border Protection (CBP) requires upon entry of goods imported into the United States.

CBP is also responsible for collecting taxes and fees from other federal agencies, such as the Consolidated Omnibus Budget Reconciliation Act (COBRA) outlines.

In cases where additional tax collection is mandatory, it is stipulated according to the class to which the imported goods belong.

Imports of alcoholic beverages and tobacco products, for example, must collect federal excise duties. The Internal Revenue Service (IRS) is responsible for stipulating the tax amount, and CBP is the designated agent for collection.

The type of fee and the corresponding amount are functions of the entry category and means of transportation to bring goods to the United States. For instance, the obligation to charge according to the Merchandise Processing Fee (MPF) applies to both formal (the goods have a value greater than $2,500) and informal entries. There is also an obligation to pay usage fees for imported goods.

There are taxes on formal operations, with an ad valorem rate of 0.3464%. The charge has maximum and minimum amounts that can change over time.

To calculate the rate, import value, excluding freight, ancillary expenses, and cargo insurance, serves as the basis.

The MPF for informal operations is pre-established with minimum and maximum values that also change.

When transport is by sea, a Harbor Maintenance Fee (HMF) is collected by CBP, which represents 0.125% of the value of the cargo transported through the ports. There is no incidence of HMF in cargo transported by air or the expression of courier services.

In addition to taxes, there are costs such as domestic sea or road freight, which may be necessary before and after the goods arrive at the port. Depending on the business transaction, the customer may bear a payment.

Dealing specifically with transport, it is worth listing a small number of common acronyms in this field:

FOB - Free on Board: freight paid by the customer from the port of origin, without insurance included	FAS - Free Alongside Ship: loading of goods and freight paid by the customer from the port of origin without insurance included
C&F - Cost and Freight: freight to specified destination paid by the seller, without insurance	CIF - Cost, Insurance, Freight: freight and insurance paid by the seller to a specified destination
ETA: Estimated Time of Arrival	ETD: Estimated Time of Departure

In transporting goods, events may cause damage to the buyer, justifying the contracting of cargo insurance from the origin to the customer's door. This is an acceptable cost since damage or loss of cargo generates a much more significant expenditure.

Importation involves situations hardly present in local purchases, which entails specific costs such as port fees, storage fees, and payment of customs clearance services.

Purchasers who are unfamiliar with import activities can ignore these differences. However, over time the steps become habitual.

23.2 Aspects to consider

Refusing materials other than those purchased is a fundamental import measure, and verification must occur before boarding.

Sending an employee of a client company to the port of origin is often not a realistic option. Nevertheless, hiring a company specializing in inspection, testing, verification, and certification at the starting point is possible.

Ensuring that the available material corresponds to the desired one compensates for the cost of the service.

The possibility of damage and the occurrence of transport delays deserve attention. Numerous types of insurance can minimize the effects of these setbacks.

Another frequent cause of headaches is bureaucracy, such as issuing inaccurate documents, filling out forms incorrectly, or not complying with the procedures stipulated by legislation and official entities.

Unlike domestic purchases, importing requires extensive documentation verified by port authorities, customs, and government agencies.

Failure to comply with documentation requirements or presenting documents with incorrect information can significantly delay the receipt of the material or generate unforeseen and unwanted fines and costs.

Researching in advance which documents and authorizations are mandatory at the origin and destination is the best action to avoid setbacks.

Unexpected or wrongly calculated taxes can occur, mainly if legislation is not fully studied. International agreements reduce import tax and thus generate mutual benefits for countries or economic blocs.

Before concluding any import, it is imperative to verify the existence of the agreements, check their validity, and ensure that they support a particular purchase.

23.3 Is importing better than buying in the domestic market?

Replacing a local supplier with another one abroad should not follow trends or copy competitors' strategies. The decision to import must result from a detailed analysis of the company's possible gains and potential risks.

Studying local and external alternatives involves defining objective parameters. The first focus is on the cost of storage, which is unequal in imports.

Actions to ensure security in serving users and optimizing storage are antagonistic. Deciding to import and provide a level of supply that reduces the chances of failure requires the maintenance of larger quantities stored, a result of a more extended replenishment period, and planning well in advance for the same reason.

Significant risks of delays are present, and as a precaution, the safety stock, whose purpose is to meet consumption in case of supply failures, will also be resized to a larger volume.

Therefore, the main effect is the higher cost of having stock when importing compared to domestic purchases.

An indispensable part of the preliminary assessment is to identify a substitute product to replace the imported one in case of delay in delivery or rejection by quality control. If there is no alternative material, the recommendation is to question the validity of importing or developing Plan B if there is an interruption in the import flow.

Finally, we suggest purchasing locally as a decision criterion for cases with a slight difference between the cost of the imported product and the national option unless there is a legitimate justification. The previously exposed risks justify the prioritization of security.

CHAPTER 24

STRATEGIC SOURCING

"If you decide that you're going to do only the things you know are going to work, you're going to leave a lot of opportunity on the table."

Jeff Bezos[96]

As a rule, every professional wants to participate in new projects for personal appreciation and opportunities for future promotion. However, excessively prolonging the planning phase to prepare the work and obtain more reliable results compromises the project.

Regardless of how good a plan is, it will only have merit if its implementation occurs and produces results.

The company's supply of materials and services depends on purchasers. Currently, the recognition of purchasing is increasing. In the past, purchasing activities were exclusively operational from the perspective of other areas. Their mission was to ensure material or service delivery with the commercial conditions of the purchase in the background.

The evaluation of the purchasing area's performance by the different departments and internal purchasing customers considers the service time, the selected brands, and the disbursed amount. It was common for the evaluation to be negative, as there were always high and often unrealistic expectations without valuing the results.

Shift mentality results from changing the essential conditions linked to organizations' supply.

Competition in the market demonstrates the essentiality of localizing modern products. Consequently, it increases the perception of the purchasing area as an indispensable player.

---

[96] Jeffrey Preston "Jeff" 'Bezos is an entrepreneur famous for being the founder of Amazon, the most important and celebrated e-commerce company in the United States.

Modernizing actions, redefining the objectives of the purchasing area, and training its professionals are general concepts that contribute to aligning purchasing performance goals with those of the organization.

From this set of changes, a Strategic Sourcing methodology has emerged. David Burt [97] shrewdly enunciated the importance of supplies in the broader context of the company: "The supply chain is the upstream portion of the organization's value chain and is responsible for feeding the production or conversion process."

24.1 Strategic Sourcing – Methodology

An accurate analysis of the improvement opportunities in the purchasing area leads to a Strategic Sourcing process.

In short, the methodology details a program that seeks to continually reorganize purchasing activities, improving and, most importantly, updating the area with innovative and efficient procedures.

The area's classic organizational model aims at operational efficiency without compromising day-to-day purchases. This approach produces superior results for materials of lesser value and little importance in operation, which are the majority.

In the case of significant purchases, the actions must be different. The details of this approach are as follows:

- Depending on users' needs, carefully analyze products and services that are more suitable for customization, ensuring a lower cost;
- Highlight suppliers with better performance, make partnerships official, establish the desired performance standards, and conduct long-term follow-up;
- Form a specific plan to find the most qualified suppliers to achieve your goals.

This process intends to prepare a detailed supply proposal in tactical and operational terms. Several activities still follow the traditional model, which is efficient and sufficient in many cases.

---

[97] BURT, David N; PETCAVAGE, Sheila; PINKERTON, Richard. Proactive Purchasing in the Supply Chain: The Key to World-Class Procurement. 1st edition. USA: McGraw Hill, December 6, 2011

The essential information for acquisitions deserves careful analysis, notably the description of the materials, whose details should result from discussions with the user areas, quality, projects, sales, and inventories.

It is also necessary to set cost targets, as the main objective is to be at the forefront of market share competition.

The increase in productivity depends on definitions of the activities, setting the supply's beginning and end according to the schedule. The period is estimated and subject to uncertainties; however, having a forecast provides a preview of the process.

24.2 Purchase cost

Strategic Sourcing pays special attention to cost, whereas most professionals focus on price, a behavior naturally assimilated by novice purchasers from contact with professionals with more time in the area.

Experience shows that the supplier whose proposal is at the lowest price also usually offers the lowest cost, but it is not a rule. The procedure requires extensive analysis, with price being an additional cost element.

When analyzing the cost of a good or service, the essential parameters are:

- Price;
- Existence of price adjustment;
- Payment terms and financial cost;
- Required packaging with payment for it;
- Shipping and loading;
- Tax incidence;
- Other special aspects of purchasing.

Analysis of the table indicates that price alone cannot reliably determine whom to buy from. Ignoring other criteria may lead to selecting the least advantageous supplier.

24.3 Emphasis on the importance of the material or service

Executing the Strategic Sourcing steps takes time; therefore, applying this approach to all purchases is not wise. It is more efficient to use simple and well-structured procedures.

Choosing a suitable model depends on the item's importance to the company, in which case the ABC classification of materials is helpful.

As the amount of material disbursement is the pivotal point, items A, because they allocate most financial resources, deserve detailed analysis and processing, and must be carefully studied. This evaluation results from fixing stock levels, economic lot size, and the time interval between replacements.

24.4 Assignment of Purchases in Strategic Sourcing

The Strategic Sourcing process does not only cover the acquisition phase. This method included the entire supply chain. Focusing on the purchasing function, which is the object of this book, it is worth highlighting:

- The internal customer needs are the crucial point, guiding the work to deliver the material or service in full compliance with the request. The user has the authority to define brands, models, and other essential aspects to individualize the purchase object;

- Meeting the stipulated deadline to receive the order without delays or anticipations is crucial. Preserving the performance history of suppliers regarding contracted deadlines and using this information to choose the best proposal is a prerequisite for supply to occur following the intended conditions;

- Commitment to obtaining an offer at the lowest possible cost and other conditions compatible with the previously detailed objectives for a purchasing department;

- Ensure delivery of the contracted quantity, enabling activities dependent on material availability. Use software to calculate the ideal batch, reducing storage costs and minimizing the risk of shortages.

The Strategic Sourcing concept provides tools for surviving in an ever-changing market. A way to satisfy a specific need in the present will not exist in the future, surpassed by something innovative.

Consumers demand good products without paying more, as gains from modern technologies and increased productivity allow companies to develop cost-reduction mechanisms. Purchasing is at the heart of this process. The challenge for purchasing analysts is to have the tools to operate in a constantly evolving market.

CHAPTER 25

STAFF TRAINING AND DEVELOPMENT

"Tell me, and I forget, teach me, and I may remember, involve me, and I learn."

Benjamin Franklin [98]

The training theme covers seeking to provide new skills and improve others that the professionals have. It is about preparing people to perform better in their current roles or transmitting the fundamentals to start in a new position.

Analyzing historically, the training activity encompasses ideas from the strategic management theory related to evolutionary improvement. Use scientific methods to get work done and increase productivity by organizing tasks-focused activities.

Investing in people's development generates superior operational and motivational outcomes. The company's reward comes from having better prepared employees, who improve their skills, act efficiently, diminish losses, and seek actions that reduce costs.

25.1 Historical context

Over time, researchers develop theories and concepts to increase employee performance.

Frederick W. Taylor, educated in mechanical engineering, achieved notoriety as the author of the book "The Principles of Scientific Management", published in 1911. His objective was to apply scientific methods in management and improve operational efficiency and effectiveness.

Taylor worked to methodize the actions of professionals, enabling them to perform tasks by following strictly defined instructions and becoming more productive. He believed in learning a specific activity to maximize job

---

[98] Benjamin Franklin was one of the leaders of the American Revolution, famous for experimenting with electricity. He was the first US ambassador to France.

performance. His strategy was to study the time and methods of performing a task. He conducted experiments until he found the most effective way to generate better results.

He aimed to make workers experts in specific functions and develop standardized tools to increase productivity.

In the job description, to unequivocally organize the specialization stages, the core was conducting tasks using calculations and devices to reduce execution time, an essential parameter for productivity gains.

The scope of Taylor's work was the execution of operational activities in the industry, although later, much of his work was helpful in administrative or general activities.

As an incentive, Taylor paid good salaries and stipulated performance rewards, introducing the talent retention strategy as the cost of training and qualifying a worker was high.

In addition to Taylor, another exponent of management science focusing on performance is Jules Henri Fayol, a French mining engineer and the author of General and Industrial Management in 1916.

Fayol based his research on the figure of a leader, highlighting the importance of hierarchy in the organization of teams. Another essential point was the division of tasks among the various people involved in the operation, giving rise to the figure of the specialist.

He planned the structuring to achieve the company's goals, defining the general objectives for later fulfillment. Of course, the engagement of employees was fundamental, a sine qua non condition to make the process viable, and for that, it rewarded with fair and satisfactory wages.

He inspired the so-called pyramid of power. The concept adopts the figure of a pyramid, placing the leaders in charge of planning at the top and the workers responsible for the tasks at the bottom.

As a result, the turnover (the relation between the entrance and exit of employees in the company, calculated based on layoffs and hirings) is low.

25.2 Purchasing Professional Training

In the purchasing department, training and development activities aim for professional education to reach the desired level for the performance of activities, with the transmission of knowledge and detailing of practices.

Experienced professionals receive regular training to emphasize known concepts and to learn new and better techniques.

Specific knowledge areas are strategic to improve performance and develop skills.

25.2.1 Commercial approach

If the reason for the existence of the purchasing area is to accomplish acquisitions for the organization, a professional working in it must be able to identify the offer that best meets the needs and strive to obtain the maximum benefit from the process.

Among the factors that seek improvement, it is worth highlighting the following:

- Negotiation: possibly the most critical skill. It is noteworthy that the proposals rarely contain the best conditions. Failing to trade implies wasting the earnings potential and the opportunity to optimize the company's results. The pivotal point is the purchaser's ability to extract concessions from the supplier, bringing the proposal closer to the best possible commercial condition. Determining the limits of those who sell is impossible, but getting closer with technique and competence is feasible. These are the fundamentals conveyed by good trading courses;

- Mathematical and financial knowledge: Another essential skill for analyzing incoming proposals and understanding each detail. Offers commonly differ in value, terms, transport costs, and taxation. Comparing alternatives requires performing critical calculations. An incorrectly calculated value compromises the analysis and leads to bad decisions, justifying the demand for training that offers the indicated skills to assess and decide confidently;

- Occasional, frequent, or scheduled acquisition: organizations have multiple demands for materials and services. Purchasing involves acting differently due to the particularities of each case, although this characteristic does not justify failing to comply with rules and procedures. An isolated or infrequent acquisition has a reduced information history compared with that made constantly. In each case, understanding the best approach provides more agility and benefits both financially and in terms of time and quality. The process will be different, with research on potential sources, user verification, and approval of specifications. Courses with specific topics on this type of conduct also exist.

25.2.2 Supply Source Management

Various purchasers seek to improve solely the items listed in the previous topic. This is a severe mistake, as career success and positive results also depend on other skills in training programs.

Featured are:

- Supplier Management: an efficient and effective supplier registry is essential for achieving the goals of the purchasing area and the company. However, taking advantage of the best supply sources is not a chance result. It comes from a job well done in selecting companies and maintaining information related to them. Periodically examine the history of customers, observing if deliveries comply with the stipulated, if there is evidence of activities taking place in an environmentally sustainable way, offers competitive costs, demonstrates innovation capacity and financial stability, and provides agility to the flow of products and services. There are helpful assessment mechanisms for these areas of expertise, and with good training detailing the alternatives for the job, the purchaser will improve their abilities;

- Category Management: Well-run companies often categorize materials to simplify and streamline their warehousing and purchasing processes, as discussed in section 10. The method for accomplishing this segmentation depends on the nature of the company and its intended objectives. In industry, the categories follow the application of the item as direct materials in the case of raw materials. In retail, there is the concept of the family, that is, the role played in sales. Management models have a specific design for the type of division chosen and seek to link suppliers to different classes;

- Supplier development and auditing: although essential, sometimes having a good list of suppliers does not meet all demands, as relevant purchases may be subject to supply insecurity. As detailed before, developing new options is essential for increasing the reliability of the entire refueling system. Knowing search engines for new sources is the purchaser's job. In training programs aimed at this audience, it is common to study the topic and justify the seek for recycling. However, maintaining a good track record requires constant monitoring of the company's performance. Therefore, a supplier audit is essential. This verification is standard for registered companies but will be insufficient without periodically repeating the analysis. When registering a company, a photograph of that moment is available, which will lose validity in the future. Regular audits ensure that all initial credibility and performance validation remain valid. This type of approach is present in a good course;

- Management indicators and performance targets: auditing efficiency requires specific actions, and recommended instruments are performance indicators, which are the best way to measure the qualification of suppliers. This is one of the topics with the most significant potential to create difficulties for purchasers. It involves fundamentals of mathematics, statistics, and other sciences. This knowledge is relevant for exercising this function, justifying that it is a frequent subject in good training courses.

25.2.3 Supply contracting

The finalization of the purchase occurs with the delivery of the object of the contract and payment to the supplier. In this context, simple measures are valuable to formalize the acquisition.

- Requirements Management: specifying the contract's object and the commercial conditions negotiated without incurring errors is essential. Detailing contractor obligations facilitates efficient control of purchase requirements. As the purchaser is hardly responsible for monitoring the delivery, a perfect description of the purchase conditions is essential to avoid doubts for the professional responsible for the task. Purchasers often remember details that their colleagues ignore, which requires efficient communication with those involved in the material receipt process. This is mandatory for professional training;

- Contract Management - SLA (Service Level Agreement): in acquiring services, the excellent management described in the previous sub-item requires a detailed description of the contracted service and execution conditions. SLA defines guidelines that bind the contractor to the supplier in the execution of the service. It aims to guarantee the maintenance of quality parameters during the contract term and contains the requirements for the agreement to satisfy everyone. As with other topics, there are also specific courses focused on SLA that can prepare purchasing professionals to manage this tool efficiently.

ANNEX - TRANSPORT AND HANDLING TERMS

Knowing some technical terms is useful when making purchases or hiring cargo transport. This annex lists the most frequent and/or beneficial terms to know for good performance in the work of a purchasing professional.

Acronym/Term	Explanation
AAR	Against all risks (insurance policy requirement)
Abatement	Discount arising from damage or for paying an amount above the established
Aboard	Regarding cargo being loaded onto a transport
Acceptance	The act of unconditionally agreeing to pay a bill of exchange or a draft on the due date
Acquittance	Document proving the discharge of a debt or obligation
Ad Valorem	Tax applied as a percentage of the chargeable value of the cargo
Advice of Shipment	Notice forwarded to a customer that the shipment is on its way with details on packaging, routing
Advising Bank	A document attesting that a letter of credit (L/C) from an issuing bank is available
Agent	Professional with authority to conduct business on behalf of a company
All In	The total price, including all costs, taxes, and fees, to transport the cargo from origin to destination
All–risk Insurance	Type of insurance that offers the carrier the most comprehensive coverage available, indemnifying all possible losses that may occur in transit
Alongside	It refers to the side of a ship. Goods delivered alongside are left on the pier to be loaded
Anti–Dumping Duty	Tariffs imposed to penalize foreign goods benefiting from subsidies, with artificially low prices and harmful to domestic manufacturers
Appraisement	Indication, by customs, of the taxable value of imported goods, according to the country's tariff rules

Arrival Notice	Document issued by the carrier notifying all relevant parties of the estimated or confirmed date of arrival of the shipment at a specified destination
Assignment	Transfer of rights, title, and interest for the concession of goods upon endorsement in the bill of lading
B/L	Abbreviation for "Bill of Lading."
Balloon Freight	Light, bulky goods
Bank Guarantee	Bank-issued carrier warranty that can replace a lost or misplaced original negotiable bill of lading
Barrel (BBL)	Unit of measure equivalent to 42 gallons of liquid
Base Rate	Tariff term meaning the maritime rate minus charges, that is, the basic rate of the tariff
Beneficiary	Individual or company to whom money is owed, or to whom a letter of credit is issued, or Seller and drawer of a draft
Bilateral	A contractual term indicating that both parties agree to provide something to the other
Bill of Exchange	Written order in which one party guarantees to pay a certain amount to another party, upon request or on a predetermined date, can be withdrawn and is often transferable by endorsement
Bill of Lading (B/L)	Shipping document issued by the carrier to the sender detailing the goods, quantity, and destination, serving as a bill of lading upon delivery of the goods to a predetermined destination
Billed Weight	Weight itemized on a shipping waybill or shipping note; invoiced weight
Bonded Warehouse	Warehouse approved by the customs authorities for the storage of goods with postponed payment of duties until the goods are removed
Booking	A transaction with a carrier to reserve space in cargo transport
Break Bulk	Transport of general cargo, loose or fractioned, not packed in a container, and without homogeneity

Broker	Professional who coordinates all procedures for transporting cargo for a percentage of cargo revenue
Bulk Cargo	Cargo not packed or placed in containers; loosely loaded in the ship's hold
Bulk Carriers	Vessels designed to transport homogeneous bulk cargo such as oil, ores, grains, etc.
Bulk–Freight Container	Container with front discharge hatch for loading bulk goods
Bunker	Is the fuel used in a ship's engine
Bunker Charge	Also called Bunker Additional Fuel (BAD) is a rate calculated as a percentage of basic ocean freight justified by higher fuel costs
Cost and Freight – C&F	The commercial term where the Seller pays the cost of goods and freight charges to the port of destination, also known as CFR
Cabotage	Word for waterway transport between ports of the same nation. Numerous countries, including the USA, have cabotage laws forcing nationally flagged ships to operate in internal transport
Cargo	The freight of a ship, freight of goods loaded on a vessel
Cargo Manifest	A manifest listing all cargo carried on a specific ship
Cargo Tonnage	Most ocean freight is charged by weight or tons, which can be short tons, 2,000 pounds, long tons of 2,240 pounds, or metric tons of 1,000 kilograms (2204.62 pounds)
Carrier	Individual or institution that undertakes to carry out or contract the execution of transport by rail, road, sea, air, or a combination of them
Carrier's Certificate	Certificate required by US Customs to release cargo to the correct entity
Cash Against Documents (CAD)	Payment for goods with the delivery of title transferring ownership to Buyer linked to cash payment to an intermediary acting on behalf of Seller, usually a broker

Cash in Advance (CIA)	Payment method in which the Buyer pays the Seller before the goods are shipped. Most common when products are made to order
Cash With Order (CWO)	Modality in which payment is made at the time of order
Certificate of Inspection	Document ensuring that the goods were in proper condition immediately before shipment
Certificate of Origin	Document confirming the origin of the goods
CCC Mark - China Compulsory Certificate Mark	Mandatory safety mark indicating that the cargo meets the standards required by China for various imported products
CE Mark	Mandatory safety mark indicating that the cargo meets the standards required by the European Community for various imported products
CI	The acronym for "Cost and Insurance" indicates that the price includes the cost of the goods, marine insurance, and transportation expenses but excludes ocean freight to the destination
CIF (named port)	Acronym for "Cost, Insurance, Freight" with a defined port of destination, similar to C&F or CFR, with the difference that the Seller pays for insurance until the destination
CKD	The acronym for "Completely Knocked Down" denotes the transport of parts and sub-assemblies to an assembly plant
Claim	Requirement for a carrier to pay for a loss incurred because of its presumed negligence
Clean Bill of Lading	Certificate issued by the carrier attesting that the goods were received in "apparent good order and good condition" without damage. When there is no annotation or exception made, the B/L is considered "clean"
Clip-On	Refrigeration equipment adaptable to a container without its own refrigeration unit

CM	"Cubic Meter"
Cm	"Centimeter"
COD	Collect (cash) on Delivery
Commercial Invoice	Document issued by the exporter to the importer, valid as a sales contract, indicating value, quantity and merchandise, and other commercial conditions. Essential for customs clearance and calculation of fees and taxes
Commodity	A substance or product that can be traded
Confirmed Letter of Credit	Letter of credit issued by a foreign bank with validity confirmed by a domestic bank. Ensures payment to the Seller even when the Buyer or foreign bank fails to pay
Confirming Bank	The bank that confirms the issuing bank's letter of credit and undertakes to pay the beneficiary upon presentation of the documents listed in the letter of credit
Consignee	Individual or company receiving the goods sent
Consignee Mark	Sign with triangle, square, or circle with letters, numbers, and port of destination, placed on the packaging for identification
Consignment	Inventory of merchandise provided in advance to a reseller who stores it at its location, but with ownership remaining with the supplier
Consignor	Individual or company mentioned on the bill of lading as a sender
Consolidation	Cargo containing goods from two or more shippers. Container load shipments may be consolidated for one or more consignees to maximize container utilization
Consumption Entry (CE)	Procedure for declaration of import of goods for consumption in the USA but manufactured abroad
Container	Resistant cargo storage structure for transport in trucks, ships, etc. They can be ventilated, refrigerated, flat rack, open-top, or bulk liquid, among other options. Sizes range from 20 feet, 40 feet, 45 feet, 48 feet or 53 feet in length, 8'0" or 8'6" in width, and 8'6" or 9'6" in height
Container Booking	Agreement with a shipping company for containerized cargo transportation

Container Manifest	Legally required document detailing the contents and order of loading and the points of origin and destination of a container
Container Terminal	Location intended for stowage of cargo in a container; accessible by truck, rail, or sea transport, where containers are collected and stored
Contract Carrier	An unusual carrier that, by contract or agreement, transports passengers or goods
Contract of Affreightment	An order from a shipping carrier granting cargo space on a particular vessel at a specified time for a defined price
Correspondent Bank	The bank that manages the business of a foreign bank locally
CPT (Carriage Paid To ...Place of Destination	The Seller pays for the transportation of the goods to the destination. Still, loss, damage to the goods, or additional costs for occurrences after goods are delivered to the carrier is up to the Buyer. In this condition, the Seller must clear the goods for export. CIP is an acronym that considers the inclusion of cargo insurance in the CPT condition
Cube Out	The situation where a container or ship has filled the volumetric capacity although it has not reached the permissible weight limit
Cubic Foot	Unit of measure corresponding to the volume of a cube measuring one foot high, one foot wide, and one foot long, totaling 1,728 cubic inches
Customhouse Broker	Individual or company hired by an importer to act in the entry and customs clearance of goods
Customs	A government department that administers charges fees on imported products and ensures compliance with rules related to import and export revenues
Customs Entry	Declaration informing the entry of foreign goods that the importer must compulsorily fill out and, generally, pay the tax on the goods. Ensures that all imported goods are declared

Customs of the Port (COP)	A common term in freight contracts, informing local rules and practices capable of impacting the costs incurred by those involved in the transaction
Cut–Off Time	Last time for goods to be delivered to a terminal for loading on scheduled transport
D&H	Acronym for "Dangerous and Hazardous" cargo
DAF (Delivered At Frontier... Named Place	Sellers have responsibilities for delivery ended when the goods are made available and cleared for export at the place established at the border, but before the custom in the adjoining country
DDC	Abbreviation for "Destination Delivery Charge", this charge is calculated as a function of container size and added to ocean freight
DDP (Delivered Duty paid... Named Port of Destination)	The Seller's responsibility ceases when the goods are available in the location of the importing country. It is also responsible for the risks and costs of delivering the goods cleared for import, including fees, taxes, and other charges. If EXW is the minimum obligation for the Seller, DDP is the maximum
DDU (Delivered Duty Unpaid... Port of Destination)	The Seller completes its delivery obligation when the goods are placed in the port of the importing country, being responsible for the costs and risks involved in the delivery of the goods (except duties, fees, and other import charges) and those arising from the fulfillment of formalities customs. The Buyer will pay for additional costs or risks caused by not clearing the goods on time
Deadweight tonnage (DWT)	The measure of the total weight of cargo that a ship can carry
Deconsolidation Point	A place where a loose or non–containerized cargo is disassembled for delivery
DEQ (Delivered Ex Quay... Named Port of Destination)	The DDU condition is over when the goods are available to the Buyer at the destination port and cleared for import. It is up to the Seller to pay for all risks and costs, including fees, taxes, and charges for delivering the goods to that location

Deficit Weight	Weight less than the minimum established for a shipment
Delivery Instructions or Shipping Delivery Order	Order usually issued by the exporter for collection of goods at an established location and delivery to a pier
Demurrage	Penalty charged to the shipper or consignee for exceeding the free time allowed for carrier's equipment or ship. Demurrage applies to cargo
DES (Delivered Ex Ship... Named Port of Destination)	The Seller's obligation ceases when he delivers the goods to the Buyer on board the ship at the defined port, ready for import. The Seller assumes the costs and risks involved in placing the goods there
Detention	Penalty charged to the shipper or consignee for delaying the carrier's equipment. Detention applies to equipment
Discrepancy Letter of Credit	When the exporter does not comply with the deadline or the documents presented are not following the content of the letter of credit (L/C), a "discrepancy" occurs, and the banks do not process the L/C, returning it to the Buyer or Seller and will wait for further instructions
Dock	Cargo handling area parallel to the pier location where the ship lands or truck loading and unloading platform in an industrial area or transport terminal
Documents Against Acceptance (D/A)	Instructions given to the bank by the sender specifying that the documents should only be delivered to the Buyer after it accepts the draft
Documents Against Payment (D/P)	Item in the draft stating that attached documents should only be released upon payment
Door–to–Door	All cargo movement from the exporter's location to the importer's place
Draft	Formal order, issued by one of the parties (drawer) and destined for the other (drawee), requiring the payment of a fixed amount to a particular person at a stipulated future date

Draft, Bank	An order issued by a seller against a buyer; determines payment, usually via an intermediary bank. Bank drafts are usually negotiable
Draft, Clean	Draft without an attached document
Drawback	A partial refund of an import tax, usually due because the goods are re-exported
Drawee	The individual or company that issues a draft and is entitled to receive the payment
Dry Cargo	A non-liquid cargo that does not require temperature control
Dumping	Import of goods at prices below market or production cost, usually with the benefit of subsidies granted by the exporting country, to gain more significant market shares
Dutiable Value	The base amount for calculating Ad Valorem or a customs duty
Endorsement	A legal signature placed on the back of a draft authorizing the transfer of the rights from the holder to a third party
ETA	Estimated Time of Arrival
Ex Dec	Shipper's Export Declaration - Occasionally required to ship goods worth more than USD 2,500 or that require a license or license exception
Ex - "locality"	Price term such as "Ex Works" indicates that the value is valid only for the highlighted location
Exception	If the cargo received at the carrier or shipped on a ship has any damage or the packaging is not in good condition, it is necessary to prepare an exception note and attach it to the bill of lading
Expiry Date	The information included in documents, such as letters of credit, to notify that content and authorizations will expire on a specific date
Export Declaration	An official document attesting that the related goods will be shipped abroad. Completed by the exporter and filed with the United States Government

Export License	A government document granting permission to the "Licensee" to export specific goods to established destinations
(Ex Works)	Incoterm of sale indicates that the Seller makes the goods available at the specified location and, from that point, the Buyer will bear the handling, costs, and risks of transporting the goods
FAS	Free Alongside Ship is a term stipulating that the Seller will deliver the goods alongside a specific ship at a particular port
FCL	Full Container Load is a term that characterizes maritime shipping in which the cargo occupies an entire container
F.D.A. Food and Drug Administration	It is a government agency responsible for protecting public health, ensuring the safety and efficacy of medicines, and the security of the food supply
FOB	Free on Board is a commercial condition in which the Seller's obligations end when the goods are placed on board the ship at the indicated shipping port
FOR	Acronym for Free on Rail, a commercial condition in which the Seller bears the costs until the goods are delivered to a railway station and loaded onto a train
Foul Bill of Lading	A goods receipt issued by the carrier notifying the finding of damage to the goods at the time of delivery
Free Carrier (FCA)	The Seller delivers the goods to a destination specified by the Buyer
Free In and Out (FIO)	The charterer/shipper pays the cost of loading and unloading a ship
Free Port	The restricted area of a seaport or airport where goods from abroad can be brought in tax-free with the requirement to be sent to another country when they leave that location
Free Time	The period that an operator's equipment can be used without charging extra costs

Free Trade Zone	Port qualified by the government of the country for tax-free receipt of non-prohibited goods, which can be stored, used for manufacturing, etc., within this area and re-exported without fees
Freight	It designates a cargo in transport or charges incurred for the transport of goods
Freight Bill	Document issued by the carrier according to the bill of lading data and other information; necessary to account for a cargo transport both operationally and financially
Freight Forwarder	A professional whose activity is to act as an agent on behalf of the shipper, and often makes reservations for the cargo transportation
Full Containerships	Ships equipped with permanent container cell structures, with minimal or no space for other types of cargo
Gateway	The point at which, regularly, there is a change from one mode of transport to another (such as from sea to land), performing an intermodal function
GATT - General Agreement on Tariffs and Trade	A multilateral convention aimed at reducing trade barriers between signatory countries and stimulating trade through the application of tariff concessions
General Cargo Carriers	Vessels designed to transport heterogeneous cargo, such as bulk products, cars, cattle, palletized goods, etc.
General Order - GO.	A status assigned to imported goods without the required documentation when it is not possible to release it quickly due to other inaccuracies, if taxes, fees, or costs have not been paid if the owner has not provided the documentation correctly, or if the invoice is not legally compliant
Gross Weight	When ready for shipment, the total weight of the merchandise, with packaging and container. Containers generally have an 80,000-pound limit for road transport.
Groupage	Consolidation of small cargoes in container
GVW - Gross Vehicle Weight	The combined total weight of a vehicle plus the container

Harbor	A place where ships can stay, load or unload passengers or goods, obtain fuel, water, or supplies
Harmonized System of Codes - HS	An international commodity classification system that describes cargoes in a single commodity coding scheme. The code is a product nomenclature containing about 5,000 titles and subtitles, 99 chapters (covers industry materials and products, such as Chapter 50, Silk), and 22 sections (covers an industry, such as Section XI, Textiles and Textile Articles). The basic code contains four-digit headers and six-digit subtitles, although several countries add digits for customs and statistical fees (the USA uses eight digits for tax rates and ten digits for statistical suffixes)
Heavy–Lift Charge	The calculated rate for lifting weighty goods, which exceed the capacity of the ship's usual equipment and require specialized machinery such as cranes
House–to–House	The same condition of Door–to–Door
House–to–Pier	Cargo is loaded in a container by the shipper in his unit and exported for unloading on a foreign pier at the destination
IE - Immediate Exit	Customs IE Form is used in the US when goods are brought there and are immediately re-exported without being moved within the US
IMCO - International Maritime Consultative Organization	Forum that brings together most of the major maritime nations to issue recommendations for the transport of dangerous goods, bulk goods, and maritime regulations that became internationally recognized
Import	Process intending to receive goods from a foreign country
Import License	Document required and issued by some governments authorizing the import of certain goods into the country
In Transit	Goods in transit
In–Transit Entry	Consent for the in-bond transport of foreign goods arriving at one port to another, in which a superseding entry is filed

INCOTERMS	Abbreviation for the International Chamber of Commerce Terms of Sale, a standardized regulatory norm for the different aspects of international trade, making clear the distribution of risks, costs, and responsibilities of those involved in a transaction of purchase and sale of goods
Inducement	Allocate a port in a ship's itinerary, as the volume of cargo in that port offsets the cost of detouring the ship
Inherent Vice	Insurance term relating to a defect or feature of a product capable of resulting in damage to the product without any external cause (chemical instability, for example). Insurance policies may contain clauses to exclude losses in such cases
Inspection Certificate	Certificate issued by an independent agent or company attesting that the quality and/or quantity of the goods shipped match those specified
Installment Shipments	Successive shipments are allowed as long as they are linked to letters of credit, and it is common to have a time limit for them to occur
Insurance with Average–clause	A clause that covers the goods if the damage is equal to or above three percent of the insured value. Losses are fully covered if the vessel burns, sinks, or collides. In marine insurance terminology, the average describes partial damage or loss
Insurance, General–Average	In maritime transport, it refers to the deliberate sacrifice of part of the cargo to make the ship safe for the rest of the cargo. Those who share the remaining load proportionally cover the loss
Interline Freight	Shipping service from origin to destination with the participation of two or more carriers
Intermodal	The transport of containers interchangeably between modes of transportation, for example, rail and sea, with the equipment being compatible with the systems used

International Ship and Port Security Code - ISPS	Amendment to the Convention for the Safety of Life at Sea (SOLAS), which deliberates on minimum security measures for ships, ports, and government agencies and prescribes the responsibilities for all involved to detect threats to security and take preventive measures
Inward Foreign Manifest – IFM	Complete list of all shipments entering the country for unloading. Mandatory document in all ports around the world and the main cargo control matrix against which the receiving government assesses tax
Irrevocable Letter of Credit	Letter of credit with specified payment guaranteed by the bank if all obligations and conditions are fulfilled by the drawee, not being revocable without the joint agreement of the Buyer and Seller
ISO-International Standards Organization	International non-governmental organization that brings together specialists to study and develop International Standards based on consensus and relevant to the market
Issuing Bank	A bank that issues the straight or negotiable letter of credit and undertakes to pay the bank or beneficiary if the documents presented comply with the terms of the letter of credit
Issuing Carrier	The issuing carrier of the transport documents
IT - Immediate Transport	Document issued by the carrier to allow shipment to go on from the US port of entry for customs clearance at destination with customs procedures taking place at the destination
Joint Rate	Tariff applicable from one point of a transport line to another point, on a different line, established by agreement and unified by all transport lines for which it applies
KT	Kilo or metric ton. 1,000 Kilograms or 2,204.6 pounds
Kilogram - Kg	1,000 grams or 2.2046 pounds
Knocked Down (KD)	Components are disassembled to reduce the volume or to optimize dispatch, which will be reassembled later
Known Loss	Loss identified before or at the time of delivery of goods of a shipment
L/C	Abbreviation for Letter of Credit

Lading	Goods carried by a vehicle or the act of loading such goods
Landed Cost	The total cost of a good to the Buyer, including the shipping cost
Landing Certificate	Certificate issued by consular officials of certain importing countries at the place of export and required if these goods are exported on bond
LAYCAN – Lay days Cancelling (date)	The expected time interval for the start of the hire agreement
LCL - Less than Container Load	The amount of cargo is lower than that required to apply a container loading fee
Less Than Truckload - LTC	Similar meaning to LCL
Letter of Credit - LC	A document issued by the bank following the instructions of the Buyer of the goods. Its purpose is to guarantee the Seller the withdrawal of a specific amount if it presents the documents listed therein to the bank within a certain period
Letter of Credit Back–to–Back	A new letter of credit issued to another beneficiary backed by a first L/C that serves as collateral for the bank. Used in a tripartite transaction
Letter of Credit Clean	Letter of credit requesting only a withdrawal or receipt to pay specified funds
Letter of Credit Deferred Payment	A letter of credit issued for the purchase and financing of goods, like a letter of acceptance credit (payable by a time draft authorization on or after a specified date), except that it requires the presentation of sight drafts to pay in installments
Letter of Credit noncumulative	A revolving letter of credit that prohibits later withdrawal of unused amount during the specified period
Letter of Credit Restricted	A manifest imposition in the letter of credit that restricts its trading to a specified bank

Letter of Credit Revocable	Document subject to change or cancellation at any time, without prior notice and regardless of the beneficiary's agreement. It usually includes a clause ensuring that a draft negotiated by a bank before receipt of notification of revocation or amendment will be honored by the issuing bank. Because it does not provide security to the Seller, it is practically not used
Letter of Credit Revolving	Irrevocable letter of credit issued with a fixed amount and renewable for an equal amount for a specified period
Letter of Credit Transferable	A letter of credit that grants the beneficiary the right to transfer all or part of it to other persons or entities, provided that the sum of all transfers is limited to the credit amount
Letter of Credit Unconfirmed	A letter of credit without guarantee or confirmation made by a bank other than the one that issued it. The advising bank only notifies the beneficiary of its terms and conditions
Lien	A legal claim for goods to settle some debt or obligation
Liner	A vessel that provides travel on a specific regular commercial route
Liter	1.06 liquid US quarts or 33.9 fluid ounces
Load line	The waterline indicative of the maximum cargo that a vessel is authorized to carry
Long Ton	2,240 pounds or 1,016.047 kilograms
Loose	Unpacked Goods
Manifest	The document, used for customs procedures, lists all bills of lading issued by a carrier or its agent for a voyage, detailing the total cargo of the ship
Marine Insurance	Insurance covering loss or damage to goods at sea, which generally indemnifies the owner of the goods for losses incurred by fire, shipwreck, etc., excluding losses recoverable by the carrier

Maritime Security and Safety Information System - MSSIS	A mechanism for sharing and displaying the vessel's Automatic Identification System (AIS) data in real-time to international users using a web-based, password-protected system
Marking	To simplify identification, letters, numbers, and symbols are printed on cargo packages. Also known as marks
Master Inbound	US Customs computerized program under the Automated Manifest System (AMS). He receives electronic reports of inbound foreign loads in the US.
Measurement Cargo	Type of shipping in which the calculation of transport fees depends on the volume
Measurement Ton	Unit of measure for a volume equivalent to 40 cubic feet
Meter	Unit of measure of length with an approximate value of 39.37 inches
Mile	Unit of measurement equivalent to 5,280 feet on land or 6,076.12 feet in the case of the nautical mile
Mini Landbridge	An intermodal container transport system by sea and then by train or road to a port previously accessed by water transport
Minimum Bill of Lading	The clause contained in a bill of lading establishes the lowest amount that the carrier will charge for the issue
Mixed Container Load	A container load made up of different articles consolidated into a single shipment
MSA Maritime Security Act	This 1996 law authorized the formation of a Maritime Security Fleet, included in the Maritime Security Program (MSP), to establish a fleet of commercial and military ships to act for national defense or other security requirements
MT	Acronym for "Metric Ton."
Multimodal	The exact meaning of Intermodal
Multitank Container	A multimodal container frame designed to enable the transport of different liquids
Nautical Mile	About 6,076,12 FT or 1,852 meters

269

Negotiable Instruments	A legally transferable document from an individual or company to another person or institution (such as a draft, bill of lading, etc.). A straight consignment is a non-negotiable bill of lading, while an order b/l is a negotiable one
Nested	Items packaged together, one being placed partially or entirely inside the other, minimizing the total space occupied in cubic feet
Net Tare Weight	The weight of an empty cargo transport equipment with all components permanently attached to the structure
Net Tonnage (NT)	The carrying capacity of the carrier ship is, in some instances, the basis used to calculate a ship's fees or taxes
Net Weight	Weight of the goods alone, without packaging or any other element of protection or conservation
Non–Dumping Certificate	Mandatory presentation certificate in some countries to protect against dumping in the commercial transaction of certain products.
NOR - Notice of readiness	Document informing that a ship is available for loading
No–show	Denomination when cargo is not loaded, although there is a reserved space on the ship, due to a delay in arrival
Ocean Bill of Lading (Ocean B/L)	A transport contract between a shipper and a carrier, and it is also evidence of receipt of the cargo by the carrier
On Board	Note on a bill of lading stating that the cargo was loaded onto a ship to comply with the letter of credit requirements
Open Account	A commercial agreement that allows the shipment of goods to a buyer abroad without a guarantee of payment
Open Insurance Policy	A marine insurance policy applicable to all shipments made by the exporter during a stipulated period
Open Top Container	A container with a removable canvas or metal roof so it can be loaded or unloaded from the top

OPIC - Overseas Private Investment Corporation	A US government development agency that advises and assists US companies to invest abroad
Order– Notify - O/N	A bill of lading term to ensure that the release of the freight only occurs upon presentation of the original bill of lading, linked to a cargo guaranteed by a letter of credit
Origin	A location where the cargo starts transport
Original Bill of Lading - OBL	It is a shipment or transport contract document confirming the cargo's receipt by the carrier. Its validity depends on the signature of the responsible for the carriage. The issuer must mark the B/L as "original"
OS&D	A discrepancy in the amount or existence of damages that, in general, are noticed when unloading the cargo
Overcharge	Billing in an amount higher than that compatible with published rates
Overheight Cargo	Cargo with a height greater than 2.5 meters and therefore impossible to pack in a standard container
Owner Code - SCAC	A code to identify a carrier, Standard Carrier Abbreviation Code, combines three letters followed by an equipment identifier suffix. The suffix "U" means that it is a container, while the "C" indicates that it is a chassis
Packing List	Shipping documents that list the goods shipped in detail, such as packaging, dimensions, weight, and externally inscribed marks and/or numbers, without, however, citing values
PADAG - Please Authorize Delivery Against Guarantee	The consignee requests the shipper to authorize the carrier or agent to release the cargo against a bank or personal guarantee. A procedure used when the consignee is unable to present original bills of lading
Paired Ports	A US Customs software, in which at least two named customs ports will enter the cargo that arrives at any one of them, eliminating the need to present an in-bound document

Pallet	Structure with or without sides, commonly made of wood or plastic, for stacking packages or parts and allowing their handling by forklift
Panamax Tanker	A vessel with a net cargo capacity of 50,000 to 70,000 dwt
Panamax Vessel	The maximum size of a ship to be able to cross the Panama Canal
Parcel Receipt	A deal whereby a steam shipping company, following regulations defined in the freight rate, transports small packages at rates lower than the minimum bill of lading and issues a parcel receipt in substitution for a bill of lading
Partial Shipments	The annotation "Partial Shipments Permitted" in letters of credit authorizes that one or more shipments are allowed
Payee	Person or institution indicated in a document as a beneficiary of the values. In letters of credit, the beneficiary is the draft drawer or a bank
Payer	A person or institution responsible for the payment as described in the document. Regarding letters of credit, the payer is the party to which the draft is drawn. In general, the drawee bank
Per Diem	A charge is calculated based on a fixed daily rate
Perils of the Sea	The causes of any loss that exempt the carrier from being legally responsible essentially the dangers arising from maritime transport
Phytosanitary Inspection Certificate	A certificate issued by the US Department of Agriculture to comply with import regulations for goods from foreign countries attesting that the shipment has been inspected and is free of harmful pests and plant diseases
Pier–to–House	A shipment loaded in the container at the pier or terminal to proceed from there to the consignee's location
Pier–to–Pier	The shipment is loaded in a container at the pier of origin and unloaded at the port of destination
Place of Delivery	A place where the carrier's responsibility for the custody and care of the cargo ends

Place of Receipt	A place where the cargo remains under the responsibility and custody of the carrier
POD	Acronym for: 1. Port of Discharge 2. Port of Destination 3. Proof of delivery: document from the carrier essential to make payment
Point of Origin	The place of delivery of the cargo to the shipper's carrier
Pomerene Act	The Federal Bill of Lading Act of 1916. It was the US legislation establishing the necessary conditions for issuing a B/L. Drawing up a B/L containing false data leads to fines and/or imprisonment
Port of Entry	Port of unloading goods for entry into a country
Port of Exit	A place where goods are loaded and leave a country
Pre-cooling	The process used in the transport of citrus fruits or any perishable commodities. There is the packaging of the part and placement in a cold chamber, with gradual heat extraction. The fruit boxes are packed in thoroughly cooled containers and transported to the destination without opening the doors
Prepaid - Ppd	Freight charges must be paid by the Consignor (shipper) first for the subsequent release of bills of lading by the carrier
Pro Forma Invoice	An invoice provided by the supplier to the customer before cargo shipment detailing the types and quantities of goods that will be shipped, the value, and specifications (weight, size, etc.)
Quarantine	A restriction stipulated for an operation aimed at protecting the public against some health risks. A ship can be quarantined and cannot leave a protected point. During the quarantine period, the Q flag remains raised.
Quota	The quantity or volume of goods released for import without extra fee or import suspension during a specified period
Quotation	A proposal for the sale of goods with detailed price and commercial conditions

Ramp	Container arrival rail terminal for loading or unloading on trains. Most modern railway installations use lifting equipment to position containers on railcars
Ramp–to–Door	Freight type with cargo starting transport on a railroad ramp, and delivery set to the consignee's door
Ramp–to–Ramp	Type of freight with the cargo starting transport on a railway ramp and being placed on another railway ramp at the destination for the consignees to pick up
Rate Basis	The rate calculation formula includes specific factors or elements. Several factors, such as weight, dimensions, type of handling equipment, etc., may form the basis of the fee
Rebate	Illegal conduct of granting a discount or refund to reduce the tariff price
Reconsignment	Changing the consignee or destination on a bill of lading during cargo transportation. Diversion is similar
Recourse	Right to claim against the guarantors of a draft or bill of exchange
Red Label	A mandatory label on flammable item shipments
Reefer	Refrigerated container
RFP	Request for Proposal
RFQ	Request for quotation
Relay	A word that describes the act of transferring containers between vessels owned and operated by the same carrier
Remittance	Money transferred by one person to another as payment
Revenue Ton (RT)	A standard unit of measure in shipping and a basis for freight, whose rates generally take into account the cost per ton of revenue, being the higher of the total number of cubic meters versus the total number of metric tons
Ro/Ro	Abbreviation of the term "Roll-On/Roll-Off". Sea cargo handling method of operation in which a ship with ramps allows wheeled vehicles to board and alight without cranes

RVNX - Released Value Not Exceeding	It usually expresses the limit value of the goods transported, indicating the carrier's maximum liability in compensating for lost or damaged goods.
Sea Waybill	A document attested to loading goods on board and used when a bill of lading (b/l) is unnecessary. Often in cases where a company ships goods to itself
Service Contract	A contract between a shipper (or a group of shippers) and an ocean carrier. Through it, the shipper undertakes to provide a minimum amount of cargo or freight revenue for a fixed period. In contrast, the carrier undertakes to maintain a specific rate or rate schedule and a defined level of service (such as guaranteed space, time traffic, etc.)
SHEX	Saturday and Holidays Excluded
SHINC	Saturday and Holidays Included
Ship Demurrage	Fee charged from those who delay a steamer in relation to a stipulated period
Ship Load	The total cargo that a ship carries or is capable of carrying
Ship's Manifest	A statement detailing all cargoes carried for a specified trip
Shipment	One lot of cargo shipped by a single consignor to only one consignee in a bill of lading
Shipper	The person or company usually supplying or owning the shipped goods, also called Consignor
Shipper's Export Declaration - SED	A joint Census International Trade Administration form used to gather information about US exports, completed by the shipper, specifies the value, weight, destination, etc., of export shipments, as well as the Schedule B commodity code
Shipper's Load & Count (SL&C)	Shipment loaded and sealed by the shipper and not inspected or verified by the carrier
Shipping Order	Instructions issued by the shipper to the carrier regarding the shipment of goods, usually a triplicate bill of lading
Short Ton - ST	Unit of measure for weight equivalent to 2,000 pounds

Shrink Wrap	Polyethylene or similar thermally shrunk material wrapping multiple units, consolidating them as a single package and protecting them when stowed on a pallet
Side–Door Container	A container with a rear door and at least one side door
Sight Draft	A document that guarantees the exporter the possession of the transported goods until the effective payment is characterized by the obligation of the importer to pay, upon presentation, immediately after receiving the goods
SL/W	Shippers load and count, those clauses appear in the bill of lading, when necessary, to exempt the carrier from liability if the Consignor loaded the cargo
Spotting	Position a container at the specified location to be loaded or unloaded
SSHEX - Saturdays, Sundays, and Holidays Excepted	Related to the cargo loading and unloading procedure, complying with the charter party, specifying that the time will not count in the calculation of demurrage and dispatch
Standard Industrial Classification - SIC	A numeric code defined by the US government for the classification of products and services
Standard International Trade Classification - SITC	A numerical code regulated by the United Nations to classify internationally traded commodities
Steamship Guarantee	An indemnity guarantee document, issued by a bank in favor of the carrier, protecting it from any loss or damage resulting from the delivery of the goods to the consignee, generally prepared when the bill of lading is lost or not available
Store–Door Pick–up Delivery	A complete package of pick-up and delivery services performed by a carrier from origin to destination

Straight Bill of Lading	Non-negotiable bill of lading identifying the specific person or entity to whom to deliver the goods
Stuffing	Load the cargo into the container
Subrogate	Putting in someone else's place; to substitute someone for another concerning a legal right, for example, when the insurer indemnifies a claim, is in the same condition as the beneficiary to claim any rights against third parties
Surcharge	An extra or additional cost or fee
Surtax	An additional tax
T&E - Transportation and Exportation	Customs authorization form for a carrier to move goods from the port of entry to the port of exit in the US to export to a different country, for example, transport cargo originating in Mexico to Canada via the US
Tankers	Vessels containing tanks for transporting liquid cargo, such as oil, chemicals, liquefied gases, etc.
Tare Weight	In transports through wagons or containers, indicates their empty weight before loading or after unloading
Tariff - Trf	1. Document detailing a shipping company's charges, fees, and rules 2. Tax collected on goods and services imported by a country
Temperature Recorder	A device for recording the temperature inside a container during the cargo's journey
Tenor	Time and date for payment of a draft
Terminal	An area for preparing containers for later loading onto a means of transport or where they are placed immediately after unloading
Terminal Charge	A charge due for a service provided at a carrier's terminal
TEU	Twenty-foot Equivalent Unit
Through Rate	Total fees from the point of origin to the final destination
Throughput Charge	The fee for moving a container across a container yard or for placing it on the ship

Time Charter	A lease contract by the shipowners with the lessee, stipulating the terms of the agreement, such as the duration of the lease in years or voyages
Time Draft	A draft containing a clause defining a certain number of days after acceptance or a certain number of days after the date of the draft
Ton–Mile	Helpful in comparing revenue with shipping charges. The difference between revenue and transportation cost per ton of cargo moved over a mile
Tonnage	100 cubic feet
Towage	The charge for towing a ship
Transshipment Port	Port of transferring cargo from one carrier to another
Trust Receipt	Release of goods by a bank to a buyer, but the bank retains ownership of the goods, usually intended for the manufacture or saleThe Buyer is required to keep the assets (or the proceeds of their sales) isolated from the rest of the assets and ready for repossession by the bank
Two–Way Pallet	A pallet on which the forks of a forklift can only be inserted from two sides
UCP - Uniform Customs and Practice for Documentary Credits	Most frequent pattern for making payments in international trade. Commonly known by its abbreviated title: UCP No. 500, revised publication to incorporate recent changes in the transportation and banking sectors
Ullage	Volume not filled by the liquid in a drum or tank
Unclaimed Freight	Unsolicited or uncollected freight by the consignee or owner
Undercharge	A charge made with an amount lower than the appropriate
Unit Load	Packages loaded on a pallet or crate to facilitate handling at once as if it were a single packet
Unitization (1)	Consolidate an assortment of individual items into a single large load to simplify handling and movement
Unitization (2)	Placing one or more large items in a single volume on a pallet or similar device

Unloading	Removing cargo from a ship
US Consular Invoice	A mandatory document for goods imported into the United States
USPPI – US Principal Party of Interest	A beneficiary of earnings from an export, usually the Seller of the goods
Validated Export License	A document issued by the US government approving the export of goods listed in law that requires written authorization for specific overseas sales
Validation	Authentication of B/L and when it becomes effective
Vanning	Place a cargo in a container
Variable Cost	Type of cost whose variation is a function of the activity carried out over time, e.g., the costs of transporting cargo as a function of the distance traveled and the time spent. Costs can be variable or fixed; for a company to break even, net income must pay all fixed costs. Profit will occur if all variable and fixed costs are less than net revenue
Ventilated Container	A container with air inlets on the walls (side and/or rear and front) to allow ventilation when the doors are closed
Vessel Manifest	The international carrier must issue statements on the ship's crew and cargo at the port of departure and arrival. This document lists various details of each shipment individualized by B/L
VISA-Voluntary Intermodal Sealift Agreement	It grants the US defense community "guaranteed access" to commercial intermodal capability to move sustainment loads during war or national emergencies. When such conditions do not exist, the preference for the transport of DOD cargo (military cargo) belongs to the carriers
Viz.	Namely. Specify commodities in tariffs
VLFO – Vessel Load Free Out	Regarding the loading and unloading of cargo, according to the charter contract. The carrier pays for the cargo loading operation onboard, and the receiver pays for the discharge of the ship
War Risk	Insurance coverage for losses resulting from any act of war
Warehouse	A place for receiving, distributing, and storing goods

Warehouse Entry	Identification certificate of imported goods placed in a bonded warehouse. There is no tax charge during the time that the products remain in the warehouse, but the collection will occur when the goods are withdrawn for delivery or consumption
Warehouse Withdrawal for Transportation Immediate Exportation - WDEX	Authorizes the export without payment of taxes of goods removed from a bonded warehouse in a North American port, subject to the obligation to leave through the same port
Warehouse Withdrawal for Transportation - WDT	Authorization for the removal of goods from a bonded warehouse and transport on bail to another port, where it will file a superseding entry
Warehouse Withdrawal for Transportation Exportation - WDT&E	Authorizes goods to be withdrawn from a bonded warehouse in a port to be transported on bond by the United States for further exportation from another port, duty-free
Waybill - WB	A document drawn up by a shipping company at the location of a shipment relating the origin and destination, the consigner and the consignee, a depiction of the cargo, and the amount billed for the freight. It goes with the shipment or can be mailed to the agent at the transfer point or waybill destination. Unlike a bill of lading, a waybill is not a title
Weight Cargo	Cargo with the calculation of freight rate according to weight
Weights and Measures/ Measurement ton	40 cubic feet = 1.13267 cubic meter Net ton/short ton = 2,000 lbs Gross ton/long ton = 2,240 lbs Metric ton/kilo ton = 2,204.62 lbs One cubic Meter = 35,314 Cubic ft
Wharf	Construction on the port that prolongs into deep water for ships to position themselves alongside

Wharfage - Whfge.	Fee charged by the owner of a pier or wharf to allow handling of cargo or berthing of ships
WIBON	Acronym for Whether In Berth or Not
Windy Booking	Booking freight made by shipper or forwarder to ensure space availability without having cargo at the time of booking. Carriers typically overbook a ship by 10 to 20 percent, predicting that many of these windy bookings will not happen
Without Recourse	Expression preceding the signature of the drawer or endorser of a negotiable document specifying that, in the event of its transfer to subsequent holders, there will be no liability of the endorser in case of non-payment or delivery
WM - W/M	Abbreviation for "Weight or Measure," indicating the basis for calculating the freight, establishing that among the weight or measure of the cargo, the one that generates the highest revenue will be adopted. Another terminology is "worm". The comparison is between the number of metric tons of weight with the number of cubic meters of space that the cargo measures
Yard	An area for sorting, storing, or switching
Zulu Time	Time based on Greenwich Mean Time

BIBLIOGRAPHY

BAILY, Peter; FARMER David; CROCKER Barry; JESSOP David. Procurement Principles and Management in the Digital Age. Twelfth edition. USA: Pearson, October 21, 2021

BAILY, Peter; FARMER, David. Purchasing Principles and Techniques. 3rd edition. USA: Pitman Publishing, May 1, 1977

BURT, David N; PETCAVAGE, Sheila; PINKERTON, Richard. Proactive Purchasing in the Supply Chain: The Key to World-Class Procurement. 1st edition. USA: McGraw Hill, December 6, 2011

CECERE, Lora M. Supply Chain Metrics that Matter. 1st edition. USA: Wiley, December 8, 2014

COHEN, Shoshanah. Strategic Supply Chain Management: The Five Core Disciplines for Top Performance. 2nd edition. USA: McGraw-Hill, June 14, 2013

COVEY, Stephen R. The 7 Habits of Highly Effective People. 30th Anniversary Edition. USA: Simon & Schuster, May 19,2020

FAYOL, Henry. General and Industrial Management. USA: Martino Fine Books, August 7, 2013

FISHER, Roger; URY, William L, PATTON Bruce. Getting to Yes: Negotiating Agreement Without Giving in. 3rd Revised ed. USA: Penguin Books, May 3, 2011

FRAZELLE, Edward H. Supply Chain Strategy: Unleash the Power of Business Integration to Maximize Financial, Service, and Operations Performance 2nd edition. USA: McGraw-Hill, October 27, 2017

KLEEMANN, Florian C. Outsourcing of Manufacturing Processes: Negotiating with a Single Sourcing Supplier. 1st edition. Germany: GRIN Verlag, March 5, 2012

LEE, Lamar; DOBLER, Donald W; BURT, David N. Purchasing and Supply Management. USA: McGraw-Hill, August 1, 1997

PATIDAR, Jeet; JAIN, K C. Purchasing and Materials Management. S Chand, December 1, 2011

SANTOS, Almir G; ELIA, Bruno de S; MAGALHÃES, Eduardo; PINTO, Geraldo. Gestão da cadeia de suprimentos (Supply Chain Management). 1st edition. Brazil: FGV Management, October 1, 2014

SOLLISH, Fred; SEMANIK, John. The Procurement and Supply Manager's Desk Reference 2nd edition. USA: Wiley, May 23, 2012

STEINER, Robert. Mastering Financial Calculations: A Step-by-Step Guide to the Mathematics of Financial Market Instruments. 2nd edition. USA: Prentice Hall, 2007

STEVENS, James. Supply Chain Management: Strategy, Operation & Planning for Logistics Management (Logistics, Supply Chain Management, Procurement). USA: Shepal Publishing, June 15, 2016

STUKART, Herbert Lowe. Ethics and Corruption. 1st edition. Brazil. Nobel, January 1, 2003

TAYLOR, Frederick Winslow. The Principles of Scientific Management. USA: Martino Fine Books, February 12, 2014

TAYLOR, Timothy; GREENLAW, Steven A; SHAPIRO David. Principles of Microeconomics. 2nd edition. USA: 12th Media Services, December 31, 2017

The Bird Paper. The Essential: Purchasing and Supply Chain Management. France. Douni

URY, William L. Getting Past No: Negotiating in Difficult Situations. Revised edition. USA: Bantam Dell, April 17, 2007

ZENZ, Gary J. Purchasing and the Management of Materials. 7th edition. USA: Wiley, January 14, 1994

ANNEX - TRANSPORT AND HANDLING TERMS

INDEX

Printed in the United States
by Baker & Taylor Publisher Services